Yoga inVision 11

I0132679

arching the small of the back

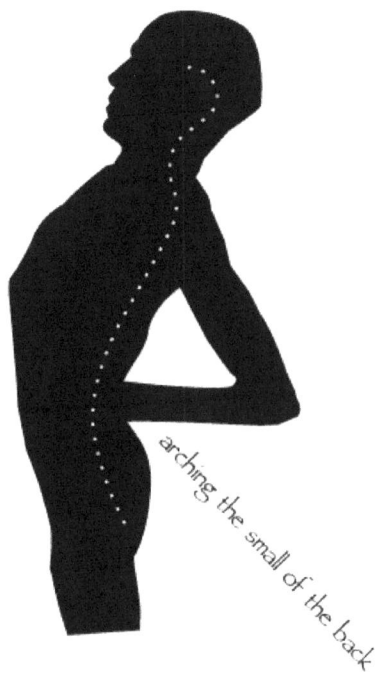

Michael Beloved

Illustrations: Author
Correspondence:
Michael Beloved
19311 SW 30th Street
Miramar FL 33029
USA
Email: axisnexus@gmail.com
                 michaelbelovedbooks@gmail.com

Paperback ISBN: 9781942887287
eBook ISBN: 9781942887294
LCCN: 2020911567

Cover:
- Yogi HarBhajan Singh Sahib, the author's teacher of breath infusion.

Mr-Beloved

Table of Contents

INTRODUCTION 5

Part 1 6

Part 2 31

Part 3 61

Part 4 98

Part 5 134

Part 6 166

Part 7 199

Index 230

About the Author 238

Publications 239

    English Series 239

    Meditation Series 242

    Explained Series 243

    Commentaries 244

    Specialty 247

    inVision Series 249

Online Resources 252

INTRODUCTION

This is the eleventh of the Yoga inVision series. It relates experiences and practices done in 2012. These give beginners ideas of the physical, psychological and spiritual experiences one may have when doing asana postures, pranayama breath-infusion and *pratyahar* sensual energy withdrawal. Beyond that is higher yoga, which Patañjali named the *samyama* procedures. He defined *samyama* as a combination of *dharana* deliberate focus, *dhyana* spontaneous focus and *samadhi* continuous spontaneous focus. During practice, these progress one into the other. If one is expert at *pratyahar* sensual energy withdrawal, one may graduate to *dharana* which is deliberate focus of the attention to a higher concentration force or person. As soon as one masters *dharana* one may slip into *dhyana* which is an effortless focus on a higher concentration force or person. Once you practice *dhyana*, *samadhi* happens as the continuous effortless focus on a higher concentration force or person.

Many persons on a spiritual path feel that they can construct a process as they advance. This idea denotes failure. After all, if the supernatural and spiritual environment, is not already there, no one can create it now. It is either there or it is not. For instance, if one intends to moves to a different country, then of course one will fail if the country intended does not exist. It has to be there prior. Similarly, what you aim for as spiritual life, must be there already, or one will find that the aspiration is incorrect. This is why I speak of a concentration force or person. I could have said concentration person or divine person, or God. I did not because I do not know how anyone's spiritual path will develop.

One may leave an island in the safest boat and still the vessel may sink. One should keep one's mind open and be willing to work with fate. In spiritual development, there is providence too. What one desires to have one may not achieve. What one wishes to see may never appear.

These Yoga inVision journals show how sporadic my course of yoga was. This is after years of practice. It gives some idea of what to expect. Once you get through the lower yoga practice, you will see advancement in a more stable way but it may be incremental, accruing little by little, with bright flashes here and there.

Part 1

Intellect Freed from Kundalini Dominance

After practicing the breath infusion into the thighs, legs and feet for some time now, for over two years and for at least eight months intensively focusing through the knee downwards, I recommend this process with confidence. It yielded results which may rarely be attained otherwise.

Three astral yogis are to be credited for showing this process. These are Yogeshwarananda, Tibeti Yogi, his friend and Pranajogi one of his teachers.

Their idea is that unless one gets the entire subtle body flushed of heavy astral energy in every part of it, one cannot be successful with the Patanjali process, ashtanga yoga. In his book, *First Steps to Higher Yoga,* Yogesh stressed the importance of many asanas and pranayama methods as if these were absolutely necessary.

Originally in India, one had to do the eight steps one by one. Later, some famous people said it was unnecessary. A famous swami ridiculed asana and hatha yoga kriyas.

My conclusion at this point is that if a person can pray and sing and cause the subtle body to be cleared of heavy astral energy, that someone need not do anything else. My subtle body did not yield to the praying method. I acquired another process.

I can confidently say that the clearing of the heavy astral energy in the thighs, legs and feet, results in a peculiar type of meditation in the head of the subtle body, where there is full silence there, where the intellect stops displaying unwanted ideas. In fact, it seems that the intellect desires and feels the need for this state of no-mind, where no-mind is no idea, thoughts or images arising in the mind space to bewilder the coreSelf. Instead, the intellect desires naad sound resonance. It welcomes the clear light astral energy which rises from the thighs, legs and feet into the trunk and then passes through the neck into the head.

This new attitude of the intellect is a sigh of relief for the coreSelf which was belabored restricting the intellect from its machinations, jumping from thought to thought, idea to idea, memory to idea on and on, endlessly in a protracted struggle to meet the standard for yoga set by Patanjali. Yoga is best done when there are no theatrical activities by the intellect.

Yoga is best done when the kundalini is divested of polluted subtle energy, when it is aroused by an intense session of breath infusion (*bhastrika* or *kapalabhati* pranayama), which ignites and energizes its reserve energy. The intellect lives in fear of the kundalini lifeForce mechanism. As soon as the yogi can cause the kundalini to be activated through the entire subtle form the intellect is freed from kundalini's influence and no longer has to cower in fear of kundalini's survival and pleasure procurement demands.

Distribution of the Bliss Aspect

For breath infusion practice, this morning, I worked on the inner thighs, legs and ankles. These are remote areas which even the best yogis may neglect because of the amount of endeavor it takes to target these zones. The inner thighs are deadly for preventing one from attaining the siddha status. The thighs hold sex-impetus force, lust enhancing energies, which divert energy to the sex organ chakras, and cause the lack of distribution of that energy to other zones.

A student, once he/she attains the required determination, should consistently target the inner thighs until the mood of the energy in those regions change so that the lusty charge disappears. It should spread evenly through the subtle body and not pool in those places.

The ankles and the feet are resistant to clearance. When the embryo is formed, kundalini has interest in these areas but once the body develops in infancy, the kundalini gives these areas little attention. This is bad for an aspiring siddha.

In as much as we get interested in sexual pleasure and spend most of the adult years being focused on it, when one first does kundalini yoga practice, one aspires for spinal and brain pleasure through the arousal of kundalini through the *sushumna* nadi.

However, enough is enough. At some point a student should realize that the extremities like the feet and hands should also have infused energy saturated into them to the extent of feeling the bliss aspect there, the same bliss aspect which is felt in the spine and head on occasion.

Is the whole subtle body in bliss or is it only the *sushumna* nadi and the crown chakra?

Should the hands and feet of the subtle body have a heavy astral energy while the head and spine have a high grade of bliss force?

What if the whole body itself converts into one *sushumna* nadi?

What if the bliss aspect which is sometimes experienced at the crown chakra is felt evenly in every part of the subtle body?

Prohibitions

Breaching prohibtions *(yama)* is problematic. Patanjali wrote that there is the great vow. He insisted that it should not be breached under any circumstances. Other yogis said that one should not worry about the *yamas*. They have the opinion that it is sufficient to meditate.

Patanjali is correct. As one advances one finds more and more the necessity to return to fix the breaches because they weaken the practice. However, it is not easy.

अहिंसासत्यास्तेयब्रह्मचर्यापरिग्रहा यमाः ॥ ३० ॥

ahiṁsā satya asteya

brahmacarya aparigrahāḥ yamāḥ

ahiṁsā – non-violence; satya – realism; asteya – non-stealing; brahmacarya – sexual non-expressiveness which results in the perception of spirituality; aparigrahāḥ – non-possessiveness; yamāḥ – moral restraints.

Non-violence, realism, non-stealing, sexual non-expressiveness which results in the perception of spirituality (brahman) and non-possessiveness are the moral restraints. (Yoga Sutra 2.30)

जातिदेशकालसमयानवच्छिन्नाः सार्वभौमा महाव्रतम् ॥ ३१ ॥

jāti deśa kāla samaya anavacchinnāḥ

sārvabhaumāḥ mahāvratam

jāti – status; deśa – location; kāla – time; samaya – condition; anavacchinnāḥ – not restricted by, not adjusted by; sārvabhaumāḥ – relating to all standard stages, being standard; mahāvratam – great commitment.

Those moral restraints are not to be adjusted by the status, location, time or condition. They, being the great commitment, are related to all stages of yoga. (Yoga Sutra 2.31)

Control of Kundalini

During breath infusion, the student should be attentive. Otherwise, if kundalini is aroused, he will fail to notice it until it is beyond his control. The application of the attention with the compression locks, keeps kundalini confined such that if it is aroused, the yogi can direct it. Forceful concentration should begin in the spine. The student should not wait until kundalini gets into the head to apply the focusing control.

The yogi should look down through the body, into the base chakra. He should exert mental control, so that at the initial move of kundalini, he compresses and controls it.

Route of Sex Energy

For inSelf Yoga™ the concern is to first infuse the breath energy into the navel region, then to the groin area and then push it across to reach the base chakra. Once it reaches the base with sufficient energy, the impetus moves it up the spine.

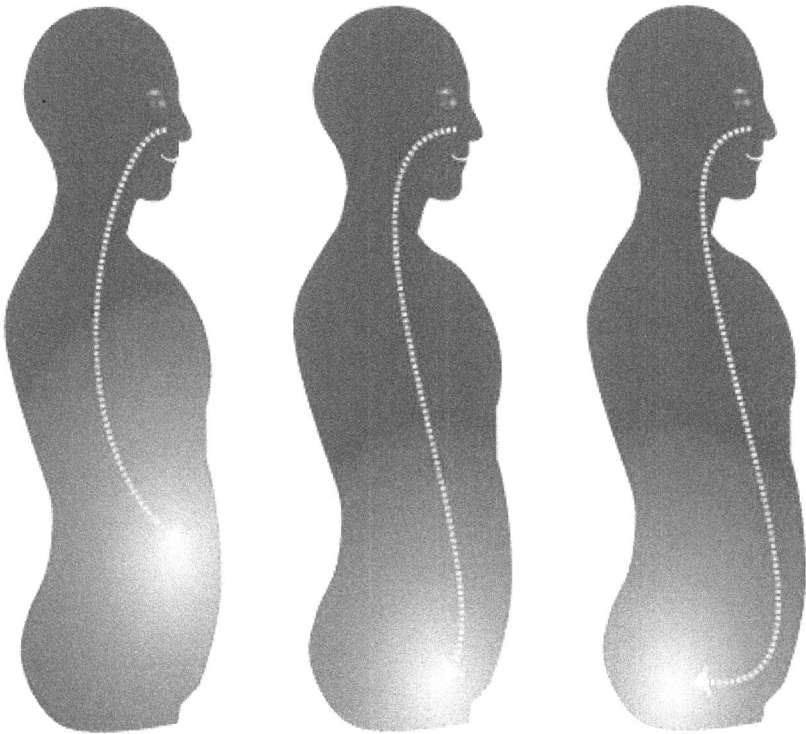

There is no lingering to do anything with the energy at the sex organ chakra, nor at the sex chakra on the spine which is different to the sex organ chakra.

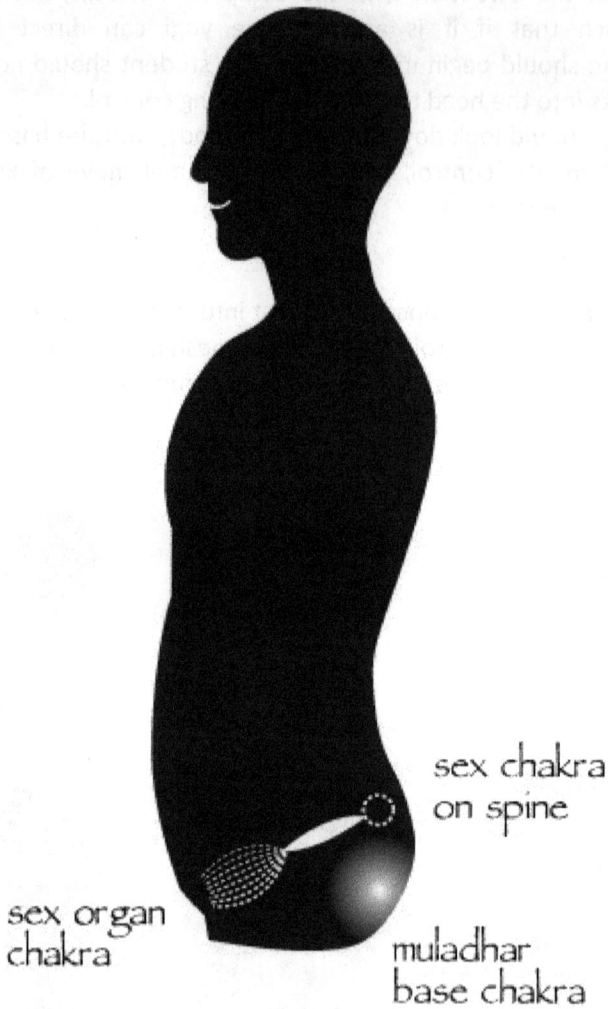

sex chakra
on spine

sex organ
chakra

muladhar
base chakra

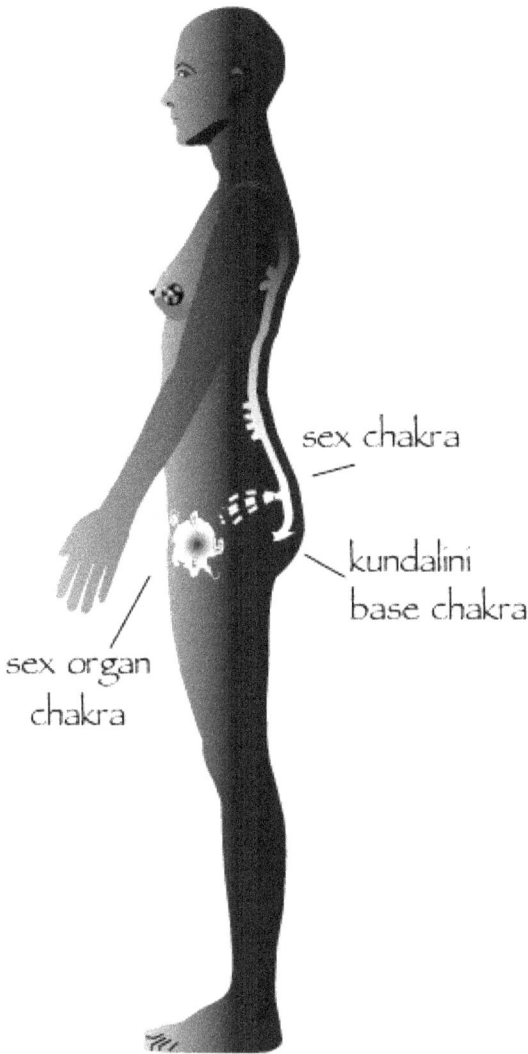

sex chakra

kundalini
base chakra

sex organ
chakra

The energy from the sex organ chakra is infused with the breath energy which came down to it but that energy is then channeled to the base chakra and then it moves through the sex chakra on the spine and travels through *sushumna* nadi into the brain.

That is the route. There is no interest in the sex organ chakra, none.

There is a more advanced practice but that is done in a more advanced stage where the energy which pools in the sex organ chakra is pulled through the middle of the subtle body while doing breath infusion.

It is not used in reference to sexual pleasure at any stage. In fact, the idea is to forget about that and to avoid that by making the system forget that and not polarize the energy for that.

In a more advanced stage, the last step in this is to destroy the authority of the thighs. The thighs are really the power in sex, not the sex organs. The thighs which have the longest bones, supply the raw material in the form of bone marrow for the creation of the sex hormones. Hence a yogi goes into the thighs in the subtle body and changes the configuration of the energy there removing from it the impetus for serving the sexual organs.

Unless he can change its purpose and distribution, sex energy distracts the yogi. It is the enemy of beginners. So long as it controls the psyche, there will be no completion of the practice, because it undermines progress.

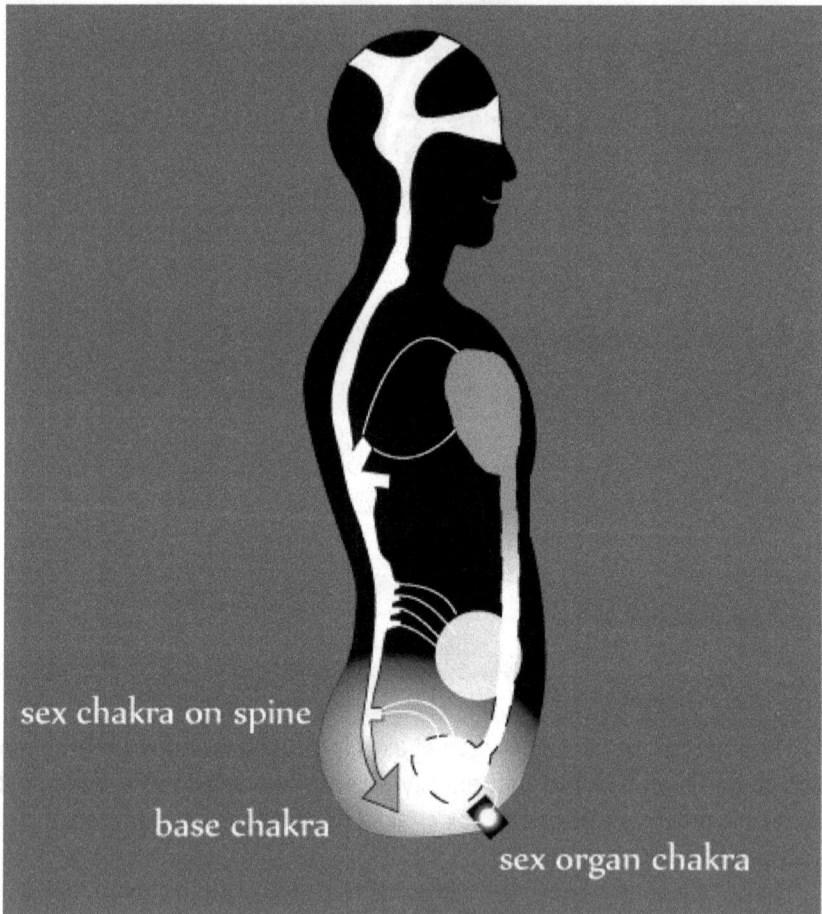

sex chakra on spine

base chakra

sex organ chakra

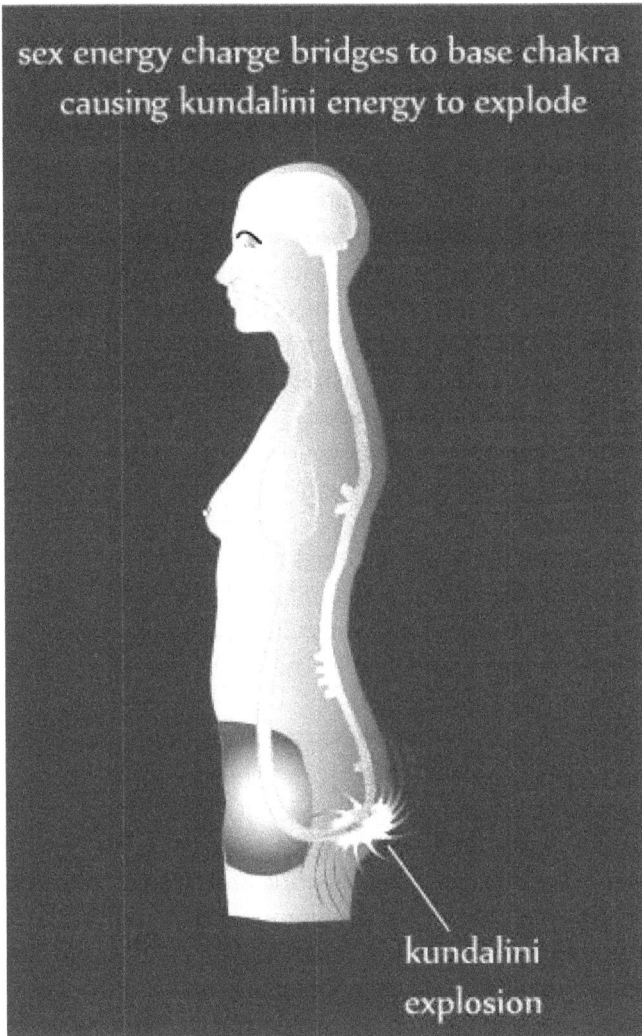

sex energy charge bridges to base chakra
causing kundalini energy to explode

kundalini
explosion

Paradise-Bypass Kriya

On the astral side, Pranajogi gave a special procedure. This is simple but it is amazing that one may never discover this by oneself. This method is for those who intend to bypass the Swarga angelic paradise worlds and join the assembly of yogis in *siddhaloka* after leaving a physical body at its death. This is a totally internal process between the yogi and his psychic adjuncts within the cavity which is called the subtle body. When doing kundalini yoga, if a student can cause kundalini to rise during the practice, something happens where angelic beings come to take the amrit nectar bliss energy which exudes from the pores of the yogi's subtle form.

This energy has a bliss aspect which is greater even than conjugal sexual exchange energy which this world continually craves. When this energy exudes from the body of a yogi, it comes out of the astral pores of the subtle body, and forms a whitish subtle cream. Using psychic perception, angelic beings perceive this. They rush to take it. They rub it on their bodies. The contact of it on those subtle forms produces a pleasure which is legendary, beyond even the most exhilarating sexual climax experience in this world.

The success of kundalini yoga to that point where this nectar bliss energy exudes from the pores of the astral form, is the bane of a yogi but as a student one cannot realize this. It is a handicap because so long as this energy will come from the subtle body, it will attract angelic beings and the yogi must deal with the attraction which it causes.

This is what happens to student yogis who pass from physical body after mastering kundalini shakti to the extent that this nectar bliss cream exudes from the astral form:

The student sees many astral beings approaching.

These astral beings wipe the cream from the student's subtle form.

They rub this on their subtle forms. It produces an ecstasy feeling.

More astral beings arrive there. They take this bliss cream from the yogi's body.

The student feels an irresistible sexual attraction to some of the angelic beings.

The student feels that he/she is conveyed through the astral atmosphere by the attractive angelic beings.

The student transits to a paradise world and resides in fabulous locations with astral gardens, luxurious accommodations, ambrosial foods and pleasure saturated objects.

The student indulges in sexual relationship with those angelic beings and remains in that place for a time according to the intensity of former yoga practice and social contributions during the last earthly life.

The student wakes up in the lower astral regions which are adjacent to the physical world near a place where there could develop an opportunity for rebirth into a physical body.

This means that the student never reached the level of the siddhas. Until there can be another attempt in another physical body, his or her yoga progress is suspended for the time being.

Pranajogi gave this method for avoiding this circular route hereafter.

- master *sushumna* nadi kundalini yoga.
- master *brahmrandra* expansion kundalini yoga.
- master *front of the body* kundalini yoga (*sushumna* is not involved in this practice).

- use *bhastrika* pranayama to draw kundalini into the brain, making it abandon muladhara chakra. In this kundalini takes a stub configuration which hangs from the brain in the back of the head.

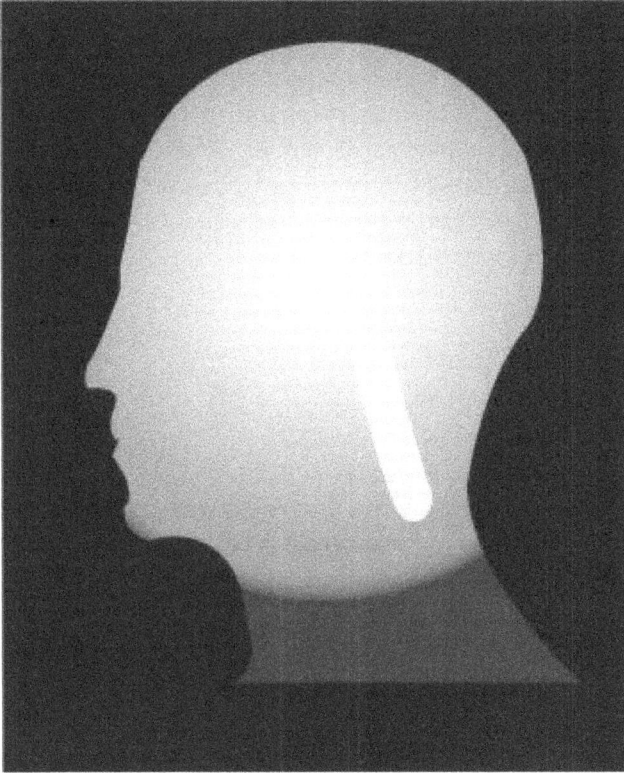

Without the assistance of kundalini or of the *sushumna* nadi passage, the student should clear all heavy astral energy from the trunk of the subtle body.

The student should blast energy in the thighs as far as the knees while pulling heavy energy up from the thighs.

Blast energy into the legs.

Blast energy into the ankles and feet.

Search for the bliss force which develops and expresses itself during the practice.

Whenever this force is found, look near it in any direction for any areas which have heavy astral energy. Throw the bliss force into those areas

Compress the bliss force into the center of the area in which it initially arose. Do not allow it to exude through the pores of the subtle body.

This last step is the action which causes a yogi to bypass the Swarga angelic world. If this is done successfully, there will be no nectar-bliss energy exuding from the subtle form. Hence no angelic beings from Swarga will be attracted. That will free the yogi to attain the association of the siddhas.

While initially one should work on *sushumna* nadi, once that is permanently cleared and has no more blockage or heavy astral energy, one should work on *brahmrandra* to study how kundalini reaches that place.

This is important because the intellect organ is involved in that and one's objectivity hinges on the condition of the intellect. The relationship between kundalini, the intellect and the coreSelf must be studied carefully, in order to crack the puzzle of why one becomes unconscious in some of the experiences where kundalini either hits the *brahmrandra* chakra or enters the head and one is uncertain of its whereabouts.

Origin of Bliss Force

Bliss force comes from three locations:
- student's psyche.
- higher dimension.
- someone else's psyche.

In the previous discussion the bliss force was generated in the student psyche by doing breath infusion where the infused energy caused the subtle body to jump to higher planes in which the energy in the personal psyche on that plane is experienced as a bliss force.

To understand how this is possible, consider that the food one eats can be converted into pus or sexual fluids. As sexual fluids it is experienced as a pleasure energy, as pus it is experienced painfully. This happens in the physical body. In the subtle body a similar situation may arise.

There is also physical experience where one gets happiness by touching another person. Or one may get pleasure from someone's sex activity. One may get pleasure from the environment, like from cool water or from a pleasant climate. There may be pleasure from eating a fruit, where its juice gives pleasure to the tongue.

Kundalini Gold Out

Gold out means that the yogi entered what is called the brahman effulgence (brahmananda). Black out means that he entered the mula prakriti state which is the dissolution of manifested matter into nothingness.

The loss of the sense of "I" occurs because the rim of the coreSelf makes contact with trillions of other core-selves which are in the brahman effulgence in undifferentiated consciousness which is reality (sat), and where there is no spiritual objectivity (chit). There is existence (sat) but no objective reference (chit). There, one self does not know where it begins or ends even though its influence is limited nevertheless.

When the chit feature surfaces, when the being is aware of itself and also of the blissful *(ananda)* nature of its isolated self *(kaivalyam),* that self has spiritual objectivity. Isolated means being isolated from the psychic adjuncts which causes the self to focus on levels of awareness which are lower than the energy spread of the self.

Samadhi

Samadhi is both known and unknown. In some *samadhi*s one has objective awareness. In other experiences, one has objective awareness after the *samadhi* occurred where there is a slight impression but no objective integration of it.

To understand this one should over time, over months if not years, make a study of the shift from *dharana* to *dhyana* and then from *dhyana* into *samadhi.*

The best thing to do is to abandon the word *samadhi.* Just hearing the word, just sounding it in the mind, causes the mind to be erratic and excited. This is because some yogis idolized *samadhi* and cause a great misunderstanding and an unjustified excitement about it. Instead of thinking of *samyama* as being *dharana* progressing into *dhyana* which shifts into *samadhi;* think of it as *dharana* into *dhyana* into long-lasting relaxed *dhyana.* This will banish the excitement which the word *samadhi* causes. This will result in objectivity to know when the effortless contact with a higher level is sustained.

In time as soon as the student sits down to meditate, he/she will know if there will be a *samadhi.* The duration of deep meditation is potentially there as soon as one sits to meditate. In time one can tell by the feel of it as soon as one sits, if the *dhyana* will be sustained and if it will convert into *samadhi.*

Kundalini Down-Flow

This morning's meditation was changed due to questioning by Pranajogi. The conversation began during breath infusion just before I sat to meditate. Pranajogi harped on the fact that when kundalini is struck severely by compressed breath energy, it tries to move. If the locks are applied successfully, the kundalini frequently moves upwards and not downwards or sideways.

All the same if the student does not apply the locks successfully, kundalini may ooze through the base or sex chakra. It may rise upwards or strike unawares. The student may lose control of the body, which falls. He may experience a white out, gold out or black out.

Pranajogi was not interested in the experiences of those students who hold the locks inefficiently. The conversation concerned those who do. His question which I could not answer on the spur of the moment, was this:

Why does kundalini not go downwards when it is struck by the infused compressed breath energy?

In the meditation I contemplated the reason for this. Perhaps I will write something later when I have a conclusion. In the meantime, study these diagrams.

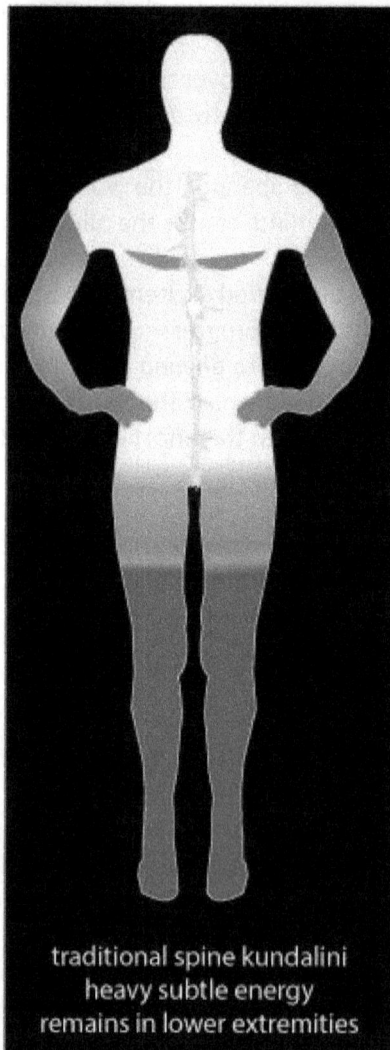

traditional spine kundalini
heavy subtle energy
remains in lower extremities

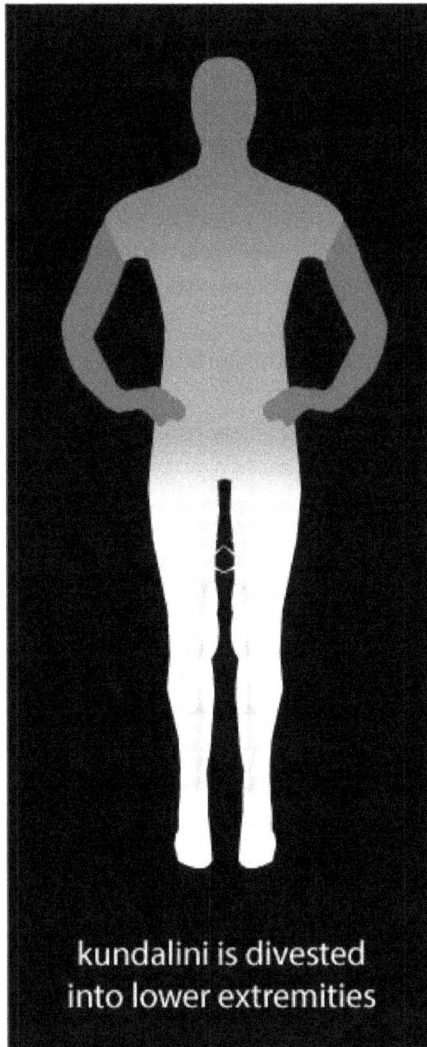

kundalini is divested
into lower extremities

Once kundalini is trapped and cannot go through the base chakra or cannot express itself in the sex organ chakra, it cannot get out the psyche unless it goes through the navel chakra. If that is locked, it must go through the throat. If that is locked, it must go into the head, where the student may lose control if he/she is inattentive and has not perfected the mind lock.

The question remains as to why kundalini does not go into the thighs, legs and feet. Why does the student have to practice for months if not years, to master kundalini to the extent of forcing it to first go into the lower extremities and then rising from there, instead of neglecting the extremities and leaving heavy astral energies in the lower parts?

Yogi as Enjoyer or Monitor

This morning during breath infusion, Pranajogi, questioned as to what the coreSelf was in fact, as to if it is an enjoyer of the sensations or a regulating principle. He said that in the advanced pranayama practice, one honestly assesses the dominance or lack of it for the coreSelf.

In the psyche there is a privacy matter which may limit the progression of a student and keep him on a lower level of development. Hence at a certain point the student should regard this question about the core being either the enjoyer or the monitor.

When is the enjoyer role appropriate? When it is preferred to be the monitor?

Is there any danger in impulsively remaining as the enjoyer at all times and in all places where one can do so?

How does the coreSelf detach itself from its fusion with the intellect and kundalini lifeForce?

Is the psyche the self?

Is the self the psyche?

The termites enjoy wood. They get satisfaction from eating it. Is the enjoyer mentality the mission of the coreSelf? Should the core abandon its impulsive needs, to become detached from the enjoying mentality which it exhibits?

The child enjoyed the ice-cream. The father enjoyed seeing the child enjoying the ice-cream. Is either the posture of the coreSelf?

The young adult enjoyed the night club and casual sex. The elderly one enjoyed financial security and the privilege of authority. Is that the mission of the self?

Pranajogi said this:

Within the psyche there is energy which creates a bliss aspect. In an efficient pranayama practice, this bliss is secreted within the psyche. What should the yogi do with it? Should it be enjoyed the way people enjoy sexual pleasure or the way the children enjoy sweets? How should the face of the yogi be turned to it?

Squeeze Down Reverse Kriya

Pranajogi showed a squeeze down procedure which involved working in the thighs one after the other in various poses where one naturally focuses on the thighs from pelvis to knees. The thigh bones generate bone marrow. In the subtle body it creates a misty subtle energy which is made heavier in the fleshy parts of the thigh. Traditionally in the method used by the kundalini, this energy is drawn to the groin area where it is used to create a compound sexual energy.

In Pranajogi's procedure this system of sexual energy is demolished. The student pushes through the center of the thigh and pulls all the energy which accumulated there. He causes it to turn into a fine mist by the breath infusion practice. When it is misted it does not move to the groin. Instead it is pushed through the center of the thigh into the knees.

Looking down through the thigh, this looks like a white cylinder which turned white-hot and which has a hole at the knee. After a time, bliss energy radiates. This is when Pranajogi said to compress it down and not to allow it to reach the head.

These instructions may seem contrary to most yoga aspirations but these are for persons who want to develop a yoga siddha body, in which all parts of the body are in a highly energized state, not just the subtle spine or head.

Pranajogi is a yogi who gave instruction to Yogeshwarananda in the Himalayas. This yogi disappeared because Yogesh and another student pulled his body from a river when the yogi did pranayama practice.

This incidence was cited in the books Himalaya Yogi Ka Part 1 and First Steps to Higher Yoga. Pranajogi's guru is Atmananda who is also Yogesh's guru. These persons are deceased.

Pranajogi was a leading master of pranayama during the time of Yogesh. There is hardly anything he does not know about pranayama practice.

Pranajogi's Special Head Kriya

This morning breath infusion had many little phases of energy which accumulated and scattered through various parts of the psyche, especially in and around the middle part of the subtle trunk, in the thighs, legs and feet.

One special event was the rise of bliss energy which came from various parts and then dropped in droplets into the center in a cylindrical area just on the inside of the lower trunk near the spine.

As the energy beads deposited there, I continued the infusion and cause it to dissipate upwards. It evaporated and then appeared in the subtle head and went through the top part of the subtle head but a little to the back instead of at the *brahmrandra* which is usually located at the top but a little to the front top.

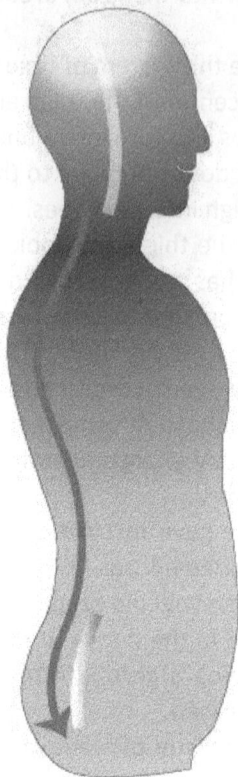

Yogesh and Pranajogi, checked the practice. Pranajogi is an expert on various subtle head procedures which if practiced eventually lead to the complete accomplishment of Patanjali's second sutra, regarding the shutdown of the vrittis interference vibrations during meditation.

Looking through my subtle body and checking to see the passages of the infused energy, Pranajogi suggested that I should pull energy to the top of the head but a little to the back from center avoiding the front area completely.

Near the end of this session, I worked on the slant passage taken by kundalini in its subversive operations when it influences the intellect without having the permission of the coreSelf. The system is that kundalini has the authority to bypass the coreSelf and convince not just the intellect but the senses as well, to do its requests in the creature survival world.

Instead of arguing about this arrangement which one cannot change, one can influence the process by purifying the passage used by kundalini when it attacks the intellect. If this passage is cleared, if the energy in this passage is a higher grade of subtle force, kundalini will send harmless messages since the passage will itself recondition kundalini's energy which moves through it.

This is supposed to be higher yoga in the area of *samyama* practice but it may be rated as higher higher yoga. *Samyama* is the system of the three higher stages of yoga as one sequential practice.

This begins with *dharana* linkage into higher concentration energies, then graduates into *dhyana* effortless linkage into the same. It develops further into continuous effortless linkage which is *samadhi*. There are various types of *samadhi* depending on the application of the linkage to specific higher concentration energies, environments, dimensions or persons.

Kundalini Overpowering the Intellect

If during breath infusion, the student suddenly finds himself in an intense golden background or foreground, it means that kundalini was aroused in full blast before that condition was perceived. Kundalini already overpowered the intellect organ before the yogi realized it.

The application of locks after this happened will not be executed effectively by the system because the coreSelf already lost grips of the intellect. That organ already lost command. On any sea-worthy ship there is a captain, just as there is a coreSelf and an intellect. If from the engine room, the chief mechanic (kundalini) decides to commandeer the ship, the captain can do nothing if the mechanic comes from behind and puts a gun to the captain's head.

At that point to say something about reaching to ring the alarm is nonsense because the mechanic will be smart enough to blow the captain's head off before he can reach the lever.

Once this happens unless you are a kundalini yoga master like Yogi Bhajan, you cannot control anything because every hand on deck is under the orders of the chief engineer. As the captain you lost control of the ship. Your token control which was used before the mutiny, is suspended by the real captain who operated the engine which is the kundalini.

Unless one is a master one cannot control kundalini once it blasts its way into the brain after it is hit by a forceful surge of breath infusion. Once that happens all attempts to gain control of the psyche are mere gimmicks.

The idea of applying full locks at this stage is nonsensical. At this stage the power to do that is not there with the coreSelf. It cannot act at this stage because its agent of action which is the intellect, was put out of commission.

Kundalini Spontaneous Arousal

Kundalini may not be aroused at someone's command. It does not have to rise at the time when the yogi expects it to or at a certain time during a sequence in a specific posture.

Because of clinging to preconceived notions or clinging to a plan of when kundalini should rise, the student may not realize when kundalini ascends spontaneously. Subsequently if he applied the locks after kundalini spread through the system, having taken control before the locks were applied, his willpower order for the locks will be ignored.

Morality of the Subtle Body

The value of the human body as compared to the angelic forms in the subtle paradises, is that the human can develop and utilize morality. The subtle body is inconsistent with morality. It has little regard for it. Because of reproduction on the physical level, morality comes to fore. It faces one and makes one realize responsibility. One has to use the physical body to cause the subtle one to adhere to morality. It is not an easy achievement but it can be done.

Because of the subtle body, the physical one makes moral breaches. Because of the physical body, if one can reform it, the subtle one may be adjusted.

In the story of the Ramayana, Rama tells Sugriva, "I had to cut you down because you sexually indulged your brother's wife."

This means that the divine beings come down and try to show us the path of responsible social behavior. It is a hard lesson to master because of the subtle body.

Reverse Lotus Posture

Recently as instructed by Yogeshwarananda on the astral side, I did a reverse lotus posture *(padmasana)*. This was to be done some years ago but somehow, I neglected the practice. Yogesh stipulated it in a way where I did it once and for all. It is a wonder how one may get an instruction either physically or psychically, and for no reason, one does not execute it because the suggestive energy from the guru does not anchor in one's psyche. The psyche is unresponsive to certain vital instructions which would result in much advancement if complied with.

The reverse lotus posture is when one begins the posture with the foot which one regularly folds in last when doing the posture. In my case, when doing lotus, I begin by putting the right foot on the left thigh. As soon as I do this, I make sure that my spine is erect and not crouched over. If it is crouched, I correct it so that I sit perpendicular to the floor. It is important when sitting in lotus posture that the pelvic cage of bones be square on and not be with a collapsed construction.

After properly situating my right foot on the left thigh, I then place the left foot on the right thigh. I support the lower part of the back, to be sure that I support the lower spine if I am against a wall.

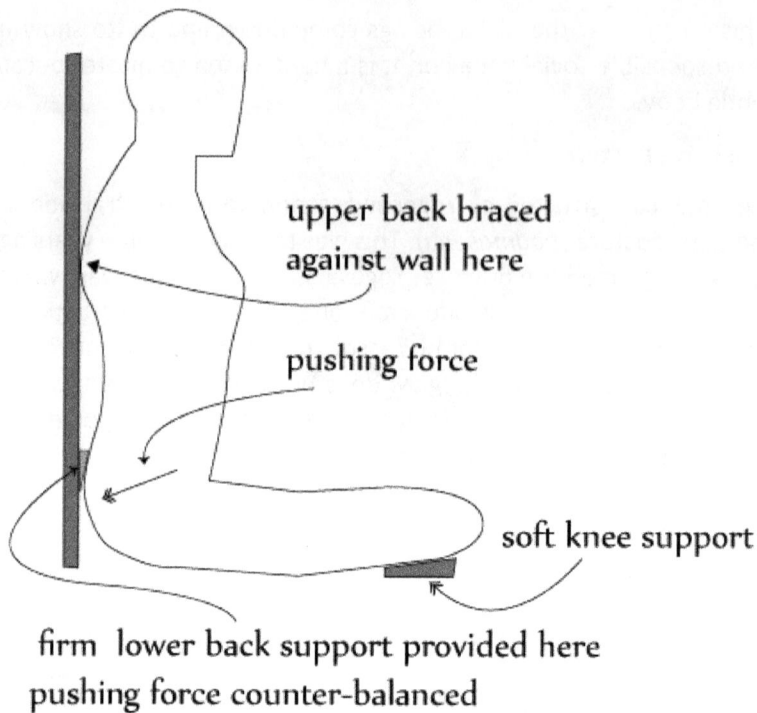

upper back braced against wall here

pushing force

soft knee support

firm lower back support provided here
pushing force counter-balanced

I practiced this posture since 1970. When I first began doing this, there was strain and pain. Because of years of assuming it for meditation, this is an easy posture. There were periods when I used to do the easy pose which is not as strenuous as the lotus.

Reverse lotus means that the student does a lotus where he/she begins with the opposite foot, placing that on the opposite thigh. This is strenuous if one became habituated to doing the lotus with one foot first repeatedly and never using the other foot first.

In difficult postures, hard to reach areas in the subtle body are easily accessed. When doing breath infusion in this posture, I can pull polluted astral energy from some hard to reach regions of the subtle body. I can compress fresh light-weight psychic energy. That is the wonder which I found with the mix of postures and breath infusion techniques.

Postures do not do the trick, and breath infusion by itself can only do so much. The combination is the technique. The postures disturb and shift the pollutions, while the infusion targets and pulls those shifted pollutions out of the subtle body.

If I wanted to clean the physical body, the method is a bath. To clean the heavy astral energy from the subtle body, the method is breath infusion in various postures.

I could sit and used visualization and mantras, except that I have no confidence in those methods. The breath infusion during *bhastrika* pranayama is effective to shift the subtle body to a higher plane.

When I did that reverse lotus posture, all of a sudden, inside the subtle body, there was this tube-like area in the hip of that form. It had a hormone storage compartment. I pulled that energy out. I diffused it out of the subtle body, thus bringing fresh pranic energy into that area. This is the first time I saw into the left hip in that way.

Squeezing the Bliss Aspect / AnandaSamkocha Kriya

On the astral side, Yogeshwarananda showed a process which is used for siddha applicants in training. This allows them to bypass the allurements of the Swargaloka angelic realms.

Because of failure to transcend the celestial allurements, many yogis who do not go through this training never make it as siddhas. These energies are pleasure forces which make even sexual intercourse in a human body seems undesirable.

After leaving the physical body for good, if a yogi practiced sufficiently, his subtle body will assume a high energy astral state. He will feel as if he rises in the astral atmosphere. If he was versed in internal yoga, he will feel as if he is propelled through an inner space.

At a certain point there will be with him angelic beings and even deities from the higher astral world. However, in that association he will be touched with a pearly atmospheric substance which is called amrit in the Vedic literatures. For most of these students, this amrit is the cause of their return to the lower astral regions but some go into the Swarga angelic world of the Indra supernatural, who controls the paradise astral domain. There, such student yogis pair with an angelic person of the opposite sex. They enjoy heavenly delights.

Needless to say, the sexual intercourse there is legendary. It last for days with no end to the pleasure derived. It is so intense that sexual intercourse as we experience it now is considered in comparison to be like a syrup which has urine, pepper and sand mixed into it.

Unfortunately, student yogis, who are not prepared for this, become overwhelmed by the amrit energy in the subtle body. They lose the vision of being a siddha. They no longer experience the desire to be with advanced yogis.

After sometime when the effect-force of their austerities in the last life, are exhausted, they find themselves in the lower astral world and feel drawn to a birth environment on earth. Such yogis, fallen brats, come out again as someone's infant. They struggle again to master yoga.

To avoid this circular passage of again becoming an embryo, a yogi should do the squeeze out practice. This is where when the kundalini energy rises during pranayama practice, the yogis applies the bandhas, special locks, and compress the bliss aspect of these energies. It is especially useful as a practice when a yogi evaporated the kundalini *sushumna* nadi. Then the tiny nadi channels can be discovered, when the infused energy flushes those nadis and one bleeds bliss energies. The yogi should apply inner psychic locks and compress the energy emanating from the aroused kundalini.

This causes an increase resistance to the bliss aspects, so that later after leaving the body, the yogi is not overwhelmed by the paradise atmosphere of the Swarga angelic world. The yogi bypasses that zone and transits to siddhaloka.

A student yogi who is attracted to the amrit pleasure energies postpones his advent to the siddhaloka place. But it is doubtful that in the next physical body, he/she will complete the necessary austerities.

Power of Sexual Attraction

Attachment to an individual could cause the attached person to transmigrate through one or more lives, just to be with that individual. There is a story of Pururavas who became attached to the goddess Urvashee. This was not an ordinary woman but a person who emerged from the body of God *(Narayana)*. Under the circumstances it is understandable why Pururavas was crazy for her to such an extent that he spent thousands of years moving from one dimension to another tracking and meeting her.

That story is told in the Srimad Bhagavatam. Once in the Uddhava Gita which is from that book, Uddhava asked Krishna about the location of Pururavas, as to whether the guy finally broke the sexual spell that the goddess had on him.

Many siddhas knew what happened to Puru. They were frightened by it, because Krishna had many times in the past swore that he monitors the devotees and does not allow them to get lost in these creations. When they heard what happened to Puru, they were concerned that something like that could happen to them.

After all, no matter how powerful one is as a yogi, one is still not God, not Krishna, not Shiva, not Brahma. Unless one gets help from either of these persons, a male may not resist a goddess woman.

One should not get any hair raising ideas about resisting every woman. A yogi may resist one or two but there is a limit. There are some women whom one cannot resist no matter if one gets oneself in spiritual order. Hence unless one remains under the shelter of the divine males, one's situation is questionable. One may transmigrate forever chasing after this or that sexually-attractive female.

Past Life Perception

Information about many previous lives is retrieved in deep meditation but sometimes in the usual morning meditation session, one may have a flash back to one specific past life from even thousands of years prior.

Some insight into this is given in the life of Gautama Buddha in the Pali canon reports about what he experienced during meditation. At a certain stage he experienced past lives, including those in lower species, many of them, in a compressed memory form.

To get to that level in meditation one must transfer completely to the causal plane, then stay there for a time, and then cross back to the subtle world, as one crosses, one may see the sum total subtle memories which one had in the present duration of the universe.

Usually this happens in a flash or it is experienced as a cross point like crossing just one lazer beam. Buddha lingered there and experienced records of lives to that point in that birth.

If one reads Patanjali, there are verses which reveal how one could get that experience.

परिणामत्रयसंयमादतीतानागतज्ञानम्॥ १६॥

pariṇāmatraya saṁyamāt atīta anāgatajñānam

pariṇāma – transformation change; traya – threefold; saṁyamāt – from the complete restraint of the mento-emotional energy; atīta – past; anāgata – future; jñānam – information.

From the complete restrain of the mento-emotional energy in terms of the three-fold transformations within it, the yogi gets information about the past and future. (Yoga Sutras 3.16)

संस्कारसाक्षात्करणात्पूर्वजातिज्ञानम्॥ १८॥

saṁskāra sākṣātkaraṇāt pūrvajātijñānam

saṁskāra – the subtle impressions stored in memory; sākṣātkaraṇāt – from causing to be visibly present, direct intuitive perception; pūrva – before, previous; jāti – status, life; jñānam – knowledge.

From direct intuitive perception of the subtle impressions stored in the memory, the yogi gains knowledge of previous lives. (Yoga Sutras 3.18)

coreSelf Turning

There are essentially two ways to get to the back of the subtle head. One is the default automatic method which means that the yogi will retreat but with the coreSelf facing the front as it was before.

The psyche is designed for the coreSelf to be oriented towards the intellect and the sensual orbs. This means that the core is positioned to look forward.

Think of the driver of a car with seat belts secure. He is oriented towards the windshield. Going to the back of the head is as if the driver's seat was moved into the back seat but with the driver still facing forward. He has no tendency to look through the back window.

Besides this default configuration, the driver can do two things. He can sit in the driver's seat and turn his head so that he can see what happens in the back seat. Or he can unbuckle the harness, turn around and jump into the back seat with his face towards the back window.

To be oriented to back of the head meditation, a yogi should work on jumping into the back seat while looking out the back window or turning the head around and looking through the back window. The effect of this is that he will find that the coreSelf is no longer compelled to remain in the default configuration.

The coreSelf is spring loaded to face forward. If it turns to the back, it immediately flies back to its default position. The same thing is experienced with the head of the subtle body, where its default position is to be situated like the physical one.

This means two actions: one is the subtle head with its components turning backwards as one object, and the other is the coreSelf alone turning not the subtle head. In either case, there is resistance.

Part 2

Resistance Energy

At times when practicing postures and/or breath infusion, I noticed a resistance energy which limits how much I practice. This is a psychic force which limits how long one practices and how frequently. This power is evident during some meditation sessions, where in meditation, one gets a compulsion to stop a session even though prior one did a productive infusion practice.

What is that negative force?

Who or what is the source of it?

Why does it have the authority to stop or limit the practice?

Those influences come from the lower dense astral energy but it is funneled through individuals whom one associates with.

Regarding the siddhas, when they come below a certain astral plane, they are affected by that influence. When they are above that they are not influenced because those energies do not penetrate the higher levels.

In chapter one of *Meditation Pictorial*, the sensual energy withdrawal practice for the coreSelf is explained in a series of diagrams. That however is the first stage of the practice. For a student yogi, there is no such thing as a coreSelf by itself. It is not a fact that a student yogi can reach the level of the coreSelf directly. The capability is not there initially.

What is shown as the coreSelf in those diagrams in the *Meditation Pictorial* book, is the core surrounded on all sides, spherically, by the sense of identity *(ahamkara)*.

But there is also another adjunct which is the intellect. This usually does not surround the coreSelf as the sense of identity does but rather remains in the frontal part of the head and regulates the coreSelf's use of the senses or memories.

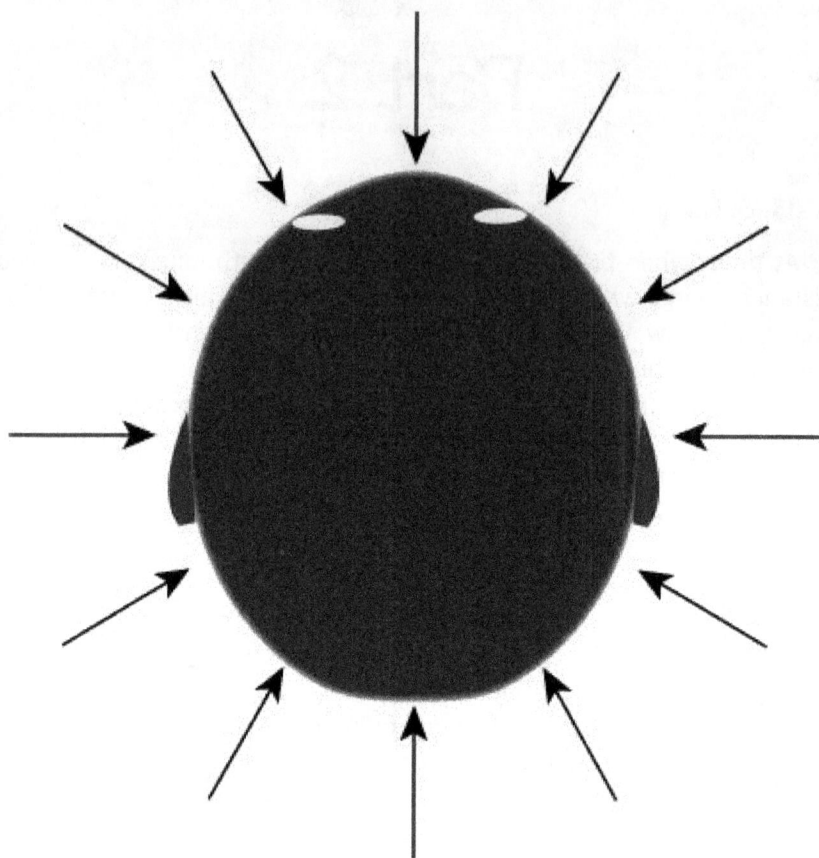

retraction of invested interest
from physically related objects
there is a general idea of self
which is based on physicalness and sensation

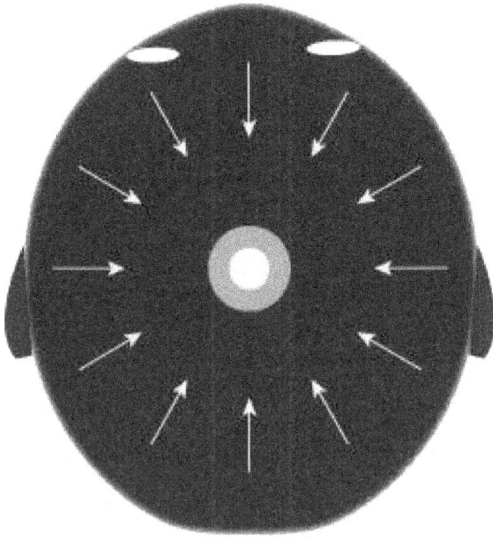

retraction of psychic interest
into coreSelf (white center)
which is surrounded by
sense of identity (grey)

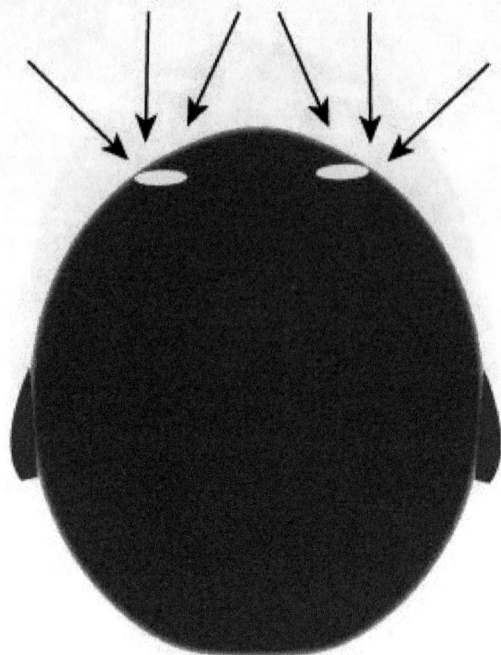

retraction of visual interest
into subtle eyes

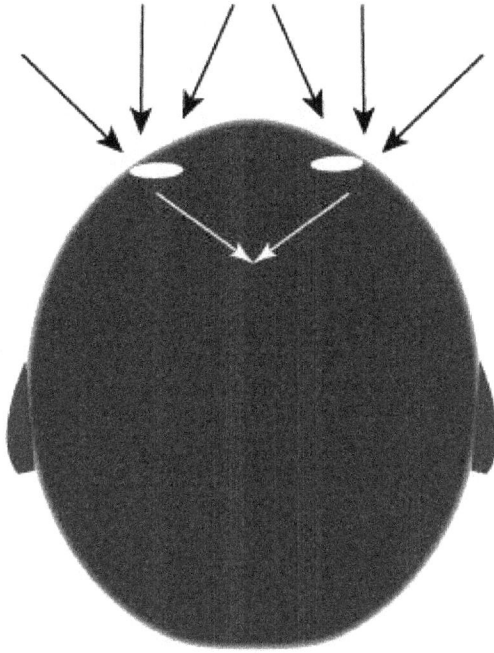

retraction of visual interest
into optic channels
which merge

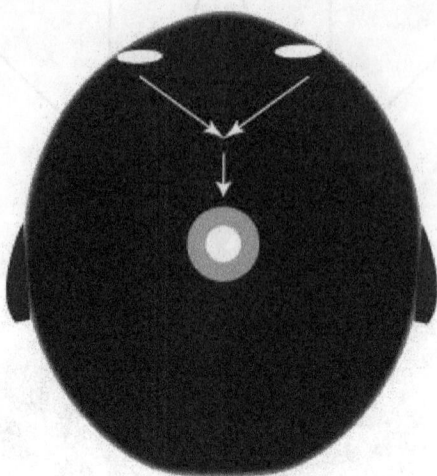

retraction of optic energy
into coreSelf

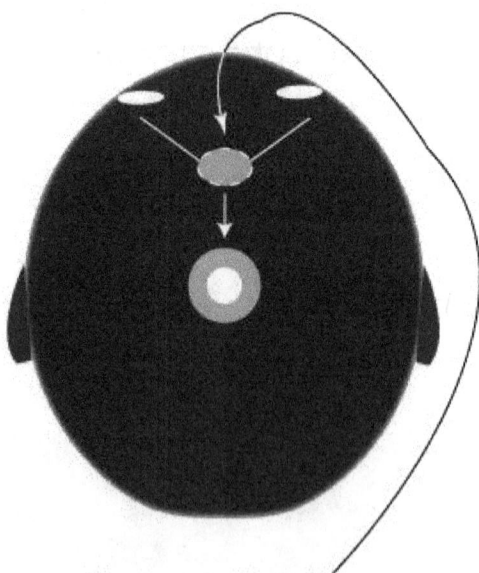

discovery of intellect
where optic energy splits

In the effort to pull the energy back into the coreSelf what really happens is that the energy, if it is obedient to this desire, will travel into the intellect or better if one really masters what it says in chapter one of *Meditation Pictorial*, into the sense of identity.

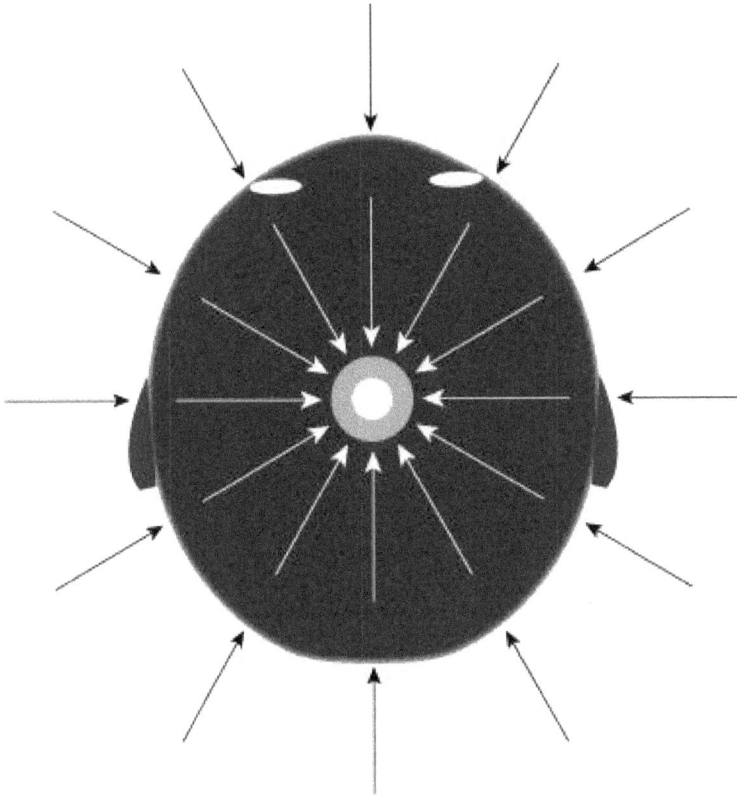

out body and in body sensual withdrawal

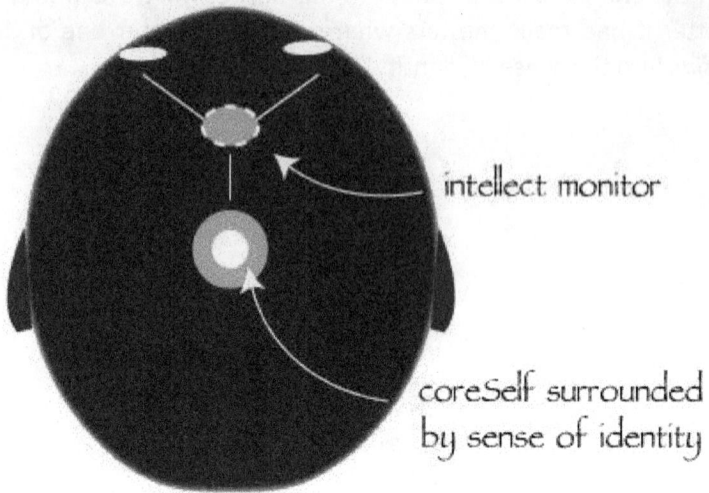

intellect monitor

coreSelf surrounded
by sense of identity

By retreating to the back of the head, the coreSelf experiences itself in isolation. There it is free from the intellect's influence.

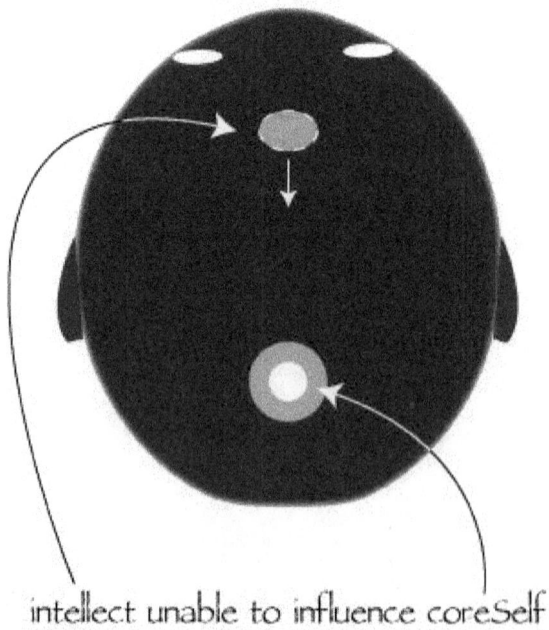

intellect unable to influence coreSelf

As soon as the self abandons its needs for the sensual facilities of the subtle body, that self is released from the extortion plan of the intellect. But that is temporary, because the student will again resume the subordinate position.

Meditation at the back of the head is a more advance retraction practice because it shows the student that introspection, as a withdrawal from the material world, is an elementary practice. It is an important practice but it is elementary nevertheless.

Instead of pulling back the energy one invested in the physical world, why not terminate social affairs? The practice of going to the back detaches the yogi from social concerns.

Types of Supernatural Vision

Usually in visionary experiences, the supernatural objects are present, but they disappear just as magically as they appeared. There are times when these experiences are frequent. There are periods when they do not occur.

Sometimes at the third eye, there are scenes passing one after the other in a steady flow but the yogi has no control over it. He sees it as if he looked through a bay window into another world. Then he perceives a scene from elsewhere in that or some other dimension.

Some visions may not be third eye experiences. Those may be higher perceptions either of the intellect or the sense of identity. One can identify a perception by its location. Third eye vision happens just outside of the forehead in the frontal part of the head. Intellect vision happens inside the forehead, say about two inches in from the skin of the face. Sense of identity vision is three or more inches in from the skin between the eyebrows.

To determine which is which, one should know the locations of the perceiving adjunct. There is also another lower vision which is vision through the astral eyes which are two psychic eyeballs like the physical ones.

Third eye vision, intellect perception and sense of identity vision are uniVisions, except that the third eye is perception looking through the window of the third eye, looking out of the psyche, while intellect vision and sense of identity vision occur within the psyche. There is no peering out like in third eye vision.

To understand this, one can consider someone who lives in a house which has three windows. Two are matched and they work together. Those are the eyes of the subtle body. But there is another window which if you look from the outside of the house you will not see it. From the inside of the house it is not seen also except under special circumstances. Then one can see through that single opening which is like a bay window.

Besides these three windows there are two other ways of seeing outside by remote viewing. These are a surveillance viewing, so that without going outside, without looking through a window one sees what others do from within a closed house, a closed psyche.

In some experiences one is not equipped with the observational capacity to know how the supernatural object came into purview. Some supernatural objects are just that and that only, while some others have a physical counterpart. For instance, our bodies are physical realities but there is a psychic copy existing as the astral form. There are people in the astral world who have no physical bodies to match their subtle forms. Of course, when this body dies, I will be in a similar situation.

A yogi may see a scene from an astral realm. His intellect may range into that territory at a time when the inhabitants of that place do something. This is a chance occurrence like if one walks through a forest and finds a castle except that when one goes into it no one is present but one knows that people must be there because of arrangements.

The intellect can do this without moving to the other place. It can range into a supernatural location. It can see events which are millions of miles away, either dimensionally or physically.

Third eye vision is perception of supernatural objects by looking outside the psyche. If it is in the psyche, meaning in the subtle head or in the subtle body, it is not third eye vision.

Just as we peer through a window which is on the surface of a building, third eye vision is peering through an opening which is at the edge of the individual's psyche. If one sees something inside the subtle head (or subtle body), it is not third eye vision.

Because of being unfamiliar with these visions, and their locations, and also the interactions of the various means of supernatural perception, it is difficult to determine where the vision takes place. There are other types of supernatural perception which have nothing to do with using the brow chakra (third eye).

Understand that something can be outside of the psyche and still be seen from inside of the psyche.

If there is an intruder on my premises. I may see him through a window, I know that he is outside the house. If I go into a closed room which has no windows, I see the intruder through a special technology. If there are no windows in that closed room how can I see the intruder through that technology?

The intruder is outside the house, outside the individual psyche and yet he was seen by looking out through a window and also from within the house without looking through a window.

But there was another intruder in the house. I became aware of that later. How did I see him since the third eye is an opening which permits vision outside the house?

With a technology, within the house, I may see someone in or out of the house. One cannot know it by the location of the percepton tool. It should be determined by the location of the organ of perception and its capability.

Memory

The practice of forgetting is like the concept of no clinging, where psychologically the student does not cling to an impression which forms in the environment of the mento-emotional energy.

Patanjali instructed for the cessation of those mental and feeling events. One of these is memory.

Memory operates a guerrilla warfare in the mind of the yogi. Sometimes it takes the role of a suicide bomber, where it comes into purview and then explodes inside the yogi releasing ideas which he is forced to deal with as he is pried loose from the meditation objective and is kept occupied with the trauma even during the other times of his waking and dreaming hours.

Memory has positive and negative aspects. The self becomes addicted to these. The negative ones give undesirable trauma which in Patanjali language are *kleshas*.

Memory has negative aspects which are interpreted by the weak mind of the student as pleasures. These are spearheaded by sexual climax experience, which causes the yogi to become spiritually stunted and hypnotized.

If the student can train the self to stop clinging to both negative and positive experiences, the memories will no longer have the student under control.

Breath Infusion Increase

On the astral side this morning during breath infusion practice, Yogesh, instructed for 200 breaths. This meant 200 counts during breath infusion practice. This is a count in addition to whatever was done to get the trunk, thighs, legs and feet full of light (as in sunlight).

A certain amount of practice should be done before a yoga guru can help one to get to a more advanced stage. Sometime after breath infusion to the trunk is completed, a reluctance may be experienced. One feels that one should cease the practice.

To go to higher practice, one should resist or ignore this reluctance. Help with this resistance may be acquired from a yoga guru, not by speaking to him about it but by stating to oneself that one has an obligation to do this as it was insisted by the teacher.

When one gets an instruction to increase austerities, there is with that an energy of empowerment which is deposited into one's psyche. One must utilize that energy to activate it.

Special Note:

I do not count the number of inhales or exhales during *bhastrika* rapid breathing. I count to a certain number as the breathing proceeds. This causes the counting not to restrict or control the breathing.

I may do say about 30 breaths in a 20-number mental count or even 18 breaths. I do not count the breaths. The counting is done sequentially in the mind irrespective of the rate of breathing.

Naad Absorption

The process is to use naad sound, to link to it. If one links to naad and remains in naad effortlessly and is not pulled out of it or ejected from it, one should remain with naad.

The first effort is to:

- Go to back of head
- Link to naad there
- Remain with naad if one can effortlessly do so and one is not ejected from naad by a compelling force.

If this linkage into naad deepens, one will be in naad for a time as if one is frozen in a chamber. Then one will find oneself looking forward into the frontal part of the head. This will be beneficial because one may see the third eye open or some other supernatural event. One may see that the front is devoid of images as if the image maker (intellect) was absent, as if it no longer exists.

If that fails, if one finds that when one links one cannot remain there as if one is pulled out or repelled from naad, give up the effort for linking to naad. Instead, make the effort to remain at the back of the head while hearing naad. In this process naad will be in proximity or distant, depending on how well the breath infusion session was.

When one remains in the back of the head, with a link to naad which is near or far from the coreSelf , one should notice if one is relocated to the front part of the head or if one's attention jumps or channels through to the front of the head to be under the influence of the image making intellect.

Take note of the force which pulls one from the back of the head. Resist it.

Take note of how long it takes for one to lose control and then find oneself in the front of the head or looking into the front of the head under the spell of the image maker.

This observation is vital. Over time, one will develop the power to resist the image maker.

Infused Energy Pitched into the Subtle Head

Breath infusion practice this morning was great with no reinstatement of the usual kundalini in the spine. For the first twenty minutes it was infused energy and kundalini flashes in the trunk and thighs of the subtle body. Energy fired left and right, up and down, with many colorful energy micro-pixels of light.

The trunk of the subtle body had this energy diffused evenly everywhere. No area had a special pleasure charge which was distinct or intensified in reference to any other area.

After that twenty minutes when the entire trunk and the thighs were saturated with energy, energy began to move through the shoulders and the fleshy part of the neck. This was like tiny pearl beads shimmering upwards with a bliss aspect.

When some energy moved through the neck in this way, there was a cool heat in the neck like if one rubbed a menthol cream.

As I did the infusion, Yogesh sent an instruction which read:

"Throw it in the head!"

This was an instruction to take the energy which reached the neck and pitch it into the head, the way with the throw of a hand one may pitch a coin a distance.

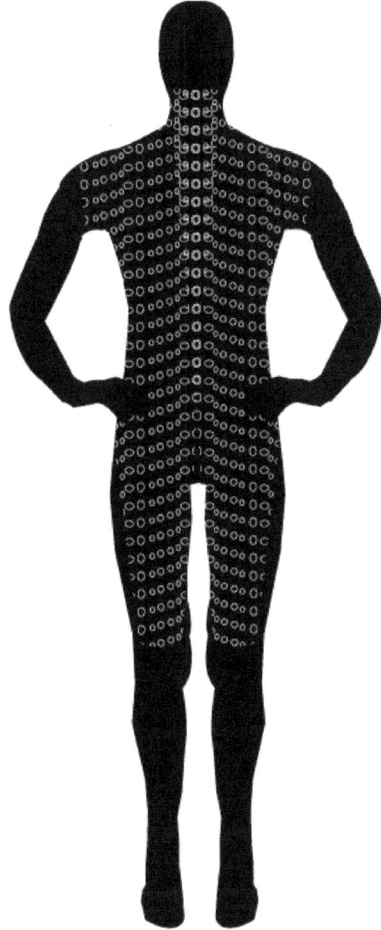

Doing this, I found that the energy went up in the head and then subsided as if one threw water in the air, where it rises and then gravity pulls it to the ground.

Subtle Body Configuration Changes

After taking help from two astral yogis, Tibeti Yogi and Yogeshwarananda, I made changes in the configuration of the subtle body, especially in the survival lifeForce mechanism, the kundalini.

In this method, having no more use for it, the *sushumna* nadi is cleared. The trunk of the subtle body is filled with astral lights of varied color due to the infused subtle energy.

Once this is achieved consistently, day after day for some time, the yogi gets the energy into the thighs. Usually in kundalini yoga, the interest is to get the energy into the head but this practice is contrary to that. The head is of no concern

The main concern is to cause the energy to get into the thighs. When that is achieved for some time, the yogi aims for getting the energy down to the ankles. When that is accomplished, he targets the toes.

The thighs, legs and feet become filled with fresh subtle energy. The polluted subtle force is expelled. This is not imagined or visualized but done by doing intensive breath infusion.

This morning soon after I began the infusion, about fifteen minutes into it, the infused energy into the toes fired through the body upwards through the legs and thighs. It ejected into the trunk like tiny coiled springs being jettisoned at a rapid rate with bliss sparklets being scattered through the trunk.

The big change is this:

Instead of reaching no further than the pubic area and dead-ending there, the energy was not attracted there. It went through the thigh into the right and left sides of the torso, not even being

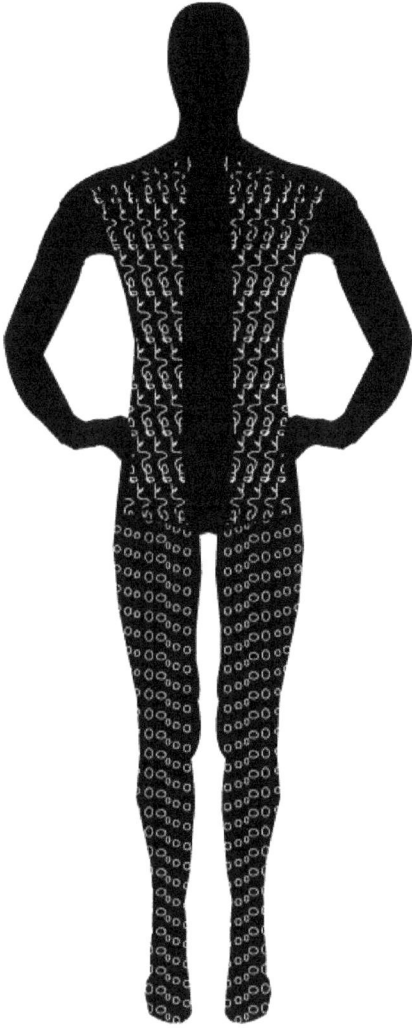

attracted to the pubic system, nor to the kundalini spinal system.

Kundalini's Creature Survival Calculus

Breath infusion practice is in a special phase where there is no kundalini system in the spine. The energy in the subtle body is random rather than being organized under the control of the kundalini lifeForce.

Of course, a yogi would be a fool to think that the kundalini is absent. Until one can forego the advantages of this creature existence, one should not indulge hair-raising ideas about eliminating kundalini. Without kundalini doing its creature survival calculus one would be in a lower species stuck somewhere as potential food for a predatory species. Kundalini rendered wonderful service to us individually to get us up the totem pole of material existence, where we dominate the other species from the platform of being human beings. It is exploitation for sure. It is vicious how we keep animals and plants for food, taking their life to maintain our own. But that is the game here. Play it expertly or perish.

And yet, a yogi must seriously consider giving up these hard-earned accomplishments while transmigrating through various species. In yoga in the advanced stages one should make the decision to do that, so as to be exempt from the survival game.

In yoga there are phases in practice where a former accomplishment loses prominence. One starts again with a new system, which at first seems chaotic.

I did a split body process which is when each half of the astral form arches around and up and make a curl in the direction of the head, remaining connected to the head. See a diagram below which is different to that posture but which is another astral arc posture.

split subtle body - astral practice

These astral poses come to mind as soon as the yogi removes the prominence of the sex pleasure function in the psyche.

During the meditation I made the effort to move naad to the frontal part of the subtle head. This was to gain control of that area putting it under the influence of naad. This washes out the compelling thought/image display which naturally flashes in the frontal region of the subtle head.

Taking Power from Kundalini

The pressure to sexually engage to provide an embryo comes from the kundalini energy. In a sense the yogi has nothing to do with it. It is independently engaged by the various kundalini forces in response to each other.

Even if the yogi is sincerely renounced, that will add up to nothing if the kundalini force is still present with survival needs. It is important to understand this intellectually. The core is not the kundalini which has totally different interests and is relentless in pursuing its aims.

It is important to study one's nature after getting some basic intellectual views about kundalini. By studying one's nature one can at least understand the percentage of power one has in the psyche. One can take up the task of increasing the coreSelf's authority and decreasing the kundalini's command over the physical and subtle bodies. Once a yogi sees that he is not in control and that the psychological adjuncts are dominant, he can plan to change the way the psyche operates.

If the rebellion fails one has nothing to lose. Some who decided to wrestle control from kundalini were taken to a psychiatric ward. The best plan is to keep the rebellion a secret so that even the kundalini, which is so dear, has no idea of the plan. Little by little, one should take power from kundalini.

Kundalini may not be rated as a person, as a self, but that does not in any way affect its control of the psyche. It has one thing going for it which is instinctual intelligence. It is sentient in that sense.

One person who ruthlessly suppressed kundalini was Gautama Buddha but he had a supreme determination which no limited entity can have. Another person who did the suppression but not as well as Buddha was Hiranyakashipu, who had ulterior motives. There was the boy Dhruva of Srimad Bhagavatam fame. He wanted universal control. When he got control of kundalini, he realized that his objectives were childish.

It is not possible to do what Buddha did because he is a Personality of Godhead. The value of his life is that it gives an inside view of what it would take to wrestle full control from kundalini. Taking hints from what he did one can avoid certain pitfalls and get ready for challenges from kundalini.

Cranium Light Kriya

Today I did a cranium light procedure. This was part of the tiny package which Tibeti Yogi left. In this practice with the subtle body split, with each half being connected only through the top of the cranium, energy is infused into the system while doing *bhastrika* pranayama in a downward thrust from the very top of the head.

There seems to be about a six-inch thrust of air while one does this. These are practices of the siddhas, which are designed to disrupt the reptilian nature of the kundalini.

Split Subtle Body / Tibeti Kriya

During breath infusion I realized that Tibeti Yogi had left a small package of instructions. This astral material was a tiny package wrapped in a small piece of paper which I was not to open. This was about one-inch square, wrapped in unprinted newsprint paper, tied with a silk cotton string.

The small package I opened today was fragrant with his energy. It was an instruction to do the splits. This meant completely splitting the energies from either side of the body. This process of Tibeti is the destruction of *sushumna* nadi and its related distribution.

The energy configuration from the toes up to the torso maintains its integrity and does not join at the inner thighs where the thighs meet the torso.

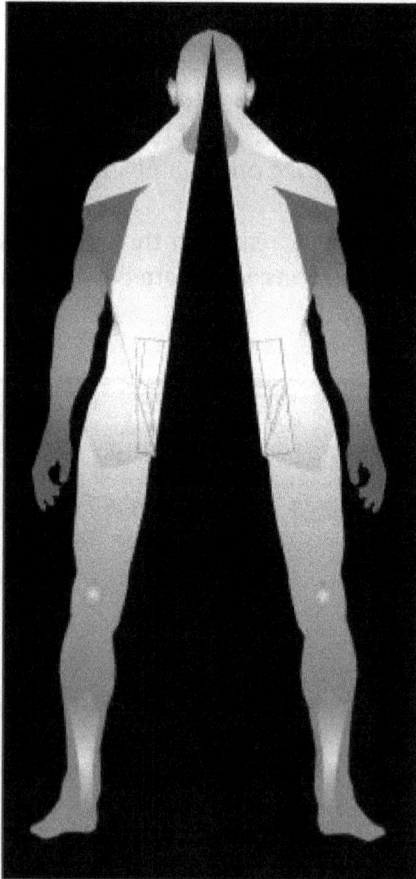

Tibeti's procedure for this is that one no longer allows the energy from the right thigh to merge and fuse at the genitals with that of the left thigh. Instead the energy fuses at the crown chakra top of the head. This means that the energy does not connect at any other points along the way from the toes to the crown.

Practice Method

The procedure is to do breath infusion as efficiently and tightly as you can. Then sit to meditate. This sitting to meditate should be immediately after the infusion session, with no break in time between the two.

One should check for two things:
- the effect of the infusion
- the location of naad sound

If there is an effect of the infusion observe it. Link to it

As soon as this effect subsides locate and link to naad sound.

Rectum in Higher Yoga

The rectum is important in higher yoga. If it does not operate as it should, it will cause the kundalini to be inefficient. It will make the kundalini remain attached to muladhara base chakra.

What to do if one is in old age and the rectum malfunctions beyond repair?

One must live with it but realize what its best condition should be. Perhaps when one gets the next body or in the afterlife, one may do something to change the behavior of this organ.

The rectum like the mouth is so important that to neglect it is a fool's way. The mouth is the entry gate. The rectum is the exit. If either malfunctions, one is distracted. Of course, we are more concerned with the mouth because it provides the pleasure of taste, the expression of speech and it helps with breathing. It even helps in the spectrum of sexual happiness.

The rectum?

Few care about that obnoxious part of the body?

In first steps to higher yoga, the rectum has importance. If waste can get to it as quickly as possible, and if it functions efficiently, it will collect and expel waste efficiently.

Left to its own devices, the kundalini will operate the lower intestines and the rectum which is collectively called the bowels. This means that the waste gases in the tissues are collected by the kundalini and used for operating some functions like jettisoning waste, urine and sexual fluids.

When by doing breath infusion or any other effective pranayama method, the waste gas is efficiently eliminated from the body, then what?

How will the rectum operate? How will the bowels process food efficiently? If the queen of a palace dismisses her chamber maid, who will sanitize the potty? Obviously, the queen will be inconvenienced. She is not familiar with menial tasks.

What happens when a yogi expels waste gases from the blood stream during breath infusion?

Then, the infused energy must do the evacuation but that happens only if the yogi works at supplying enough of it. In the natural system of letting the kundalini take waste gases from cells and use it for evacuation, no extra effort is required. But in the yogic method of using fresh air to help with evacuation, that will happen only if extra effort is applied doing much breath infusion to compress that fresh air into the trunk of the physical and subtle bodies.

Then the evacuation will be efficient. There will be less and less negative energy in the subtle body which will cause that form to be filled with more energizing astral energy, which in turn will enhance meditation and afford the yogi higher supernatural perceptions.

Evacuation / Meditation

Yogeshwarananda requested that I continue the first steps of higher yoga regardless of the success I would have with higher yoga. Higher yoga is *samyama* which are the three highest stages in one sequential progression as meditation.

Why bother with the first steps?

Why keep doing postures and breath infusion when one can meditate which is the ultimate objective?

For me the answer to this question is simply that I do it because I was instructed by a yoga guru.

A simple practice like the nauli stomach pumps combined with the agnisara abdomen infusion should be continued daily even if one advanced to higher meditation.

Why?

Because the system tries to regress. If one is inattentive, kundalini will reestablish its primitive habits. Slowly but surely kundalini will sneak back to the base chakra. It will reestablish its domain controlling digestion, hormone formulation, sexual excretion and waste formulation.

While the yogi is happily and confidently doing *samyama* or doing what he/she thinks is *samyama*, kundalini will again take the psyche downwards to the animal kingdom but this will not happen if one is attentive to the first steps to higher yoga during practice.

How much time per day should one meditate?

How much of that time can one switch and devote to an aggressive effort for completing with efficiency the first steps to higher yoga.

Let us take the example of evacuation. Using Western commodes, human beings sit to evacuate but that does not allow as efficient propulsion of the waste outwards as squatting. In using the advantage of modern toilets, we lost some propulsion power which we exerted while squatting and evacuating. We sit and wait. Sometimes nothing comes and we are helpless except to take laxatives and enemas.

How does this impact meditation?

Is there a connection between efficient evacuation and meditation?

What does higher meditation have to do with the physical body?

Use of Locks

The application of locks during the breath infusion is a practice for a student up to the stage when kundalini no longer has the inclination to remain at muladhara chakra.

There will come a time when kundalini will lose physical interest in this chakra. It will go up even when one does not practice. When this happens, the physical locks lose significance.

In a simple hydraulic system, there is no need to pull a liquid downwards. Gravity does that. There is only need to pull a liquid upwards to counteract gravity.

Thus, when the kundalini exhibits an anti-gravity attraction and comes up by itself and loses its downward tendency, the locks become redundant.

A yogi should be attentive to what happens in the subtle body. For instance, a student may be told to apply ashwini mudra anal sphincter muscle pull-up. He may do that physically with no corresponding subtle action. In contrast, an advanced student may have no sphincter muscle pull-up physically but may have the lock applied in the subtle body. Ultimately it is the subtle locks which are important.

Problems with Testes

Problems with pain in the testes which comes from semen in the tubes which connect with the testes, may be caused by a disease in the body or by lifting heavy objects. These causes have to be dealt with in a medical way. When however, there is pain in the tubes due to sexual agitation, the yogi should know the cause of the agitation and should avoid that association in the future.

If there is sexual agitation, fluids will flow from the testes towards the seminal vesicle, if these fluids keep flowing and are not emitted, that will cause pain because the tubes will swell.

Males who do not have female sexual partners and who expose themselves to sexual stimulation either through videos or by exposure to sexual suggestive objects, may get swollen tubes which cause pain in the groin and testes. The solution is to avoid the sexual associations.

Apana Removal / Strange Method

Yogeshwarananda shared details of a yoga siddha body which does not have the usual kundalini circuit of the subtle bodies which carry the mundane survival impulse in them and which always require the person to take rebirth in a physical species.

Of course, there are times in the universal break down when there are no opportunities for physical bodies and then what? When there is no species of life to enter or when the species one is adapted to is no longer manifested as in the case of many extinct lifeforms, what happens to a living entity who uses a subtle body which requires that type of physical form?

The problem with existing as a subtle body and not getting an opportunity for a physical one is the feeling of frustration. This in turn causes one to become desperate when one does get such a body. One likely, misbehaves or acts in a vicious way to fulfill the desire for physical life.

If one has a subtle body which needs physical forms for fulfillment, it is beneficial if one reduces the desperation when there are no physical species available either because the universe is scrapped physically or there are no suitable species forms due to extinction. But a greater accomplishment is to qualify for the yoga siddha body which has no need for a physical form corresponding to it.

Yogesh showed a system of subtle pollution energy withdrawal which is different to elementary kundalini yoga practice. In that system there is no kundalini circuit in the subtle body, no *sushumna* nadi. Instead when one looks down through the subtle body one sees nothing but spatial energy scattered like trillions of micro-pixels of multicolor.

When one does the breath infusion, the multicolor become transparent. At a certain point, it shows as a clear color, a see-thru translucent color.

In that subtle body there would be little pollution. The yogi pulls that energy up. It comes up like tiny bubbles rising from the bottom of a lake. As the yogi does the infusion, that pollution is extracted. There is no pushing down of the infused compressed force in order to pressure that energy to route through or around the groin area and hit muladhara chakra and then go up the spine into the brain. This is an advanced practice which one could do when one has mastered kundalini and removed the small-of-the-back blockage.

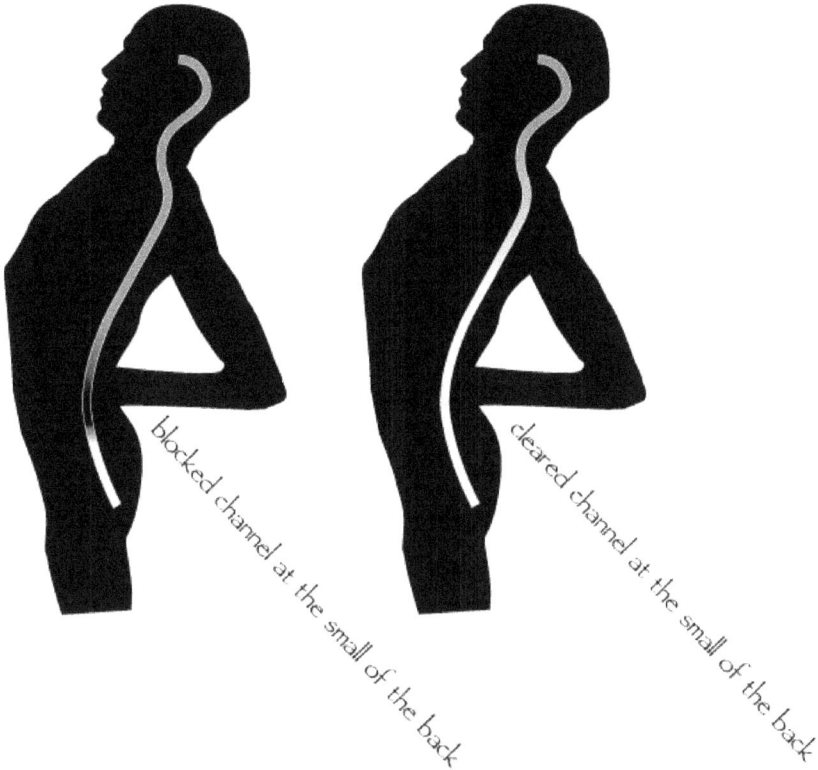

blocked channel at the small of the back

cleared channel at the small of the back

The micro-pixels are always in the subtle body but it is their quality of energy and configuration of shape which is of concern. If possible, the yogi should change the quality to a higher one. If they are heavy, that is not good because that indicates that the subtle body uses energy from a lower plane.

Through the breath infusion there should be a combustion of the heavier pixels and an increase in the proportion of the lighter pixels.

Doing the holding down of the ocular orbs is the classic and routine way of seeing these pixels. However sooner or later one should abandon this method and look down through the body using pranaVision and some other types of supernatural perception. The main one is pranaVision, but one should begin by using the ocular orbs because these are specifically designed to permit mystic sight.

pranaVision is the big event but it is subjective perception. It causes doubts in a student's mind as to whether it is imaginary or real.

Here is one verse which indicates the ocular perception between the eyebrows.

स्पर्शान्कृत्वा बहिर्बाह्यांश्

चक्षुश्चैवान्तरे भ्रुवोः ।

प्राणापानौ समौ कृत्वा

नासाभ्यन्तरचारिणौ ॥५.२७॥

sparśānkṛtvā bahirbāhyāṁś
cakṣuścaivāntare bhruvoḥ
prāṇāpānau samau kṛtvā
nāsābhyantaracāriṇau (5.27)

sparśān — *sensual contact; kṛtvā* — *having done; bahir = bahiḥ* — *external; bāhyāṁś = bāhyān* — *excluded; cakṣuścaivāntare = cakṣuḥ* — *visual focus + ca* — *and + (eva)* — *indeed + antare* — *in between; bhruvoḥ* — *of the two eyebrows; prāṇāpānau* — *both inhalation and exhalation; samau* — *in balance; kṛtvā* — *having made; nāsābhyantaracāriṇau = nāsa* — *nose + abhyantara* — *within + cāriṇau* — *moving*

Excluding the external sensual contacts, and fixing the visual focus between the eyebrows, putting the inhalation and exhalation in balance, moving through the nose. (Bhagavad Gita 5.27)

This is slightly different to using the ocular orbs which are two. Third eye vision is an univision but it is related because it occurs when the two ocular orbs are abandoned and their split ray becomes one ocular blast.

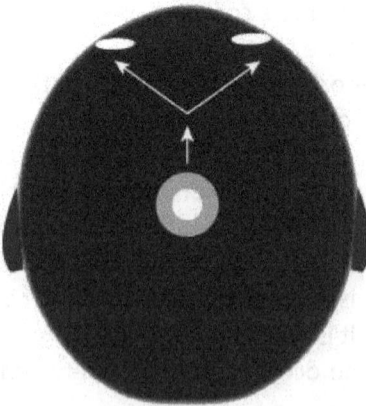

split optic energy   non-split uniVision

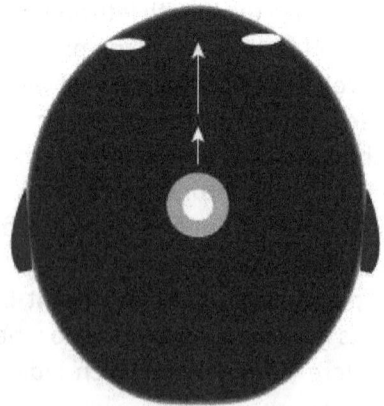

Physical nature endowed us with split vision. By her grace, we became addicted to that but as a yogi one should push on and abandon the grace. pranaVision is different because it is not a visual focus. One must practice it for some time and grope in the dark with it. Then it will become a solid means of perception.

The subtle body is based on this split vision but even though there are two eyes in the spiritual form, the spiritual body has nothing to do with the subtle one. In the spiritual form, the two eyes have no sharp focus like the two physical eyes. This is because all parts of the spiritual body are capable of vision.

To transfer into a spiritual body, one must come to the stage where one is completely dependent and trusting of pranavision.

Teaching Students of My Students

Recently a student solicited my help with someone who asked for assistance. More or less I refused to assist because this student who was asked by another person, should deal with the situation.

One idea which I convey is that I am not free to begin teaching at the behest of a student. I do not take teaching directions from students. If I show someone a technique which I learned from a particular teacher, that is done on behalf of that teacher and at the teacher's convenience.

I cannot proselyte students nor take students which my students attract.

If you attract a student you should care for that person. Why refer that someone to me.

If someone attracts students the attractor should teach those persons. If you find that you are not qualified to teach, you should desist. Hide from people so that you can practice more, read spiritual books, do more meditation and gain the advancement which will qualify you as a teacher.

I cannot take a student based on the desire of my students. That is insensible. I take students based on the desire of advanced yogis who want me to serve their behest while I have this body.

Preliminary Kundalini

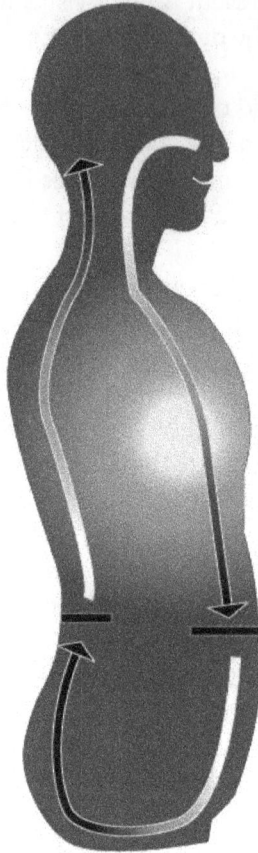

This diagram above was shown by Yogeshwarananda. The explanation is in the diagram below. This completes the neophyte stage of kundalini yoga, which though it may take years to complete is the beginner's achievement.

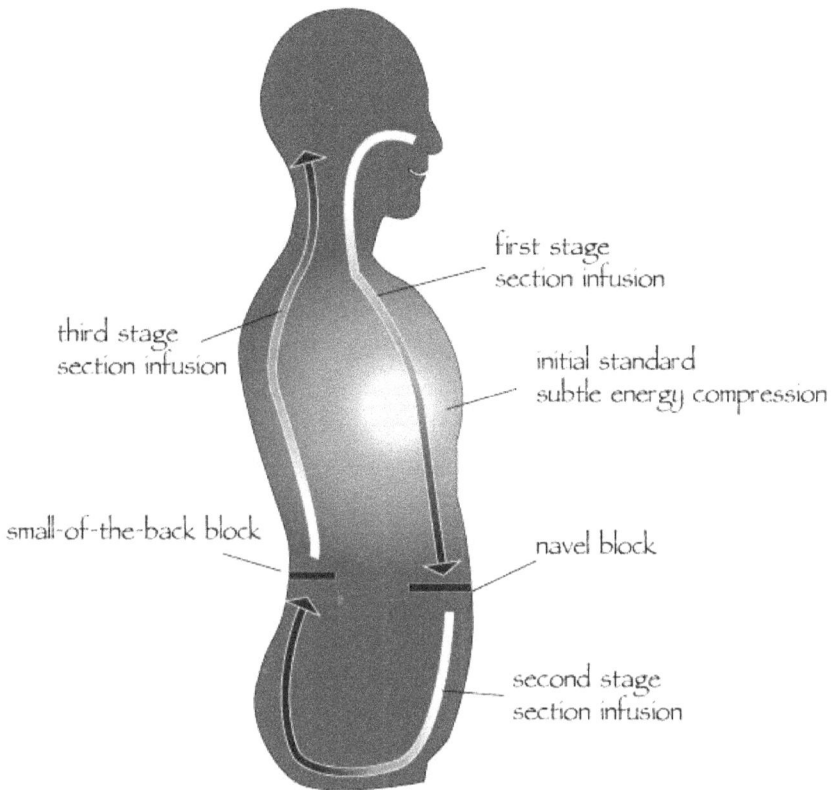

first stage
section infusion

third stage
section infusion

initial standard
subtle energy compression

small-of-the-back block

navel block

second stage
section infusion

In the diagram there are two blocks. The first is the navel block. Until the student bores through it, shattering its power and causing it to disintegrate, he/she must confront this block repeatedly. It must be shattered and diffused on the molecular level. This may be compared to using a nuclear explosive rather than using dynamite.

In dynamite there are many fragments going there, demolishing anything which does not have enough hardness to resist it, but with nuclear substance, there are no fragments left; even on the molecular level there is disintegration.

Initially the student will attack the navel block using a compaction process but after repeatedly challenging that block the student will go nuclear and will have lasting success. Otherwise the resistance is reestablished daily soon after the student practices.

In the second block which is the *small of the back* block, the yogi learns that the psyche is designed to stop the kundalini from ascending beyond the *small of the back*. There is a choke-hold which stops the kundalini energy from rising through this point. The student experiences the release of this choke-hold when suddenly kundalini penetrates and goes into the brain. That causes a black out, white out or gold out. Soon after kundalini retreats to the base chakra. It leaves the student with the usual lower consciousness as before.

While dong *bhastrika* pranayama if the student is not vigilant and does not efficiently apply the neck lock, stomach lock, sex lock, anus lock and mind lock, if the student bends the spine in a certain way even accidentally, kundalini will, on occasion, rush through this block. That will cause loss of control of the physical body.

However sooner or later, the student will master this. Eventually he will eliminate this block so that kundalini comes into the head at every moment and does not linger below this block with a reserve energy for sexual intercourse and/or reproduction of the species.

The first stage infusion is the initial stage of kundalini yoga. It may take months, or years even, to master this. This concerns focusing the inhaled subtle energy at the navel.

The second stage infusion is when energy passes behind the navel and is accumulated in the public area. It passes to the base chakra and moves to the *small of the back* block. The student should regulate this. If he/she fails the sex drive will increase. The yogi may become a sex maniac. This is because the accumulated energy must be used in some way. If the small-of-the-back block is not penetrated, the energy will pressure in the downward direction which will cause sexual enthusiasm. This will make the student become a phony tantric yogi, who having failed to transmute sexual energy rationalizes that the excessive sexual pleasure is rightly justified.

The third stage infusion is when the energy passes the *small of the back* block. Once this is attained the student is on his/her way to higher yoga. The pleasure vices, which the lower chakras sponsor, are no longer predominant. The yogi comes under the influence of the siddhas.

The initial standard breath compression is the holding area of the lungs. This is the initial compression. The yogi must command this place to distribute the accumulated breath through the subtle body.

Assistance from Shiva

When subduing the sex drive, a yogi should settle with the ancestors as indicated in the *sex you!* book.

Even though kundalini will again subside and descend to its grotto at muladhara chakra, the yogi should bore through the spine so that kundalini bursts into the head at least once per day.

Study the attachment to sex attraction by understanding the advantage which it affords and the pleasure energy which it generates.

Admit that one fights a losing battle against sex potency. If one is continuously challenged by it, one must at some point indulge. This will cause one to take more shelter of advanced yogis and supernatural beings like Shiva. Stop chanting *Shivoham (Shivah Aham)* which means *I am Shiva* or *I am like Shiva*. The truth is that one is not like Shiva because one does not have the power to snap off the penis and discard it. One cannot resist females as much as Shiva. The only way out is to take help from the real God who is Shiva. With his help one can muster the resistance, otherwise one must indulge. The appropriate mantra is *jivoham (jivah aham)* which means I am a limited self. One cannot escape from this prison by oneself. One must be assisted by Shiva.

Soft Bones in Pranayama Practice

Yogeshwarananda had me work on what he termed as the soft bones in the body. That is the intestinal track of tubes which processes food.

The great yogi considered this as the soft bones in contrast to the bones in the body which are mineral structures which produce bone marrow. In diseases like leukemia, the bones malfunction, the person becomes anemic. The blood no longer serves the purpose of providing energy to operate the body. The person feels pooped both physically and psychologically because the subtle body which is the composite psychology is affected due to de-energizing subtle energy.

During this session, Yogesh showed how to directly infuse the intestines. This is a specific breath infusion practice. It consists of introspectively reaching inside near the center of the coiled apparatus, and then infusing energy through the intestinal tubes so that the heavy negative energy is extracted.

When this is done one feels heavy dark energy at the intestinal mass. This converts into a globule of dense energy. It rises. Before it reaches the center of the chest it disappears.

In a yoga siddha subtle body there is no counterpart of the intestinal tubes. Thus, in the subtle body one must burn-blast this zone out of existence. If this system remains, one will inevitably take another embryo since the kundalini will feel the need for physical nutrients and will be attracted to the survival existence world where it can procure that.

When Kundalini is Made to Dance

Buddhi lila is intellectual activity, even the impulsive or compulsive types, even absentmindedness or subconscious activity. Kundalini lila is emotional sensual activities, deliberately induced or spontaneously occurring.

Kundalini being a psychic mechanism cannot be commanded fully by any limited self. By controlling its air/energy supply an indirect method is used to defeat it. It is influenced by the type and quantity of air/energy it ingests.

This is similar to starving a rebel king by controlling his food supply. Kundalini is hemmed in from all sides just as medieval kings were by building a wall around their cities and by having a wide moat outside the walls.

But there is a flaw in the ancient design which is that the king and his subjects only have a stockpile of food which will last for a certain number of weeks or months. By kumbhak breath retention one can kill the body. Some yogis use that method to junk an old body. However, because a student needs the help of the body to continue the spiritual discipline it does him no good to kill the body.

If the subtle body is not reformed before passing from the physical form, death puts the student at a disadvantage where he/she cannot control the subtle body when it has no physical form.

Kites need tails, or weighted ends, for stability. Without a tail the kite will cant in the wind and crash to the ground. The unreformed non-siddha subtle body needs to have a physical one for stability

If the student develops a yoga siddha subtle form, there is no need for a corresponding physical system. Then, he/she can do kumbhak breath retention control to kill the physical system, junking it. Hurrah for that yogi!

For others that is not a solution. To get kundalini controlled, the student should use the roundabout method of controlling the air intake of kundalini. By manipulating its air supply, the yogi can have fun watching kundalini dance when it is subjected to breath infusion practice.

In the conditioned state, the coreSelf must dance every time the kundalini expresses an urge. When the student finds an effective breath infusion method, the roles switch. The yogi becomes happy seeing that, kundalini must be subordinate.

Who is involved in this?

It is only the coreSelf and its kundalini which is involved. These are two of the principal components in the psyche of an individual living being. It does not concern others. It is inside the psyche.

Part 3

Neck *Sushumna*

Sushumna nadi as it is described in yogic lore corresponds to the central spinal column. It is not a physical channel. It is in the subtle body. When kundalini rises, it is preferred if it travels through this central channel and not be on one side or the other in an imbalance. Now however I use a process where the *sushumna* nadi is absent. The entire neck functions as one nadi channel.

In this experience, the same quantity of energy passes up from the trunk of the subtle body into the head of the form. When it passes it does so with less concentration due to being spread through the wider channel of the neck as compared to passing in a tiny passage in the central spine in the neck.

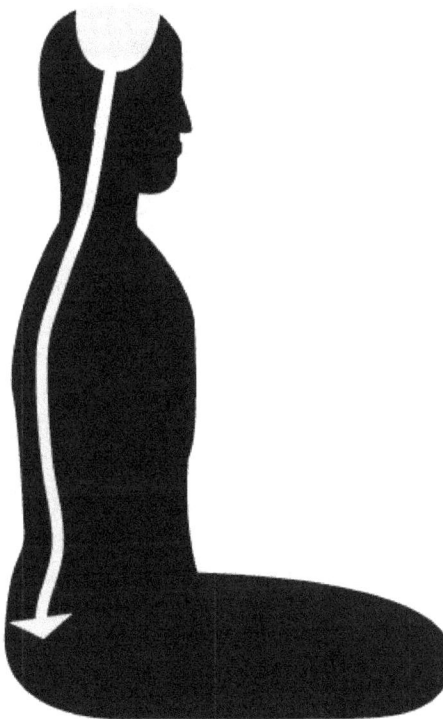

sushumna passage kundalini
through neck

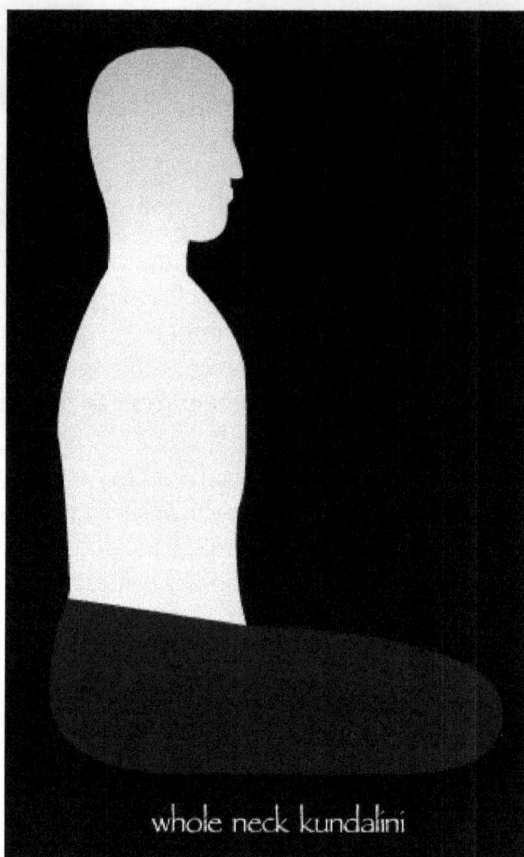

whole neck kundalini

This has a divergent bliss aspect which is like many tiny pixels of multi-colored bliss force. For kundalini to pass through the tiny *sushumna* passage, it needs infused concentrated energy. It bores its way through the tiny *sushumna* passage into the head. But in this practice the excess infused energy which is in the trunk of the subtle body overflows upwards through the neck and then enters the head.

Another difference is that when kundalini enters the head after boring its way through the *sushumna* nadi it usually fires energy to the intellect and the *brahmrandra* crown chakra. This causes a black out, white out or gold out. Later, like a serpent retreating backwards into its hole kundalini subsides and descends the spine.

When the neck itself is the channel, kundalini enters the head but it does not target the intellect or the *brahmrandra*. Instead it goes on either side of the head, up to the ears. From there it either retreats or it floods the entire head evenly without focus on *brahmrandra*.

This kundalini which is diffused evenly is not the same as the kundalini which uses the *sushumna*. It is instead infused energy. It does not have the survival characteristic of the traditional kundalini.

Relaxing the Grip on Pleasure

One hard-to-reach place in the subtle body for pulling out dull energy and replacing it with energizing energy, is the two sides of the trunk of the body. Due to a strong focus on the spine and brain for raising kundalini, many areas are neglected by the yogi. In fact, the need for pleasure is so great that a yogi gets crazy about raising kundalini in order to feel bliss or to get relief from stress.

The demand for pleasure is so intrinsic that it is an effort to integrate into and understand it. For instance, when one has a craving for sweet food, one will do whatever is necessary to justify overeating that. At some point a yogi must step out of the ring and decide to go it alone abandoning these addictions and the justifications which are required to continue unwanted habits.

After kundalini was raised over and over, again and again, each day of practice, and when the student can do so in a jiffy, there comes a time when the need for the pleasure energy no longer asserts itself. Then the yogi sees the neglected parts of the psyche.

Because he relaxed the grip on the pleasure need, his attention shifts to other areas. A new practice of breath infusion begins with the polluted areas as the new targets.

In practice this morning my attention was brought to infused bliss energy rising in each side of the subtle body, going into the shoulders and then running upwards from the armpits to where the shoulders meet the neck. I assisted this energy by infusing subtle breath energy down the center of the body to the floor of the trunk from where it gushed in a loop and came up the side into the armpits and shoulders.

Once the energy hit the armpits, it was like tiny pixels of mild bliss force saturating the shoulders.

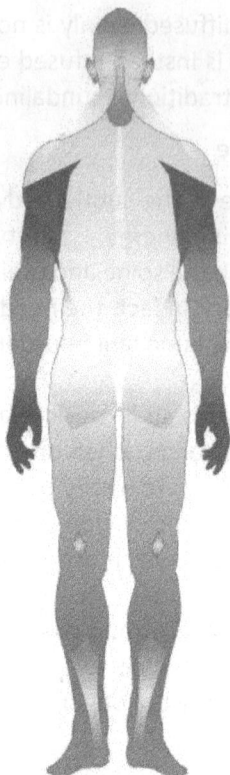

A Foothold in Siddhaloka

This morning breath infusion and meditation were routine. I worked on the base area of the subtle body. I worked on the feet, legs, fingers and forearms. These are hard to reach areas which are usually neglected as yogis focus on raising kundalini into the brain. Sooner or later a yogi is confronted with the fact that even if kundalini is raised to *brahmrandra*, if other areas of the psyche remain with low-grade astral energy, the impurities will cause a return to the lower planes of existence after there is an experience of brahmananda or spiritual bliss.

The way out is to get a method for confronting the low-grade astral energy through which one can effectively (not by imagination or visualization) expel that energy and replace it with high grade subtle energy from higher planes.

If in the subtle body, all parts are elevated before the death of the physical form, the yogi will access the siddhaloka realms where the mahayogins reside. Going there in the afterlife the student can get further instructions about securing a foothold in the spiritual atmosphere.

As a psyche, the subtle body itself is a whole domain, an environment or living space.

As a subtle body, it is used to explore a domain which is external to itself, the so-called astral world.

A subtle body is a psyche, a system with components, one of which is a coreSelf or spirit person.

Transport to Higher Dimensions

There are some factors which are required before a yogi may transit to higher dimensions permanently. Here is a list:

- association with advanced yogis on the physical and/or the astral planes.
- information from reliable yoga books like *Bhagavad Gita* and *Yoga Sutras*.
- valid yoga practice which yields the result intended.
- experience of the astral world in astral projections.
- association with advanced yogis on the physical and/or astral planes.

If one can find an advanced yogi who currently uses a physical body, that is the easiest and most definite course. Still that course is not as easy as it seems because one must submit for training under that person's tutelage. That submission is not easy. It is hampered by social obligations which may prohibit one from the association. One may be unable to relocate. One may not have the time to devout to the association because of having to generate an income for family support and other obligations.

The most difficult part is to find a yogi in the astral world who is advanced. There are many such yogis but finding them is a task. First, unless such a yogi wants to give association to a certain person, that yogi cannot be found by that person. It is not like in physical existence where if I am located at an address, you can find me there. Physically there is no way that I can transit my body into any other dimension. It remains locked into this three-dimensional world.

In the astral world if I am at a certain address and you travel there to locate me, I can give you the slip by lowering or enhancing the vibrational rate of my subtle body. It is difficult to locate superior yogis because they have the power of invisibility.

How do I locate them?

I do not. My secret is that they locate me. If the student raises the vibration of his subtle body, a yogi from a higher plane may notice and may communicate to render assistance.

To reach a great yogin, one should practice whatever discipline that person taught. As one advances that teacher will sense the improvement and may come to one's aid. This could happen even if one follows instructions from a book written by a great yogin, even if the person was deceased for hundreds or thousands of years.

The reading of books which were written by or about senior yogis or the supreme person Krishna or the supreme person Shiva, is required in most cases. There are exceptions of persons who had no access to such books and who made the progress to siddhaloka anyway. For instance, there were Taoist masters in China who did so.

The books do a double assistance: as a map and as a source of morale for disheartened yogis who face great opposition from people who are against the required austerities.

As a map these books give the yogi a sense of direction and alert about what he/she should experience during practice. Without confidence one cannot make advancement. These books can give faith to a yogi who is bogged down by social resistance which penetrates his/her mind from others who are adverse to yoga.

Valid yoga practice which yields the result intended.

A yogi must have a valid process which will yield the intended results. If one does not have this, one will spend weeks, months or years cultivating methods which cause disappointment.

The first thing one should admit is that whatever process one uses, if it was not mastered before by anyone, it will not succeed. This is because the human psyche is the same now as it was from the first instance of humans being manifested on this planet. Essentially, the layout of the subtle body is the same. The method for freedom is the same.

There is however many variations and novel ways in which a person enters into the discipline but at some point, it becomes streamlined. The course charted in the *Yoga Sutras* and *Bhagavad Gita*, must be followed.

There can be exceptions to this like for instance someone goes to spiritual perfection just by the grace of a deity (Krishna, Shiva, Devi) but you have to be sure that you were singled out for that. If you were not selected, it is in your interest to endeavor and assume the disciplines which were suggested by Krishna, Shiva or Brahma.

Once the deity makes it clear that you should strive, asking for grace is futile. Uddhava is a case of a person who asked for that but who was told by Krishna to do austerities at Badrinath.

In the Anu Gita, when Arjuna asked for a live replay of the Universal Form experience and the infusement of supernatural energy, he was upbraided by

Krishna, who refused to again indulge Arjuna. Arjuna and his brothers had to practice aggressively in the end by resuming the austerities which they left aside while enjoying the luxurious royal life.

My life is an example of yogi who got the grace of the deity in the form of instructions to complete the austerities. Grace is not always an energy for easy transit. Sometimes grace comes as an inspiration for endeavor.

Experience of the astral world in astral projections.

A yogin does not have to master astral projection or be an expert at *out of the body experience* (OBE). The accomplishment of the yogi is to be aware when the astral projection takes place.

In psychic practice, mastery of astral projection is a must but in yoga, the yogi must gain mastery of objective awareness when astral projection takes places. Take the example of a train. There should be a conductor in the first section, the engine body. Then there should be passengers in the powerless carriages.

The psychic people want to take the position of the conductor. A yogi has no interest in that. There is already a conductor of astral projection which is the kundalini. The yogi will let the kundalini perform its function, while the yogi stays alert as a passenger.

A yogi's concern with the conductor (kundalini) is with its training and inclination. The yogi does kundalini yoga to achieve control over the conductor. In time the yogi develops the authority to say this to the conductor,

"You can perform tasks but only in my interest. Do not take the train to locations which are contrary to my aims."

Kundalini however is a wayward force. It will not do what anyone says, even the coreSelf, unless that core mastered kundalini yoga by any which means.

Funnel Chakra

Breath infusion practice today was productive, one special event was a funnel shaped chakra which pointed downwards. This is the lung chakra which is on the spine. When seen visually this chakra is shaped like a funnel which points downwards. As it operates it sends a wave motion downwards through the chakras on the spine which are below it.

In operating this chakra with breath infusion, the infused energy which is compressed in the action of rapid breathing, moves downward in a wave motion and then draws up energy from the lower trunk of the subtle body.

From time to time while doing breath infusion one may as one looks down through the subtle body, see various chakras, but the form and configuration, colors and vibrations of these, may not correspond to what is written in the classic literature.

In some experiences there would be correlation with the literature however. It is best to jot notes of these experiences and draw diagrams showing the location of a perception.

Nonyogic Association

Expect that any nonyogic association will produce a downgrade in practice. Yogic association from advanced persons will produce an upgrade. This includes mental or psychic association as well as physical relation. Teach the mind how to make physical association with non-yogic people, superficial, so that the mind does not make strong impressions when in contact with such folk.

There are so many things which the student must do. God will not do everything for anyone. Nor will the yoga guru. Advice will be provided. Example will be set. Methods must be demonstrated but that is all one will get from God and guru. Guru cannot uplift anyone permanently unless that effort is reinforced by the student's sincere endeavor. Some students complain that God or Guru does little but they are reluctant to put the best foot forward in practice. And yet, if one follows a student for say a week one will discover that in other areas of the life, that person puts the best foot forward.

Why does the student cry for help from God or guru, when the real problem is not the lack of assistance but the unwillingness to exert in the direction of progress? Besides, when the student does have the power to practice, he may use that energy in another area of the lifestyle?

The answer to this is that the student is under more than one influence. A particular influence prevails and uses the student's exertion power to further its ends.

Being under the influence of a yoga guru is not everything. It is only part of the range of influences which prevail. In the privacy of one's mind, of one's emotions, of one's psyche, one should investigate and see what it is which confiscates and uses the exertion power.

In many instances God cannot help and the guru can do even less, simply because the student does not invest in himself/herself. The student's action reduces/prevents the divine grace.

Managing Lust

Whatever one eats certainly will form into sex hormones which will provoke lusty expression and attraction. However, even if one gets the diet under control, so long as the subtle body has the tendency to store energy for sexual expression, it will be inclined to lust. Even one grain of sugar can cause the tongue to remember previous sugar binges and drive the psyche into craving.

Never think that only a little lust is safe and only much of it is dangerous. A little is the friend of much. A little is the gateway to much.

Before I took this present body, in the last physical body in India, I completely curbed lust but when I took this body, just by contact with the people from whom I got the embryo, I again resumed the lusty interest with such a force, that it took over forty years to come to terms with it.

Recently someone asked for the reason of forty years. In the *Bhagavad Gita*, Arjuna asked about it.

अर्जुन उवाच

अथ केन प्रयुक्तोऽयं

पापं चरति पूरुषः ।

अनिच्छन्नपि वार्ष्णेय

बलादिव नियोजितः ॥ ३.३६ ॥

arjuna uvāca
atha kena prayukto'yam
pāpam carati pūruṣaḥ
anicchannapi vārṣṇeya
balādiva niyojitaḥ (3.36)

arjuna — Arjuna; uvāca — said; atha — then; kena — by what?; prayukto = prayuktaḥ — forced; 'yam = ayam — this; pāpam — evil; carati — commits; pūruṣaḥ — a person; anicchannapi = anicchan — unwilling + napi (api) — even; vārṣṇeya — family man of the Vṛṣṇis; balād = balāt — from force; iva — as if; niyojitaḥ — compelled

Arjuna said: Then explain, O family man of the Vṛṣṇis, by what is a person forced to commit an evil unwillingly, just as if he were compelled to do so? (Bhagavad Gita 3.36)

श्रीभगवानुवाच

काम एष क्रोध एष

रजोगुणसमुद्भवः।

महाशनो महापाप्मा

विद्धेनमिह वैरिणम् ॥३.३७॥

śrībhagavānuvāca

kāma eṣa krodha eṣa

rajoguṇasamudbhavaḥ

mahāśano mahāpāpmā

viddhyenamiha vairiṇam (3.37)

śri bhagavān — the Blessed Lord; uvāca — said; kāma — craving; eṣa — this; krodha — anger; eṣa — this; rajoguṇasamudbhavaḥ = rajo (rajaḥ) — passion + guṇa — emotion + samudbhavaḥ — source; mahāśano (mahāśanaḥ) = mahā — great + aśana — consuming power; mahāpāpmā = mahā — much + pāpmā — damage; viddhyenam = viddhi — recognize + enam — this; iha — in this case; vairiṇam — enemy

The Blessed Lord said: This force is craving. This power is anger. The passionate emotion is the source. It has a great consuming power and does much damage. Recognize it as the enemy in this case. (Bhagavad Gita 3.37)

धूमेनाव्रियते वह्निर्

यथादर्शो मलेन च ।

यथोल्बेनावृतो गर्भस्

तथा तेनेदमावृतम् ॥३.३८॥

dhūmenāvriyate vahnir

yathādarśo malena ca

yatholbenāvṛto garbhas

tathā tenedamāvṛtam (3.38)

dhūmenāvriyate = dhūmena — by smoke + āvriyate — is obscured; vahnir = vahniḥ — the sacrificial fire; yathā — similarly; 'darśo = ādarśaḥ — mirror;

malena — with dust; ca — and; yatholbenāvṛto = yatholbenāvṛtaḥ = yatho (yatha) — similarly + ulbena — by skin + āvṛtaḥ — is covered; garbhaḥ — embryo; tathā — so; tenedam = tena — by this + idam — this; āvṛtam — is blocked

As the sacrificial fire is obscured by smoke, and similarly as a mirror is shrouded by dust or as an embryo is covered by skin, so a man's insight is blocked by the passionate energy. (Bhagavad Gita 3.38)

आवृतं ज्ञानमेतेन

ज्ञानिनो नित्यवैरिणा ।

कामरूपेण कौन्तेय

दुष्पूरेणानलेन च ॥ ३.३९॥

āvṛtaṁ jñānametena

jñānino nityavairiṇā

kāmarūpeṇa kaunteya

duṣpūreṇānalena ca (3.39)

āvṛtam — is adjusted; jñānam — discernment; etena — by this; jñānino = jñāninaḥ — educated people; nityavairiṇā = nitya — eternal + vairiṇā — by the enemy; kāmarūpeṇa = kāma — yearning for various things + rūpeṇa — by the sense or form of; kaunteya — son of Kuntī; duṣpūreṇānalena = duṣpūreṇa — is hard to satisfy + analena — by fire; ca — and

The discernment of educated people is adjusted by their eternal enemy which is the sense of yearning for various things. O son of Kuntī, the lusty power, is as hard to satisfy as it is to keep a fire burning. (Bhagavad Gita 3.39)

Resuming Progress from the Previous Life

All social concerns will vanish for the time being when one loses this specific body. When one assumes another body in the same or in another family, things would have changed. One will again get involved and will again struggle in the practice.

A yogi who was advanced in previous lives, may quickly resume the practice and continue progressing from where it stopped in the previous life, but it is likely that he will struggle to resume the practice. Negative associations may impede him.

Some yogis resume the progress. Others do not. It hinges on the amount of contamination one acquires in the interim period in the astral world and also what happens in the birth environment. Usually the digression occurs in the birth environment when the yogi absorbs the influence of relatives. He must deal with negative influences in schools and elsewhere.

One can make an assessment of the degree of contamination by trying to go back to the past life in the subconscious. If one is unable to do this, it means that the contamination is major.

Subtle Body Energy Distribution

This morning for about thirty seconds for the most, Tibeti Yogi was on the psychic side. His form was barely visible being extremely subtle and made of a high-quality astral energy. He came when I infused breath energy into the base chakra sacral region. His remark was this:

"Tackle that area. Demolish it. Clear light only. All density removed."

This was in reference to the work which must be done in the base chakra to demolish and remove its density.

Yogeshwarananda sent a message.

"Small of the back removed. No reason for it. No reason to store that. Let it flow day and night. No accumulation."

That was in reference to the sex hormone energies which are formed and then stored in various parts of the body for sexual involvement.

Once the yogi removes these storage capacities, the energy flows freely and evenly through the entire subtle form. There is no more reservoir of sex hormones. The yogi becomes free of the distractions which involved using that stored energy. Consciousness becomes even and does not jolt after sensual interest.

The subtle body loses memories of favorite sensual enjoyments. It remains evenly functioning. Areas of the subtle body which were dull before loses the dense energy content while those areas which were bright before are no longer in contract to the dull areas. The subtle body becomes homogenously infused.

Success with Patanjali Yoga

The three main obstacles in breath infusion practice are the front navel region, the pubic area and the base chakra. If these places are cleared, meaning that if the heavy astral energy is removed, yoga can be practiced in earnest in terms of the second sutra of Patanjali which is a request for stopping the vritti vibrational modes of the intellect and the kundalini.

Of the five vibrational modes, two are especially challenging. These are memory and sleep. The other three are easy to tackle and target because those are realized as operations of the intellect. Those three are:

- correct perception
- incorrect perception
- imagination

If the intellect is conquered, these three will cease in one stroke but that still leaves the other two which are memory and sleep. Though memory is not stored in the intellect it is displayed by the intellect. If the intellect is silenced, then for the want of an illustrator, the memory is disabled. It will still be there but it will be dormant or subconscious.

Sleep is controlled and operated by the kundalini. That makes it necessary to do kundalini yoga to monitor the sleep impulse.

Breath infusion if done efficiently in the subtle body causes the accomplishments of kundalini treatment, memory suspension and intellect shut down and then Patanjali's request for stopping the vrittis of the mind can become a reality at least in the meditation one does immediately after a thorough breath infusion.

The frontal navel area, the pubic zone and the sacral regions of the subtle body must be conquered before one can make a claim about mastering the Patanjali meditation process. If these areas are not cleared of dense astral energy, one cannot quell the vibrational modes of the mind. In which case, these areas will continue to sponsor the disturbances no matter what one visualizes, hopes for or imagines.

Trying to control the vrittis by will power or visualization or imagination or by grace of Whoever, is a questionable procedure because Patanjali gave eight parts to the yoga system. All parts are necessary as far as I can see.

Head Infusion

Meditation yesterday was good except for little ability to note anything. Presently I am in Chicago where I will be for another week. This environment is somewhat negative in its effects on practice.

Breath infusion was great with a dry cool energy rising under the shoulders, then expanding into cool tiny droplets of bliss energy. I pushed on until the trunk of the body was filled, as well as the thighs, legs and feet, then I focused on the fingers, forearm and arm. When this was properly saturated, the energy over-flowed into the neck where it was like scattered random micro tit bits of varied colors with a bliss rendering influence.

The head was infused but while when kundalini rise fully through the central spine, it came into the head and struck the intellect and the *brahmrandra* crown chakra and caused a gold-out. This practice caused the entire head to be infused with tiny light crystals. The crown chakra was not specifically distinguished.

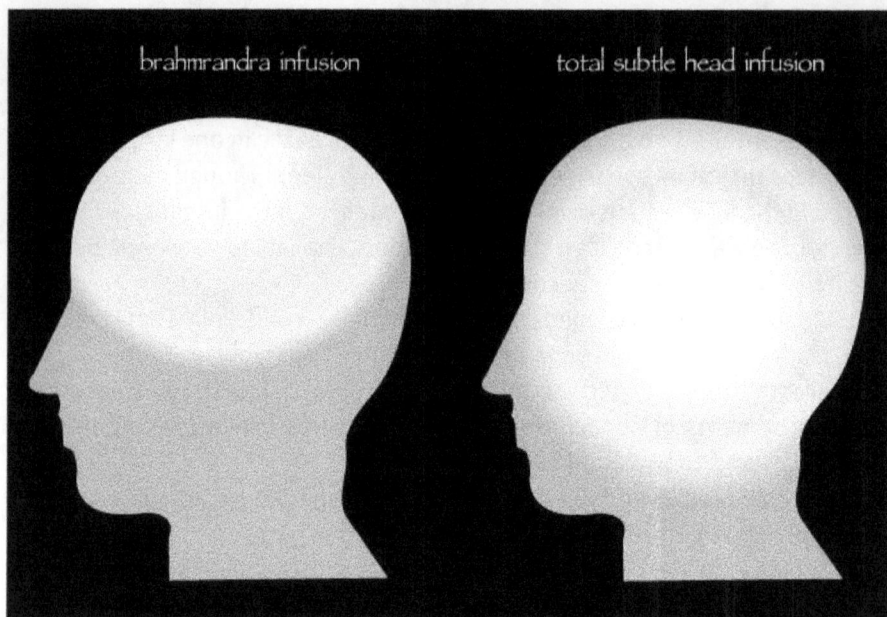

brahmrandra infusion   total subtle head infusion

Criterion on Teaching Yoga

As a teacher, I instruct in two ways. Sometimes these methods are distinct. Sometimes they are mixed. It depends on the stage of the student and the influence which prevails.

The methods are:

- teaching for a teacher who mastered a particular method or technique and who empowered me to teach on his behalf.
- teaching particular methods which I pioneered.

I prefer to teach one on one but on occasion I teach multiple students at once.

Kundalini Yoga is technical. Advanced meditation must be precisely tailored to the existential situation of the student. In a general class a teacher instructs to benefit those present. The best method is to teach students individually.

Yoga is an education too. Various levels require various disciplines and attention levels from the students.

Lalata Chakra

A throbbing light in the forehead above the line of vision, which recedes like the horizon when one tries to shift focus to it, is the lalata chakra. This may flicker like a spotlight but in bright white only, not colored.

The definite way to know this chakra, is that if you attempt to shift your attention upwards, it will shift upwards the same amount so that you cannot see it. It is rarely seen directly because it is similar to the lights miners wear which are strapped to their foreheads. If the miner raises the head, the light raises as well.

Now there is another thing to look for which is the intellect orb which is also a light if you get into the right level of consciousness to perceive it. That does not move like the lalata chakra.

Sometimes if you are in a dark room and a light is suddenly turned on, especially early in the morning, you will see the flickering white light of the lalata chakra.

The intellect organ appears midway between the centralized coreSelf and the third eye area, but it is rarely seen. Because it distracts one from deep meditation, focus on it is even more important than third eye focus.

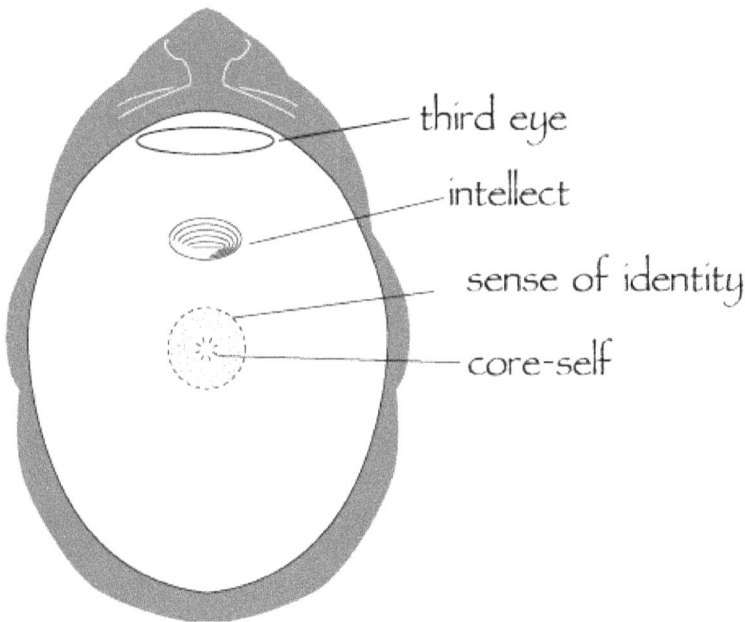

third eye

intellect

sense of identity

core-self

The Argument about Celibacy

This morning Yogeshwarananda showed two procedures which have to do with an advanced stage of celibacy. These are beyond celibacy but may be considered as more completion of celibacy. It does explain how the yoga siddha bodies transcend sex attraction for coupling of sexual organs.

Yogeshwar used to discuss having a genital just for urination and not for sexual expression. The question arises about the use of such an organ if it is designed only for urination.

Actually, this question did not arise in my mind before puberty. At that time, I never thought that the organ should be used for anything other than urination. Before puberty, the organ did not demand sexual involvement.

Sometimes when I recommend to young men that they should seriously consider retiring the organ from sex, they regard it as a very hard instruction. It seems that I do not consider the organ's demands. That may be, but if one uses the organ to the max, then one should not cry later for help when one is caught in the trap of the responsibility in a disagreeable situation.

In the Puranas, there is the story about how Lord Shiva snapped his genital organ. He threw it aside when he knew that other supernatural beings divested the physical species by propagating human beings before Shiva was prepared for that. Seeing that there were many people in the physical world, Shiva said to himself,

"What is the use of this? They already filled the creation. More children are unnecessary, I have no use for this organ."

One may wonder what the God thought. Did he not see that he should use the organ for sexual pleasure? Did he feel that the organ was only useful for sex if it produced progeny?

Yogesh showed an arc point which is where the two sides of the body connect due to the difference in polarity. They arc across the pubis symphysis gristle tendon. There is a current which arcs and stimulates sexual needs.

What happens in yoga practice is that if one is successful at dissipating the sexual energy there comes a time when one can break this arc point so that the energy no longer bridges.

First one should achieve full urdhvareta status. This means that one's sexual hormones are no longer routed for genital use. Instead, it ascends through the trunk of the subtle body. The initial stage of this accomplishment is when the energy moves from the sexual area, to the base chakra and then goes up the spine into the head.

Later the achievement changes. The energy no longer goes to the base chakra before ascending but moves directly from the pubic area into the head, moving through the center of the subtle body. There were Taoist yogis who mastered this secondary perfectional celibacy stage.

The next stage is where there is no more energy pooling in the sexual area, which means that there is no need to lift the sexual energy, because it does not accumulate there. The thighs serve a change in purpose, losing interest in sponsoring sex drive. The bone marrow created in the thigh bones no longer has lust as its primary interest.

Yogeshwaranand gave this diagram:

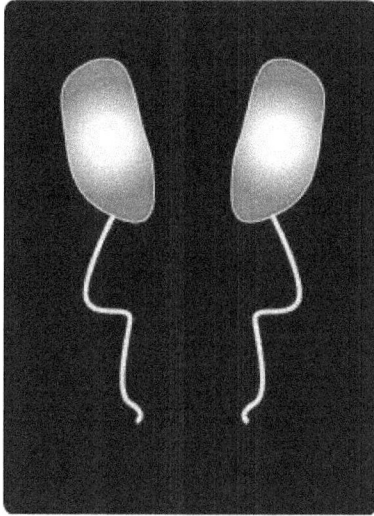

The energy from the right side of the body remains on the right. The left side does the same in full neutrality.

There are basically two types of celibacy; one static, the other dynamic. Static sexual disinterest is like the system used in monasteries. A priest takes a vow never to marry and never to be involved with sexual indulgence.

I am not a monk of either the Western or Eastern system. I do not practice the static celibacy because it does nothing to efficiently utilize the sexual energy. Subsequently, the energy accumulates a charge which causes the monk to break the vow either by self-indulgence or partner participation. In other words, the repression of the energy results in a breach for the monk.

I practice a dynamic celibacy which has for its practice a method of using the sexual energy on a daily basis by pranayama breath infusion and asana postures with special actions for hand/limb postures, muscular contractions and subtle energy manipulations. These allow that the sexual energy does not pool in the body. It is used in the psyche and is distributed evenly through the system.

One reason for this practice is that for me to associate with advanced astral yogis, I must do this. That is a requirement for the association.

The other reason is that I endeavor for a yoga siddha form. For this all energy in the system has to be reintegrated in such a way that the attraction to life in the physical plane is removed from the psyche. Part of that attraction is caused by sex energy. In curbing kundalini, dynamic celibacy is a major component for success.

Kundalini Movement Mystery (Aug 26, 2012)

Kundalini moves when there is breath infusion. It does on occasion move by other means but the most reliable one is breath infusion. By doing that one can raise kundalini. The postures help the yogi to make the infusion penetrate remote places in the body.

The postures are not a waste of time but all the same posture is not the main reason for kundalini arousal. By breath infusion alone kundalini will rise. The postures help the yogi to pilot kundalini and the infused energy to remote regions of the subtle body.

Take the example of a kinked garden hose. If you turn on a faucet to it, the hose will make an attempt to straighten but if the kink is firm, the water will access that point and go no further. If however, you shake the hose or relieve the kink the water will pass through the kinked area and invade other parts of the hose which it could not access before. In that example, turning on the water is like the breath infusion, the kink is like the blockage to a hard to reach area. Shaking the hose to remove or relieve the kink, is like doing a particular posture.

Distribution of Kundalini.

Distribution of kundalini is primarily controlled by what it finds to be an easy passage. In nature any process takes the easiest passage. What causes water to flow through gutters into the down spouts of a house? Obviously, this happens because of gravity. If you have water in the bottom of a cup however and you add more water, the water will not flow downwards until you breach the rim of the cup. Gravity is there and still the water cannot flow downwards. Kundalini does what is easy, which is to take the route through the central spinal passage into the brain. It will go up if it is forced to do so, otherwise it will go down through the genitals and anal chakra areas.

But this is not true in very case. For people who are physically focused kundalini does not go through the *sushumna* nadi. For them that nadi is totally blocked. For these people sex expression is tantamount. It is so obvious that even the least intelligent human being can describe its experience. In their physical and subtle bodies, the path for kundalini through the genitals is open. Kundalini naturally flows there.

Once a person begins to do yoga, that path remains open for a time but the spine passage also begins to open. By applying the locks, a student forces kundalini to bore the spinal passage. When this is done repeatedly, other channels which divert from the spine and some which are not directly connected, are realized. Kundalini flows through those nadis. In the human body, we know that in a healthy form blood flows everywhere in varying degrees and varying quantities. That is why the limbs are functional. The subtle body also has pathways. If one makes effort, kundalini will help in getting the system cleared.

Black outs and white outs cease if one practices for a certain length of time. The physical brain changes. One increasingly masters the locks and gets a better inner grasp on kundalini so that it takes directions and does not act independently.

One reason why kundalini overpowers the psychic organs in the head of the subtle body and thus causes the coreSelf to lose grip on reality, is the fact that kundalini is designed to match the psyche of the living entity. That means the whole psyche. If kundalini is channeled through only one part of the psyche, it may overwhelm that part.

If you request from an engineer, a generator for your appliances, he could create one accordingly. But if on running that machine, you direct its full capacity through one appliance, you may destroy that single gadget. Kundalini has the energy for the whole psyche not just for the head, or in the case of physically focused people not just for the genitals. It is found that when people have sexual satisfaction, they become exhausted. That means that kundalini expressed so much energy through the genitals, that the person must rest to recuperate.

Kundalini should be evenly distributed in the subtle body but unfortunately, it is not. If these exercises are done regularly, over time the nadis in every part of the body will be cleared. The energy will flow evenly.

In the spiritual body, the entire form, every part of it, is bliss energy. There is no stagnant/polluted part as in the physical body, where the brain and certain nerves alone are supersensitive. In the spiritual body all parts are equally super-sensitive. One must change the astral body to be similar if one is to ever go to higher worlds.

By doing breath infusion day after day, one will experience that the kundalini penetrates the body more and more.

A blocked plumbing system can be cleared if the plumber takes the time to snake a cable through each pipe. It will take time but sooner or later if he augurs, it will be cleared. Water will flow with no obstructions.

After one causes kundalini to rise through the spine into the brain during each session, the next phase is to abandon that practice and make the energy go to hard to reach places in the psyche.

One should concentrate on that. The energy will still ascend the spine because kundalini is now familiar with that passage but some of it will go to other parts. If one focuses on these other parts, one can accomplish clearance of the entire subtle body from fingers to toes.

People who have sex regularly do not have to endeavor to cause it. This is because kundalini is familiar with the sexual access channels. If kundalini is trained to go into the brain, that is what it will do. It will eventually forget the sexual access. But it should be trained not to neglect the remote places.

Positive Energy Saturation (August 26, 2012)

Preliminary breath infusion has to do with pushing, pulling, compressing and expelling gases from the psyche. Pollution is the gases which produce stupor and lack of clarity.

The breath infusion is done by aggressive or slow breathing rate for taking command of the breath actions of the body. This is not a visualization practice, where one sits and imagines that the breath penetrates. This involves physical actions of the diaphragm and lungs.

After sometime, after some years of practice, one will find that the psyche no longer hoards the negative depressing subtle energy. It will appear that the system has little interest in retaining polluted gases.

This is when the advanced breath infusion begins. Once the yogi notices that the depressing energy is no longer accumulating in the lower trunk of the subtle body, it is time to change the method of energy infusion from that of hunting down the dulling energy and removing it to that of compressing energizing subtle energy into the trunk.

The focus changes to the trunk itself and not just to the central spinal passage *sushumna* nadi. Once the negative energy is removed consistently and is no longer held in excess in the body, the kundalini's negative habits are reduced.

The complete saturation of positive energy into the trunk, thighs, legs and feet is the major achievement. This saturation results in an overflow into the neck and brain. While before all energy pooled and was stored in the trunk of the subtle body, in the pubic area of it, mostly, now the pooling and storage will occur in the neck and head. This changes the configuration of the subtle body, making it to be transformed into a yoga siddha form.

Curtail Associations

A yogi must curtail associations which do not directly contribute to spiritual progress. There must be a reduction in such association; otherwise one will never reach the advanced stage.

If the yogi absorbed much mental and/or emotional energy from others, either through physical or psychic contact, the meditation will be of low quality.

In spite of all the activity, and in spite of being attracted to physical existence, the yogi must hold the view, that the physical world is the death zone.

A yogi must perform some minimum social services, otherwise the spiritual progress will be sabotaged, and yet, a yogi must bear in mind, that the physical world is undesirable.

Pranayama through the Subtle Pores

Breath infusion practice this morning was productive of getting the pores of the subtle body to operate as an aggressive means of energy surcharge. This is something which I used to do in the early 1970s but which over time ceased because of non-yogic associations.

In the physical body there is some minor exchange of air through the pores of the skin. There is evaporation of salty liquid through the skin, but in the subtle body the pores may open and operate as the lungs and sinuses do in the physical system.

When this happens the stupor energy cannot stay in the subtle body and the effort to draw it out is greatly maximized as it can be released through the pores from the remote places. It does not have to travel through nadis to reach the subtle lungs.

In the higher configuration of the subtle body there are no lungs. It is designed in a totally different way having no accommodations for survival and for management by a kundalini lifeForce which operates on the principle of survival through reproduction and transmigration to new forms after an old form runs its course.

When the infused energy finally filled the trunk of the subtle body, it overflowed and released its excess through the neck into the head. At first this went through both sides of the neck into the jaws and felt like little tight springs being rapidly stretched and released frequently with micro bliss crystals firing.

During the practice I focused on the sacral region, particularly the bones in that area. These may be neglected by a yogin. They should be regarded. The base chakra should be considered. All polluted energy which loiters there should be compressed and extracted.

Yogi's Body made of Light (August 24, 2012)

Breath infusion was eventful this morning, with infused energy firing in the trunk of the body from the very start. The centralized effect of kundalini in the spine, is pretty much gone. The subtle body has kundalini distribution evenly through it.

Incidentally, in the spiritual body, the energy is evenly distributed. There is no centralized system as the whole body is centralized in terms of sensitivity and expression, such that in every part, the fingers, toes, everything is capable of absolute expressions. There is no special polarized part of the body as in the physical or astral forms.

In creating a yoga siddha form, one should transmute the astral form so that its configuration changes. This morning after about ten minutes, there were micro ice crystals of energy firing in the flesh of the neck? It was as if the entire neck was the *sushumna* nadi. It was ram-packed with tiny ice crystals which moved back and forth but with a heat bliss expression.

After that I got a flash appearance of Tibeti Yogi whom I have not seen in months. He was upbeat about the practice. He was happy that I made some inroad into higher yoga for the purpose of creating a yoga siddha form. Smiling, he made a remark and left. His subtle body was bright light so that I only saw his face with his checks glossy with a silver light flashing out of his light body. He said, "Full sweep! Full sweep! Complete this!"

That meant that the entire psyche was to be infused. Every bit of pollution was to be extracted. The system should be saturated with refreshing subtle energy.

Later, I did some postures which have to do with extracting energy from the lower trunk.

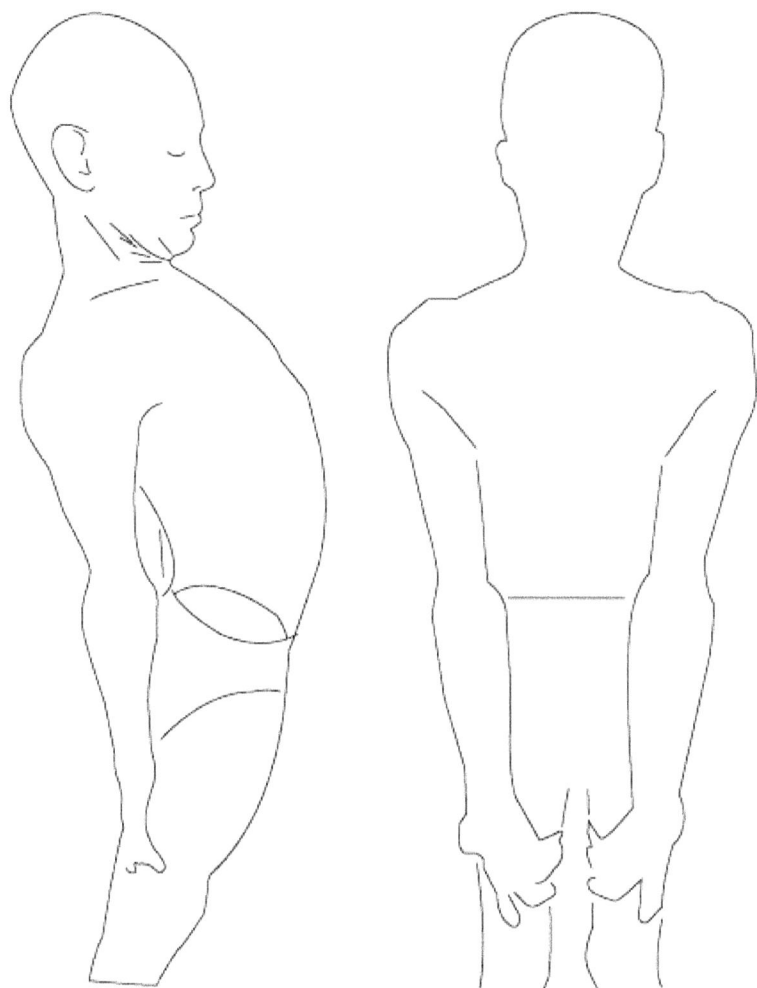

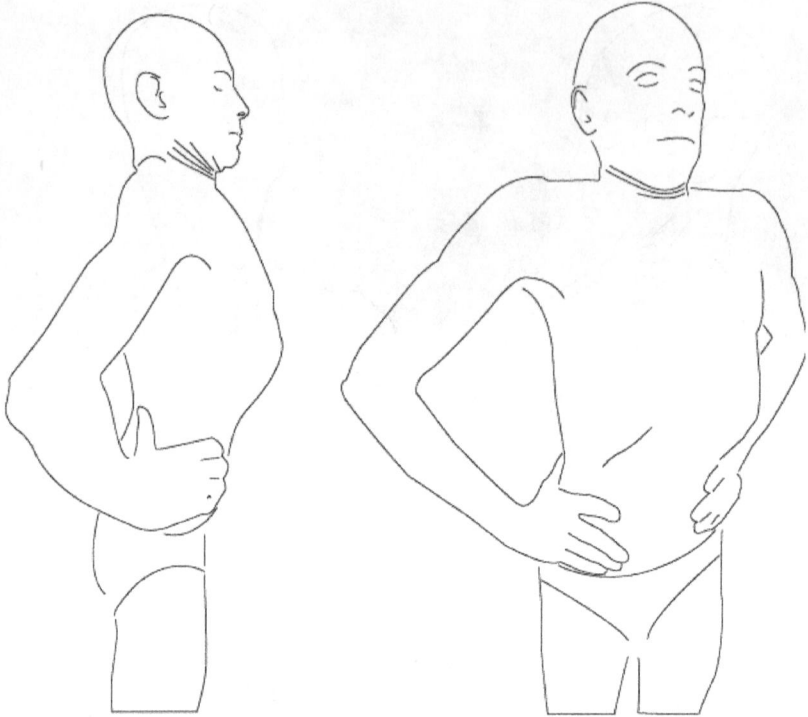

These are dangerous poses because of arching/stretching the back. If one does these one should be sure to be on the alert for kundalini to rise. During these poses, as soon as one stops rapid breathing locks should be applied.

One may do the rapid breathing in other poses, then stop, apply locks and then do these back-arch stretches, making sure the eyes are closed and the mind is centralized and alert for actions or flash actions of kundalini. If possible, wear a blindfold.

In these illustrations there is no blindfold because this is for demonstration only. One should use a complete face head cover while doing these exercises and during meditation.

Subjugation of Negative Subtle Energy (Aug 24, 2012)

The subjugation of pollution may take a yogi years to complete. That energy will resist and obstruct every step of the way. It is insistent on its place in the life of a yogi.

There are many aspects. There is the energy itself, the moods which it produces or sponsors and the places which it inhabits in the psyche. Here are details.

The pollution energy itself:

This is just the energy. In the physical world, the carbon dioxide is used by trees for energy. Certain mammalian species also use it in part or whole to fuel and assist in survival operations. In the human species, we use it to build muscular physique, and to induce insensitivity moods. The psyche feels the need for it. When a yogi begins the prospect of eliminating the negative astral energy, it is an uphill battle as the system is prone to storing that unwanted influence.

In the first years, a yogi may, time and again, work to extract this energy but he/she will find that it reinstates itself on a daily basis. After years of consistent practice, there may be a time when the yogi notices that this energy does not re-establish itself after each session. Then it is a matter of infusing the system with fresh air and to extract whatever little negative energy there is.

So long as the negative energy rules the lower part of the trunk with the thighs, legs and feet, the yogi will be stuck with the task of repeatedly extracting this energy on one day and then again doing so on the following day. This is because it re-establishes itself.

After over 40 years of practice, I successful removed this energy and conquered its territories in the psyche with the energizing force. I did this with the help of Yogi Bhajan and especially with help and encouragement from Yogeshwarananda who more or less threw me a life line.

During breath infusion, instead of pushing down the negative energy and then forcing it out of the system by extraction, I can spend more time infusing the fresh air energy and pulling up all lingering pollution which is in the lower trunk, thighs, legs and feet of the subtle body. This takes me one step closer to developing a yoga siddha form.

The efficient way to do yoga, is to practice daily. Over time one may become successful. In any case without that daily effort, no meaningful accomplishment will be attained.

- a yogi becomes elevated by association.
- a yogi becomes degraded by association.
- a yogi stagnates and makes no progress by association.

In the *Bhagavad Gita* there is a verse:

योगी युञ्जीत सततम्

आत्मानं रहसि स्थितः ।

एकाकी यतचित्तात्मा

निराशीरपरिग्रहः ॥ ६.१० ॥

yogī yuñjīta satatam

ātmānaṁ rahasi sthitaḥ

ekākī yatacittātmā

nirāśīraparigrahaḥ (6.10)

yogī — yogi; yuñjīta — should concentrate; satatam — constantly; ātmānam — on the self; rahasi — in isolation; sthitaḥ — situated; ekākī — alone; yatacittātmā = yata - controlling + citta - thinking + ātmā — self; nirāśīr — without desire; aparigrahaḥ — without possessions

In isolation, the yogi should constantly concentrate on the self. Being alone, he should be of controlled thinking and subdued self without desire and without possessions. (Bhagavad Gita 6.10)

Note the word *ekākī* which means *eka* or the number 1. It means that a yogi must be isolated. Some modern yogis reject this and think that they can be successful. It is not possible.

The deeper part of this aloneness of the yogi is that he/she has to be alone under supervision. It is not that he is alone and he becomes enlightened by himself. He must be alone or isolated and be under supervision of a more advanced yogi. If the student has psychic perception the instructor does not have to be physically present.

In taking this body, I came under certain unfavorable associations. My subtle body was totally reconditioned by entry into the parent's auras as well as in association with others and with the general social atmosphere of my birth circumstance.

Even though it is easy to go downwards, to become degraded, it is difficult to be elevated. The bad habits are not removed except after a protracted and prolonged struggle.

There is a certain inefficiency during practice. It is related to associations. According to the persons one associates with, one's practice becomes more or less efficient because the inner concentration is split between the yoga interest and the pressing needs of the associations one has. These are not only physical but psychic connections.

Unfortunately, I could not accelerate my practice because of the energy which I absorbed when I took this body. That energy had to run its course. Once you eat something, you must digest and then excrete it. Digesting it means that it will influence you. Once you eat it you must endure its effects. It will hold you until its influence is exhausted.

One can promise never to eat that diet again but whatever one eats must run its course. The influences which prevailed at my birth, became saturated in my subtle body. It took this long for that to run its course. By doing the practice, I deterred further absorption of those energies but I could not remove and had to endure what was already digested.

There was a time back in 1968 when I was in USAF tech school, when I considered to abandon this body and the mission for which it was assumed. The situation of salvaging myself from this, seemed impossible at the time. But then a voice from within the psyche suggested that such an action would result in a greater burden being carried over to the astral world and then to the next life. Subsequently, I decided that it was best to complete this, even though it meant working my way through much contamination.

A yogi is retarded by accessory association which he/she contacts inevitably along the way in trying to fulfill a mission. One will inevitably meet people. In such association, one digresses.

There is no doubt that I will reach the siddha levels. The doubt stands in regards to when and where. Will it be in this birth, or hereafter, or in some other birth? With the help of divine beings and yoga gurus, one can go to higher levels but one must be receptive.

It is a matter of absorbing a higher grade of subtle energy, and reducing one's interest in the history of the humans on planet earth.

Once one sees that this history is circular, that it is the same theme repeated with a slightly different cast each time, one begins to understand that the interest one has in it, is a ruse to keep one from advancing. One should shift interest to other dimensions.

The earth's history is like that of a play which has the same theme for each season with a little change here and a little change there but with the same basic plot. After sometime a yogi integrates this and makes the decision to be extracted.

Dream Recall

Dream recall is important. It allows one to keep track of the subtle body when the physical one sleeps. Even if one does not recall dreams, one is responsible for the actions of the subtle body during sleep.

While the kundalini is occupied repairing the physical body during the night, the astral form consciously or unconsciously wanders. One should observe it. This is done by constantly making the effort to recall its astral stunts.

Illness and Yoga Practice

In my experience breath infusion can cause influenza. If there are pathogens in the air, the infusion will result in more pathogens entering the body. As for headaches, I do not get those but one can get a headache from not applying the neck lock to control how kundalini flows into the head.

Observe the practice. Observe when an action of the practice produces an unwanted effect. It does happen however that sometimes yoga is blamed for something which was caused by something else.

Once I had a painful muscle in one shoulder. It took three months to be relieved of it. It was so bad that moving my body from a reclined sleeping position was agonizing. The muscle involved in that movement in the neck and shoulder was taut and pained terribly.

I suspected it was due to yoga asana postures but it was not.

I discovered that months after when it ceased when I used a double pillow. When I resumed using a single pillow, the pain was felt again. I understood that a muscle was pulled during the sleeping position of the physical body when my head and neck were not properly supported during sleep.

As with everything else yoga requires vigilance. One must be attentive and do what is needful to maintain a healthy body.

Lungs / Breath Infusion

It is highly unlikely that breath infusion will damage the lungs. The muscle that is involved is the diaphragm. To understand what happens physically during breath infusion, study how the lungs operates.

The lungs operate on the principle of accepting or being unresponsive to fresh air and releasing or retaining used air. One may inhale but that does not mean that the lungs absorb every measure of air. If someone has acute tuberculosis even if he is in a chamber with the best filtered air, still the lungs will not absorb the air even though it is available. The lungs have an attitude.

By doing the infusion the lungs may be influenced to change attitude and absorb more of the air which is delivered.

Observation of Practice

The benefit of poor-quality practice is the observation of what caused it. Once the student takes note, the next step is to guard the psyche from those penetrating influences.

When meditating after breath infusion one should check the spread of the infused energy. If it produced or caused a concentration force, the yogi should link to that immediately.

This linking is *dharana* practice but it is *dhyana* practice if when linked, the access stays with no effort on one's part. If the link is spontaneously sustained for more than five minutes, consider it to be a *samadhi* stage.

If you can do it with a little effort, very little, it may be rated as *dhyana*. If you can do it, but with much effort, it is *dharana*. The three events are regarded as one sequential practice (*samyama*) by Patanjali.

This means that if I am linked into a concentration force or a transcendental plane, and when I make that effort to link, the link is held by itself, I progressed from *dharana* into *dhyana*. If further, the link deepens, I get caught into that absorption fully being out of touch with everything else, that is *samadhi*. Sometimes after breath infusion when I sit to meditate, I immediately can tell if it will progress from *dharana* to *dhyana* to *samadhi*.

The only practice that one should hold on to if the infusion produced effects is the naad sound, or naad light connection, or a specific instruction given previously, or at that moment by a yoga guru.

It is important to be objective to sensation and to train the self to be patient and wait for results in meditation. If one loses objectivity that will spoil the practice and delay the advancement. It will cause one not to learn how to listen to yoga gurus who may enter the psyche to give advice.

Insubmissiveness to yoga gurus comes from one single thing which is losing objectivity when experiencing intense sensation. Do not underestimate the dominance of sensation. It is a powerful addiction. It causes the student to neglect the association of yoga gurus and to be insensitive to their psychic presence.

Sex Kanda Demolished

Even though I was two hours late for doing breath infusion, the practice was good this morning. The meditation session was good but that was interrupted after fifteen minutes. From the beginning of the session, all the way through, refreshing subtle energy went in all directions. There was a time when there was a flash of energy at the sex kanda area.

I demolished the kanda in the subtle body. That is an achievement, because once that energy does not pool in the subtle body, it means that one no longer has to deal with its influence or with its ability to attract other influences which detect it.

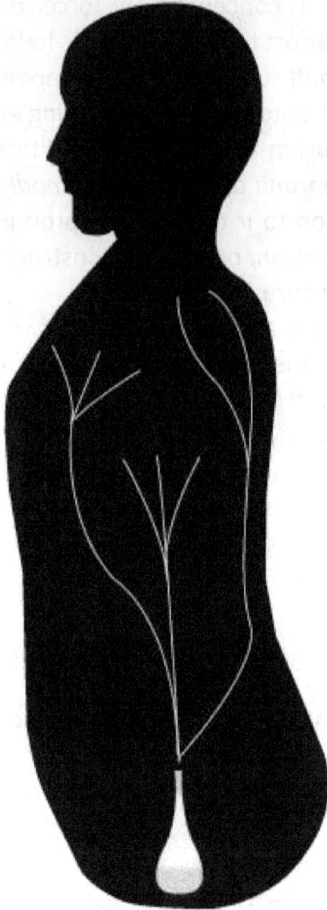

kanda reservoir

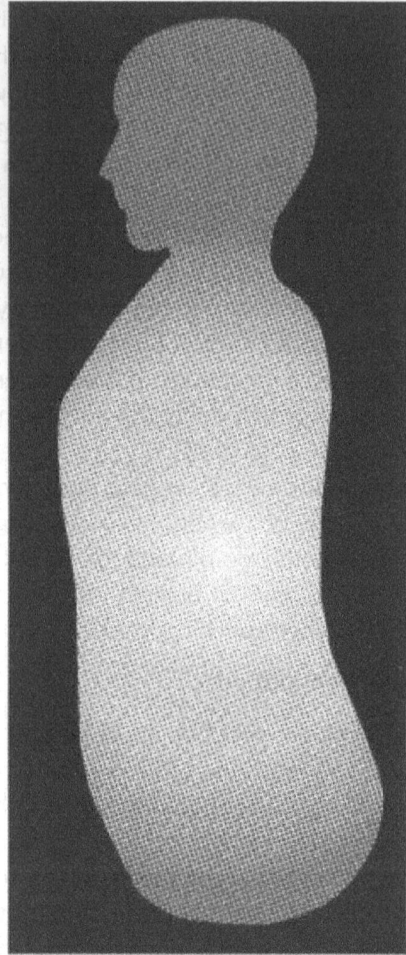

removal of kanda reservoir

subtle energy scattered everywhere

There is a parallel area to that sex kanda area which is the lower base back of the brain. Sometimes when doing breath infusion, focusing on a specific area where the energy accumulated or where it fired and produced bliss or electric sensation, one will suddenly find that one is focused on two areas, the original area and then another zone. This should be noted, as that other area is the parallel zone.

Kundalini Front Loop

This morning I worked on a new energy loop which I am in the process of creating in the subtle body. For adoption of a yoga siddha form, this is to change the way the base part of the subtle body is designed.

The initial kundalini yoga breath infusion is shown in the diagrams below. When this is completed one can practice higher processes. Study these diagrams to get a feel for the initial process which must be completed. The arrow head shows the infusion energy travelling around the front loop, then up the back loop.

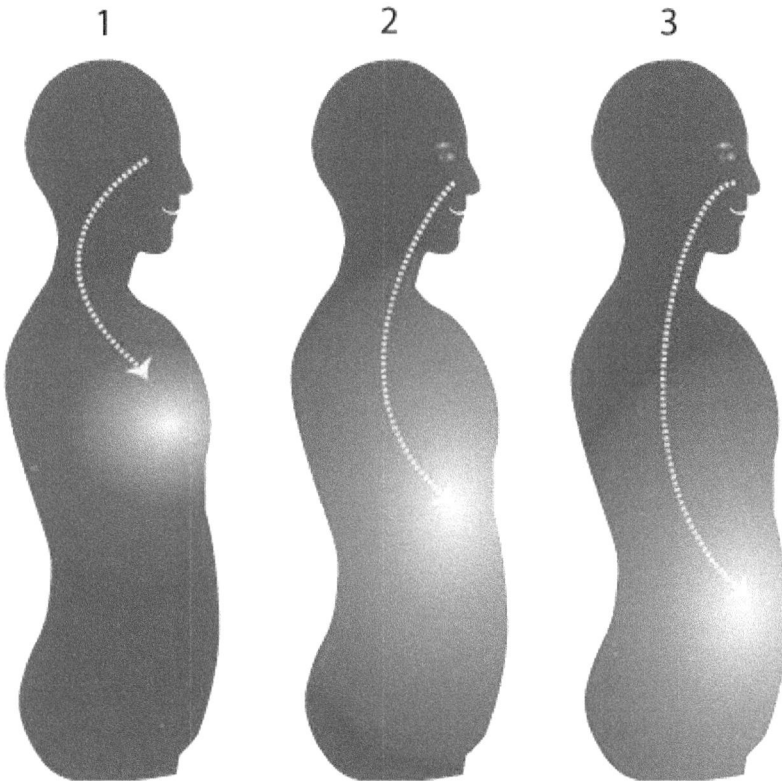

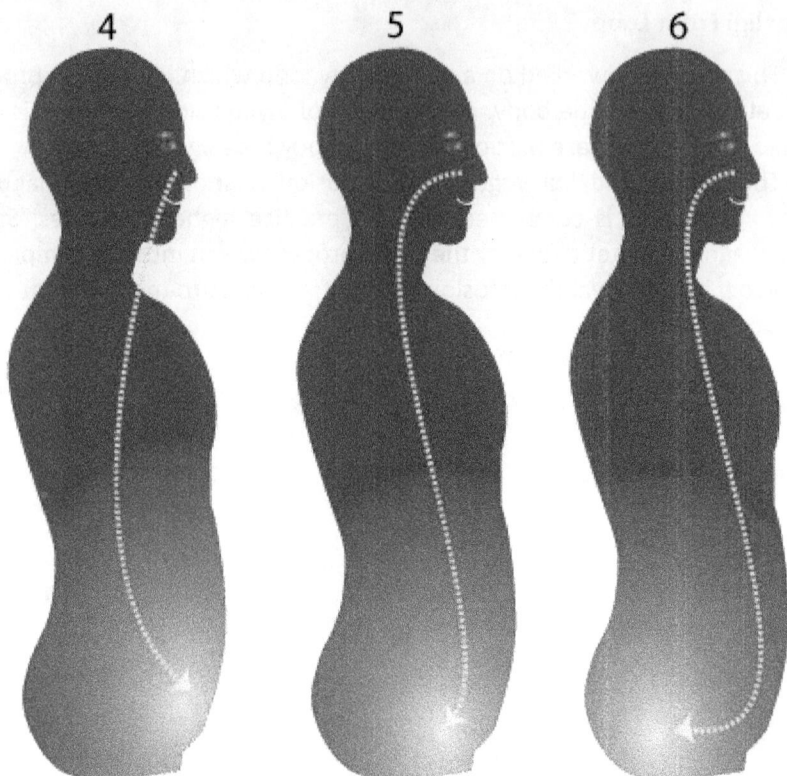

7
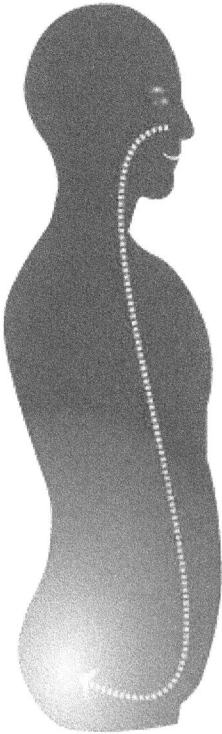

8
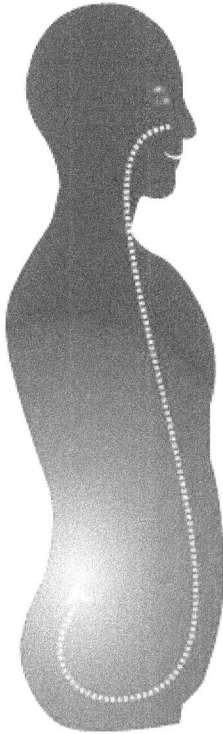

9
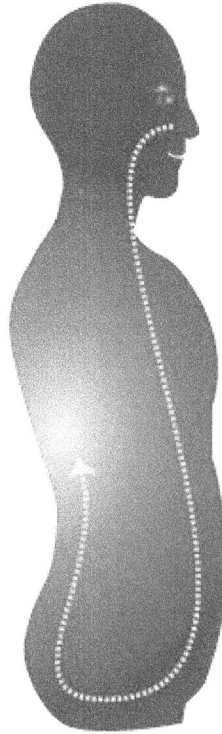

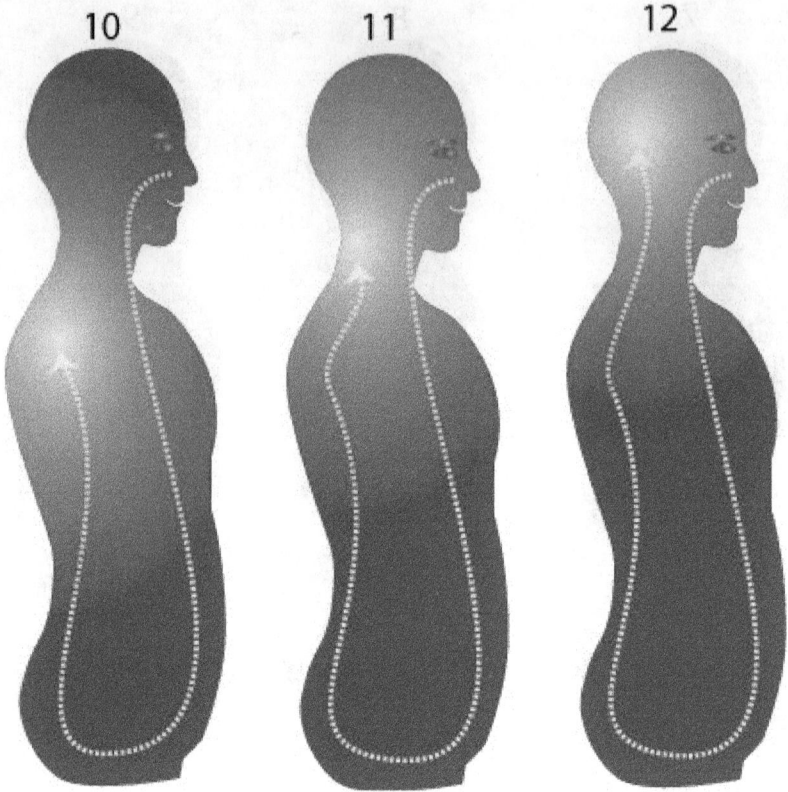

Down in the Subtle Body

Breath infusion this morning had a few unusual charged areas. One was the insteps which is normally inaccessible.

The nice thing about breath infusion is that you get to go where the train goes. Instead of dictating that the conductor takes the train here or there, you ride along, pay your fare as stipulated by the practice, and then go wherever the trains goes. Replace train with pranic energy, charged subtle breath energy.

As this energy penetrates through various nadis, it goes here and there. You follow along for the ride. Some days it takes you into the subterranean parts of the city, in the sewer pipes which run under the city carrying filthy waste. Some pipes, (read nadis) are blocked. When the fresh energy charges down there, it is like the pressure in a fire hose or in a mine shaft being filled with water which gushes or gores its way through, ripping and tearing the slush and filth which clogged after many years.

Today it hit the insteps and ankles. This felt like when you have little tiny tingling twinkies moving and moving at rapid speed in those two areas of the psyche.

It was shimmering and wavering.

Breath infusion practice with *bhastrika* or *kapalabhati* pranayama if done with full inner focus to see what happens in the subtle body (read psyche), does wonders to accelerate purification of the subtle form. It facilitates removal of stale energy which lingers in various remotes places. The result of this is that in a meditation after, one reaches higher levels of consciousness. Most of all, new subtle or supernatural perception comes into play so that what was nothing, what was void, is discovered as higher reality.

Infusion into Toes

This morning during breath infusion, I worked on the toes and the sacral cage. Sacral cage is the round bottom area of the torso. Keeping the sacral cage full of light is a special task for the yogi. Instead of focusing on getting light in the head of the subtle body, one would gain more if one made light in the base of subtle trunk.

The toes and finger, being extremities, are hard to reach areas. If there is light in the legs and forearms, one can pull the dense energy from the toes and fingers through that light.

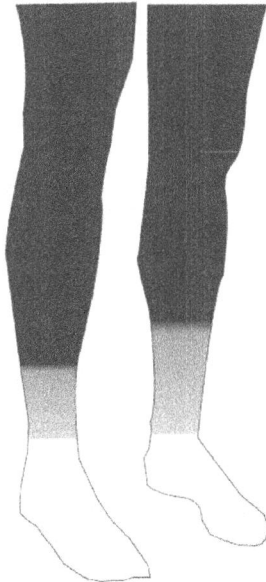

Yogi Failure

This morning on the astral side Yogesh brought to my attention that association is vital for success. He said this.

The fact is that unless one gets into isolation with very advanced yogis one cannot complete the course successfully. Other associations take one away from the practice. These associations do this repeatedly so that one may spend life after life, trying and trying and never reaching the culmination.

This reminds us of the Greek myth of Sisyphus. He was a mischievous and cruel king. He was sentenced to never achieve his aim which was to exert himself and roll a boulder over the crest of a steep hill.

A yogi cannot be involved in any fantasy about what it takes to become liberated. If you spent the last two million human births making efforts to complete yoga practice, how many more births are you willing to endure like this?

When will you be precise enough to push the boulder over the hill?

Are you addicted to the frustration of always getting near to the end and then dying to the physical world, then getting an infant body, then striving again, and then having the same partial achievement again?

The force that weakens the yogi so that he cannot make an efficient effort is non-yogic association. As long as that is in place, success will not happen.

Arrest and Throw Kundalini

The initial effort in kundalini yoga is to cause kundalini to move from muladhara chakra up the spine and into the head. That is stage one.

When this is done to proficiency and one does this at least once per day using a fail-proof method one masters kundalini to some extent. One stops being a mediocre yogi.

After this stage the next level is to curb the sex hormone energy and to work to become what is called an urdhva reta yogi, which is a yogi whose sexual hormone energy no longer moves downward. It resists gravity and comes upward as soon as it is produced. To master this, one must take help from advanced yogis who are physically or astrally present.

Because the psyche is configured with a downward going sexual energy, attaining an upward configuration of the sexual hormones is a struggle for a yogi. It can be achieved but only after steady practice of pulling up that energy using pranayama methods where the infused energy is used to evaporate the sex hormones which usually pools up in the pubic area.

Once this is achieved, the next stage is to cause all the energy which falls from the navel area to go upward. To curb this one should master agnisara practice on the subtle plane. On the physical level agnisara is done with the stomach churning exercises but this practice needs to be relocated into the subtle body.

The yogi should advance to the stage of kundalini arrest. This means that as kundalini hustles to escape from breath infusion by climbing through the spine into the head, the student should arrest it. He should throw it in a dark corner of the psyche. It should illuminate that darkness.

Why?

In the psyche, even if kundalini goes into the head, even if it reached *brahmrandra*, still if there are dense astral energies in any part of the astral body, the yogi will be influenced by that lower level where the dense energy is predominant.

This may be compared to a man who lives in a dungeon but who works in a palace. He works in an opulent place but he cannot sleep there. He must return to the undesirable environment. A yogi may go to *brahmrandra* but if any other part of the psyche has dense astral energy, he must descend to that area sooner or later.

A yogi should arrest kundalini, compress it and grab it when it tries to move up the spine. He should throw it in any dark part of the psyche. This action when done repeatedly over time will cause kundalini to stop its craze for bliss energy in the head. It will seek those dark parts of the psyche and get them into psychic brilliance.

Part 4

Bliss energy in the legs

There was an interesting development this morning in breath infusion, where for the first time since I assumed this present physical body, the legs, calves and knees of the subtle body was full of bliss energy.

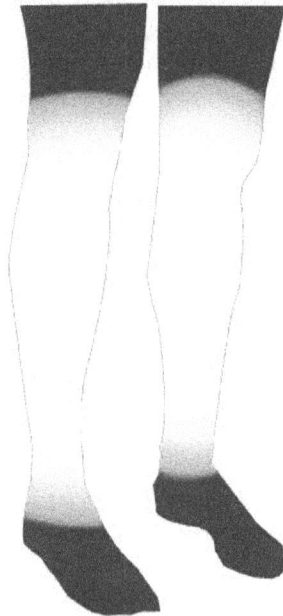

Kundalini when it fires in the head of the subtle body brings on various stages of bliss even brahmananda bliss which is spiritual energy bliss but rarely does it cause that to happen in any other part of the psyche.

This experience is good news for a student yogi who practices to achieve a yoga siddha form. This happened because of hints about certain meditation procedures which were left behind in my psyche by Tibeti Yogi. I assume that he is gone to the causal plane. All the same he left a package of practices. Gradually over time, these take root in my practice.

The bliss force in the legs was wonderful. It was shimmering glossy pearl-like microbeads of bliss force shifting through the legs. When it entered the knee, it went in a circular loop through the knee cap. It produced tingling sensations there.

There was another important development where when I was in lotus posture and did the infusion and then wiggled the bottom of the body, moving briskly from one bottom-bone to the other, there was the firing of the stub sex organ kundalini. This is from the perineum area where usually during sexual indulgence the sex pleasure emanates and goes in every direction and overtakes the psyche.

In this experience however there is no sexual flavor in the energy. It is pure bliss force. It fires sparks from a stub which is colored like white hot metal.

At first it fires horizontally from the bottom of the stub. Then it fires from the top of the stub through the trunk of the subtle body.

After this there is a flush-way which manifested without sexual interest. One remembers sex as if it is something which one knew about some billions of years past, in a distant galaxy.

This experience is realized by the subtle body in a configuration which is unlike the one used in sexual experience with the physical body and with the low-level astral form.

In that higher state, there is no comparison because it is removed from this level. It is an intense feeling but it is non-comparable.

It does not have the passionate lust flushes which occur in the sexual experience. It is a clean bliss energy, with the insight revealing perception. It lacks the passionate enthusiasm energy.

Holy Cleanliness

In breath infusion session this morning the psyche configuration was felt with the neck and limbs having the same energy. The system had one type of elevated charge.

The practice I used, is a system of pollution energy withdrawal, which was a technique deposited in my psyche by Tibeti Yogi. This is a reaching into the trunk and limbs to extract the polluted energy wherever it is hidden in various tiny nadis and in compact clusters in the subtle body.

This is a wonderful process. It removes heavy astral energy which is lingers here or there. As soon as the pollution is extracted, immediately it is replaced with fresh subtle energy that is infused by the rapid breathing.

This causes dark areas of the astral body to be filled with astral light, striking bright.

I remember when I last saw Tibeti's astral body. It was an old wrinkled Tibetan body with a slight gold orange color. It was not clean. Externally that body would not qualify for anything holy. But internally it was a different matter, immaculate within the subtle body.

I know some brahmins who are picky about external cleanliness of the physical body. This is a justified stipulation because it is a rule of ritual that anyone who does deity worship should be immaculate by taking bath and applying holy tilak clay markings.

But many brahmins are mentally unclean in that they are ever occupied planning how to exploit gullible people who attend temples and mandirs. These brahmins have no idea of breath infusion. They assume that by mantra, japa and ritual offerings their inner subtle configuration is cleansed.

Neglected Nadis

One group of nadis which may be neglected by students is the ones which correspond to the rib cage. As tradition would have, and now even more with the chakra meditation craze, students feel that objective is the *sushumna* central passage and the various chakras which are on the spine and in the head.

Getting diagrams with Sanskrit markings which they cannot read, many students of yoga, sit to meditate, after seeing images of Buddha or another mahayogin. They imagine themselves as Buddhas meditating and opening chakras. Most of this is imaginary. One cannot open chakras unless one can penetrate through the subtle body where these vortexes are located. Still, people make the effort.

There are remote nadis. Some are in the rib cage zones. This morning I targeted these. Even a yogi of worth has difficulty operating these nadis which are the subtle parallels of the bones which comprise the rib cage.

Penetrating that and making the infused energy pass through energies in the chest area, a bliss energy which sparkles and glows noticeably, will arise.

Astral Projection and Chakras

Kundalini is the psychic apparatus which operates astral projection. In fact, kundalini is a psychic adjunct which is in the individual psyche and which usually is not controlled by the individual. It is an involuntary psychic survival mechanism. It independently operates sex drive, digestion and other physiological and nervous functions.

Astral projection is not always a third eye activity. Third eye is a chakra on the subtle body. Astral projection is the displacement of the entire subtle body, to the astral planes with simultaneous de-synchronization from the physical system.

Crown chakra is not always a connection to nothingness. There can be perception, objective clear supernatural perception, at the crown chakra.

If a person raises kundalini through the neck of the subtle body, it will of its own accord go immediately to the intellect organ. If it has enough energy charge it may strike the crown. Kundalini will rarely go to the third eye chakra when it comes into the head.

Usually if it is sufficiently charged, it will first go to the intellect organ. From there if it has sufficient energizing charge it will go to the crown chakra. Usually this does not produce an astral projection of the subtle body. In fact, in this experience usually the astral body remains in the physical one but it rises in vibration while it is remains interspaced in the physical system.

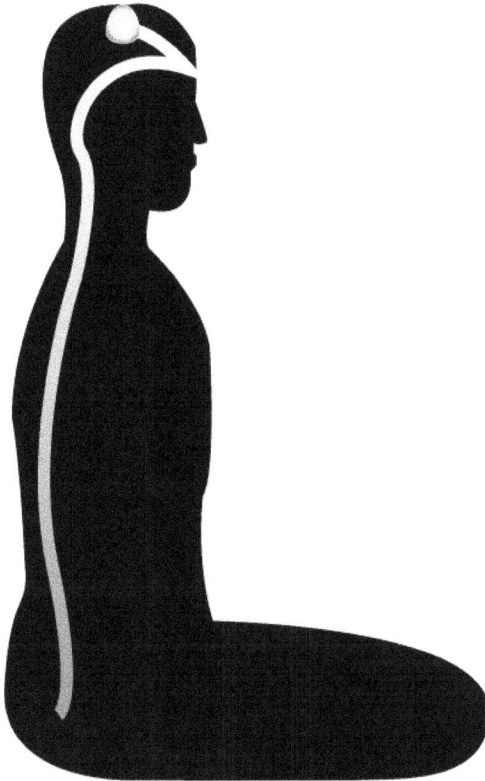

Even though the third eye serves as an entry point for thoughts coming from others, it does not create thoughts which come from the subconscious. It is not involved in the thought creative mechanism in the mind itself. To master thoughts, one should take recourse to intellect yoga *(buddhi yoga)* as explained in chapter two of *Bhagavad Gita*.

Intellect yoga as intellect + yoga, means the application of yoga proficiency to controlling the intellect organ which is the psychic adjunct which is involved in thought creation, thought recognition, thought translation, thought conversation and memory illustration.

The memory itself is impotent. It relies on the intellect organ to convert stored impressions into language and images to be perceived by the observing self which peers in the mind.

Any thought which penetrates through the third eye or which comes into the mind chamber by any other means from someone outside of the individual's psyche is helpless to do anything until it hits the intellect and is converted into something the observing self can perceive.

The curbing of the intellect is the secret to thought control. Patanjali advised in his second sutra about shutting down *chittavritti*. Even the kundalini relies on the intellect to calculate how to act and to interpret sensation and moods.

So long as the internal kundalini is not completely altered, changed, fed a different kind of subtle energy, the desire for desireless-ness and nothing-ness will never be attained because the kundalini will not allow it.

Why bother with the chakras when they are mere expressions of the kundalini. Why not attack kundalini at muladhara where it resides. Deal with it there. Reform it there.

No matter what one does at the various higher chakras (higher than the base chakra) it will be a waste of time, if kundalini retains control of the base area, and if at that place it is not reformed. But if one reforms it there, the other chakras will exhibit higher qualities.

How Yesterday Sabotaged Today's Practice

This morning during breath infusion, from the very start everything was in order with the first sequence producing a glow-bliss energy, in the trunk, neck and up to the cheeks.

Yogesh was present on the astral side. He checked to see if I would do sufficient practice, or cut the session short. When doing breath infusion, there are certain energies which influence the student to do a brief session. One should resist such suggestions.

In relation to this is the prep time for a session. The prep time for today's session began yesterday, with what I did yesterday, with whom I associated, with what was in the mind before resting in the evening, and with the persons I met during last night's dream experiences in the astral world.

Today's practice is not isolated. Its foundation is what I did yesterday. If one day was counterproductive to practice, the following day I will feel the effects of the previous influence.

I located a nadi tube which is behind the *sushumna* nadi central channel. Pushing the infused energy through this tube caused it to flatten and spread through the back of the trunk of the subtle body. This area is one which I did not discover before.

Here is a diagram of a cross section of the trunk of the body showing that nadi.

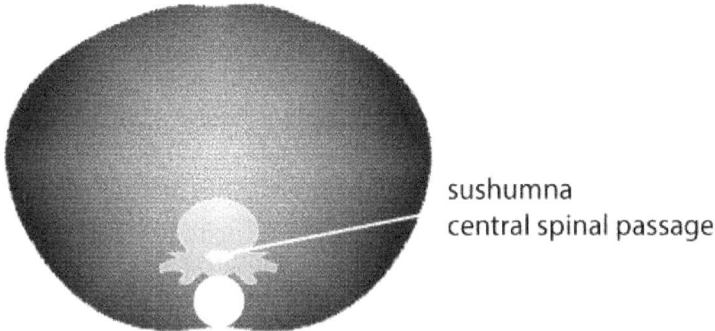

sushumna
central spinal passage

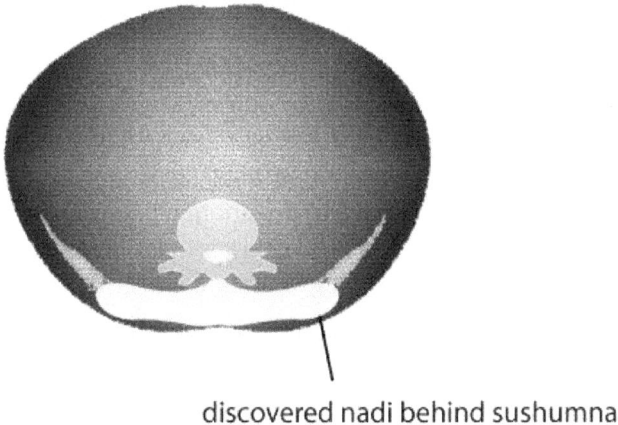

discovered nadi behind sushumna

Distribution of Infused Energy

This morning I did a double session of breath infusion. The air was not as good because due to rainfall outdoors, I was indoors at an open door. During the practice I was blindfolded. Yogesh manifested in my psyche. He directed the practice.

He noted mental distractions in the form of thought packages which infiltrated my psyche from non-yogis. These energies acted like enemy squadrons which were instructed to attack, subdue and defeat. Most attacks were warded off but a few, about three of the packages, got the better of me. When I realized that I was arrested by them, I resisted. They disappeared.

It is amazing how these influences penetrate the psyche even of a yogi of my caliber. People who do no breath infusion, who do not understand even a word of the Patanjali *Yoga Sutras*, either write or speak about their meditation being completely free of thoughts.

Who are these people fooling?

A person who cannot adopt a vegetarian diet, who cannot give up luxuries, who is attached to status, is impractical when speaking of controlling all thoughts in meditation.

The thoughts packages were from relatives mostly. Somehow their ideas penetrated the psyche and remained dormant until the time of spiritual practice when they burst in the mind to lure me into mental association.

During the session, Yogesh showed something else about pranayama. He was inside my psyche, not just inside the subtle head but inside the subtle body (head and trunk parts of it). He said that with pranayama one has several aspects to master:

1. infusion of fresh air in several postures.
2. extraction of carbon dioxide on the physical side.
3. compression of the infused energy.
4. observation of distribution of the compressed energy in specific postures while holding locks (bandhas).
5. mastership of that practice for at least two years.
6. dynamic distribution of the compressed energy, while holding locks with jerk movements and wiggling actions to vibrate nadis and make them receptive to the energy distribution.
7. noting the particular infusion charges in the psyche.
8. moving those infused charges up and out of the trunk into the head.

Previously I mastered this process up to step 5 which I practiced for over seven years. According to Yogeshwaranand, the proficiency should be gained in two years. Because of distractions during the practice sessions, in my case it took longer. Each distraction strikes off some progress and causes an increase in the time for proficiency.

These are distractions within the mind chamber, not external distractions which are detected and pursued by the senses outside the psyche. These are distractions which reside in the psyche. I progressed to the sixth stage which is the dynamic distribution of the infused breath energy.

Please be sure to note that this infusion concerns extraction of polluted air and implementation of fresh air. This is not to mix the two energies as in some other procedures.

If one is in the lotus posture doing the infusion, to do the dynamic distribution of the compressed energy, one will wiggle the bottom of the body from side to side and as one does this one should notice tingling sensations at the bottom of the body as the energy is diffused. If there is enough of it, energy will rise through the body like little bubbles rising from the bottom of a pond but with bliss feelings and electric charges exuding throughout.

As one wiggles a time will come when the distribution of energy will cease. One should begin the breath infusion again to compress and form a new charge. As soon as that is saturated, one should stop the breathing and begin the dynamic distribution of that charged subtle energy.

If one finds that the energy goes into the shoulder like bubbles which are trapped beneath a ledge under water, and that the energy does not rise through the neck and enter the head, it means that the neck is blocked. More practice over time will cause that blockage to be cleared.

Spinal Breathing

Spinal breathing was used by ancient yogis. The nadi shodana process is one such practice. Each student should try these processes as he/she is attracted to them. Evaluate their worth. Decide to practice or not to practice. I use *bhastrika/kapalabhati* process. That gives the results which I prefer.

Regarding the system of mixing fresh air and polluted gases in the body, Yogeshwarananda instructed that I need not mix these but that does not mean that his instruction is everything. These can be mixed. It is just that if one desires to go to a certain level, one must do a certain process.

For me to reach the siddha stage which I am to attain, mixing polluted air and fresh air would not serve the purpose. I am required to get polluted waste air out of the system, replacing it with fresh energy, not mixing it. In the process I use, polluted air is drawn out, identified during breath infusion practice and removed from the system.

For the siddha stage I must extract the polluted energy on a daily basis. This does not mean that I instruct everyone to do this. Instead of mixing used air in the body with fresh air inhaled I compress fresh air and use it to push out polluted used air.

The process I use is mentioned in *Bhagavad Gita*.

अपाने जुह्वति प्राणं

प्राणेऽपानं तथापरे ।

प्राणापानगती रुद्ध्वा

प्राणायामपरायणाः ॥४.२९॥

apāne juhvati prāṇaṁ
prāṇe'pānaṁ tathāpare
prāṇāpānagatī ruddhvā
prāṇāyāmaparāyaṇāḥ (4.29)

apāne — in exhalation; juhvati — they offer; prāṇam — inhalation; prāṇe — in inhalation; 'pānam = apānam — in exhalation; tathāpare = tathā — similarly + apare — others; prāṇāpāna gatī = prāṇa — energizing air + apāna — de-energizing air + gatī — channel; ruddhvā — restraining; prāṇāyāmaparāyaṇāḥ = prāṇa — inhaling + āyāma — regulating + parāyaṇāḥ — intent

Some offer inhalation into the exhalation channels; similarly, others offer the exhalation into the inhalation channels, thus being determined to regulate the channels of the energizing and de-energizing airs. (Bhagavad Gita 4.29)

अपरे नियताहाराः

प्राणान्प्राणेषु जुह्वति ।

सर्वेऽप्येते यज्ञविदो

यज्ञक्षपितकल्मषाः ॥४.३०॥

apare niyatāhārāḥ
prāṇānprāṇeṣu juhvati
sarve'pyete yajñavido
yajñakṣapitakalmaṣāḥ (4.30)

apare — others; niyatāhārāḥ — persons restrained in diet; prāṇān — fresh air; prāṇeṣu — into the previous inhalations; juhvati — impel; sarve — all; 'pyete (apyete) = apy (api) — also + ete — these; yajñavido = yajñavidaḥ — those who know the value of an act of sacrifice; yajñakṣapitakalmaṣāḥ = yajña — austerity and religious ceremony + kṣapita — destroyed, removed + kalmaṣāḥ — impurities

Others who were restrained in diet, impel fresh air into the previously inhaled air. All these ascetics whose impurities were removed by austerity and religious ceremony understand the value of an act of sacrifice. (Bhagavad Gita 4.30)

At least on this planet, we know that the vegetation (plants) use carbon dioxide as their main air for sustenance while the higher species, animals (human included) use mostly the oxygen. That is a hint that for higher dimension one should decrease the pollution and increase the energizing air.

Duryodhana was an apana yogi. He is the villain in the Mahabharata. Some ancient yogis increased apana while others increased prana.

There was an ill-intended yogi named Hiranyakashipu. He stopped his psyche from breathing. That stifled the breathing system in the creation. There was also a good yogi named Dhruva who accomplished the same feat, which is to arrest the breathing system of the planet and of some subtle dimensions. These stories are in the Srimad Bhagavatam.

Moral Breach of a Yoga-guru / Agnisara Flushway

During breath infusion this morning, kundalini-charged forces flashed here and there in the trunk of the subtle body below the neck, and also through the neck and also up into the face at the cheek bones. I had a flash from Swami Rama who directed me to infuse energy through the agnisara flushway. This is a gap place which begins in the chest of the subtle body and ends in the pubic area. This flush way is sometimes like rectangular-shaped metal tubing or it may be like cylindrical metal tubing.

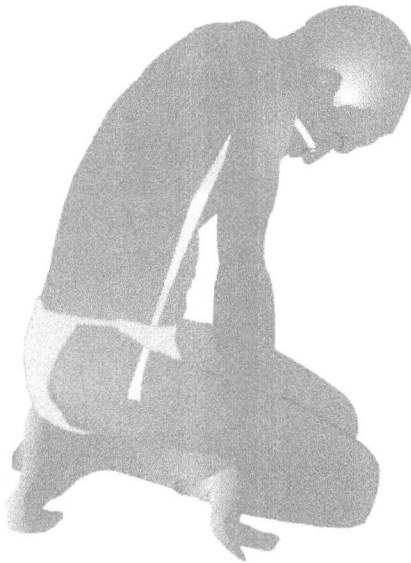

When one sees this tube, it appears to be hollow and the inner walls of it appear as grey-white. As one infuses breath using *bhastrika* or *kapalabhati,* the passage is filled with the infused energy. It feels like the exhaust from a jet engine.

One interesting feature is that Swami Rama was accused by several of his female students of sexual misconduct or abuse. If that is true how can he explain these procedures.

The answer is that whatever he achieved as a yogi, remains his achievement. Whatever he did which was out of the moral scope, is his handicap in that way. The two accounts are separate. If a man worked honestly for a wage, he will get that from the employer. But if simultaneously he performed a criminal act, he is accountable for that as well. One can get techniques from Swami Rama, provided he mastered the skill. He may not lose a proficiency because of a moral breach.

Psychic Perception with Bliss Energy

Breath infusion this morning was productive. For the past two days I did not file full reports even though I practiced breath infusion and meditation. This is due to pressing social concerns and energies from people who have no interest in yoga.

Associating with people other than advanced yogis may cause practice to be stalled or to decrease. If you mix contaminated water with purified water, you cannot truthfully say that the purified water is not contaminated. But of course, a tea spoon of sewage in a large reservoir of purified water, will not do much damage.

The problem arises when one is bogged with counterproductive social influences, these punch a hole in the spiritual practice.

This morning breath infusion began with a bang with the very first sequences of postures with breath infusion producing charged energy, kundalinis, in every part of the trunk of the subtle body. It was like when light suddenly illuminates a dark cave. For a second the darkness may hesitate to give up its space but then the harsh reality of the light faces it and smashes its territory to bits by sending flashing beams in all directions.

When I did the lotus posture, which is one of the postures I must do to secure the association of Yogeshwarananda, there was light below flashing on the pubic floor. The energy there was the same sexual energy but totally devoid of lust configuration. It was in the psychic perception mode, devoid of its usual passionate drives.

At one point with kundalini flashing down and hitting the pubic floor and then splitting off at right angles in all directions, I saw bright flashes of white light going here and there as I wiggled the torso from side to side in the lotus posture.

This is a big improvement because when I first began to do kundalini yoga using *bhastrika* way back in 1971, the rising of kundalini was only an upward movement with sexual polarity energy striking across from the sex organ chakra (not sex chakra on the spine). The infused energy would descend from the lungs, into the navel region. From there I would push it down further through the front of the lower trunk. It would strike the sex organ chakra, acquire a sexual polarity charge and then attack kundalini at the base chakra.

If the attack was successful or if the charged force, the mixture of breath energy and sex hormones, was high enough, the energy arced across to muladhara base chakra. Kundalini would try to run from it upwards through the spine into the head of the subtle body.

Once kundalini got into the head, it did one of three things:

- hit the intellect organ.
- hit the crown chakra.
- hit the third eye.

Either of these hits would cause supernatural experience in the head of the subtle body.

In that initial practice it may be said that the sexual energy was transmuted but in the practice I do now there is no transmutation because the energy does not carry a lusty charge. It is created in and remains in the clarifying mode (sattva guna). The energy is clean. It has a neutral bliss aspect, which is distinctly light producing and gives psychic perception along with bliss force.

Breath Infusion Churning / Swami Rama

Breath Infusion practice this morning was inspired by Swami Rama for the agnisara hatha yoga practice. This is a practice where the student churns the stomach, up and down, down and up, right to left, left to right, in to out, out to in, anus-rectum pull up and push down, navel in and navel out.

The classic way to do the abdomen churls was shown to me way back in 1970 in the Philippines by Arthur Beverford, my first yoga teacher. In that practice the student bends over with hands on thighs and does the churning action.

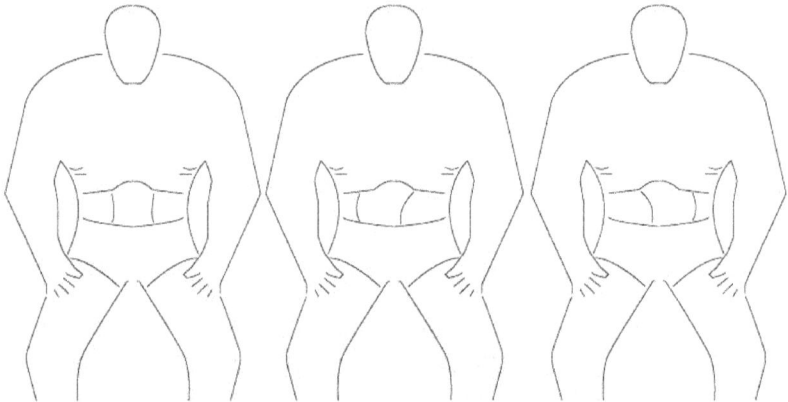

To a beginner this is agnisara in completion but actually it is only the start of the practice. For instance, when doing this, where is the mind of the student located?

Is he focused mentally into the area where the organs are churned?

Is he aware of the effects of the churning?

Does he understand the connection between digestion, evacuation and energy consumption in the subtle body?

Is he doing this for the health and beauty of the physical body?

During breath infusion, Swami Rama looked through my subtle body to observe where the infused breath energy was dispersed. He showed how to move the breath energy in the way of the agnisara churning actions. This is when one does *bhastrika* pranayama and mentally cause the air to churn in the system in exactly the way one would do physically using the diaphragm to make the churning actions. The diaphragm is not involved in this except in the action of the rapid breathing to bring the infused air into the system. Once the air is compressed into the system it is mentally handled.

Swami Rama explained the small of the back:

"Small of the back constriction is created by the posture of kundalini when it enters into fetal development. In the case of a siddha or a divine being there is no small of the back constriction in that person's subtle body, but as soon as a fetus is developed as that person, then the small of the back *is manifested because kundalini creates this.*

"It should be eliminated before one leaves the physical body, otherwise one will find that one is looped into getting another fetus immediately after leaving the body. This is because of kundalini shakti's primordial impulse which is to use physical bodies sequentially, and transfer from one old or damaged body to another newly-formed one.

"This small of the back is on the spine behind the navel. It is where energy of kundalini is constricted so that it does not go upward but remains below the navel for survival and reproduction purposes. A student has it as a task to get rid of it, to straighten that kink in the sushumna nadi. Then kundalini will always radiate up the spine continuously and the effort to raise kundalini is no longer necessary since it radiates through the spine. There is no constriction to block the flow of energy."

Nostril Imbalance

This morning breath infusion practice focused mostly on the effects of infusion using the left nostril and little of the right one. This happened because of the atmospheric conditions and the predominance of moon energy.

During some sessions both nostrils work at full capacity. During some the left one will. During others, the right one will. This happens because of the influence of the sun and moon. Moon influence causes the left nostril to be more open than the right. A predominance of sun energy causes the right nostril to have full flow.

When there is a balance of these energies, both nostrils draw in air at full capacity but even then, the fact is that the right nostril will pull in more air because the left lung is not as big as the right one. Sun influence is much more than moon influence over all. Moon will never be equal to sun even though moon can predominate under certain special conditions.

If one nostril is more open than the other, the *bhastrika* pranayama process if done proficiently will cause that open nostril to serve the whole system. After a time, one will find that after the left side for instance is open, after it is filled with fresh subtle energy, that fill will go over to the right side and when that side is filled the system will be in balance, not with equal quantity necessarily but a full integration, with each side being filled to its capacity.

Neti Pot

I used neti pot years ago when Arthur Beverford demonstrated it. Rishi Singh Gherwal showed him the method. There is also the system of holding water in the cupped-palm of the hand and inhaling the water slowly. I did that.

My finding is that it did not do anything in the subtle body. Or it had a superficial momentary effect.

On occasion if one checks one will find that even with cleared nostrils, still kundalini will rise during a posture more on one side than the other.

The neti pot method is a valid but when one shifts over to the subtle side, its value decreases. One discovers that it has a superficial effect there.

Most of the time when kundalini rises, a student will find that it raises more on one side than on the other. Of course, if there is just a slight difference, the student may not detect it. Sometimes the student will be puzzled that it raised more on one side.

Forgetting about yoga, if we go to ordinary life, kundalini makes its most pronounced expression during sexual climax. Even that occurs more on one side than on the other, even though the experience is so intense that the individual may not be objective enough to rate it.

When I practice, there may be an inspiration which dictates that I stretch to one side. When I do so, kundalini will fire into that side of the body and produce electric cramp-like sensations with a bliss aspect. As soon as I feel that it reduces full intensity, I usually stretch to the other side, but then kundalini may subside and not fire into that side.

A human body is not a balanced system. The idea that it is balanced or that it should be is mostly a mental construction based on the desire for equality. Nothing is equal anywhere in nature.

- One lung is smaller than the other.
- The heart is tilted more to one side of the body.
- One testis is larger than the other.
- One ovary has less potency than another.
- One hand does more tasks than the other.
- One foot puts more emphasis in striding than the other.

- One eye has a different seeing capacity than the other.

I noticed that the right and left hands of my body commit to particular actions. Sometimes there is an indecision regarding what one hand should do, then one hand performs the action while the other hand remains indifferent to it.

I did *bhastrika* pranayama for forty years since around 1972. There were times when I ceased it for months because of being discouraged from doing it for one reason or the other.

From that practice, I observed that when the right nostril is fully open, it is due to a predominance of sun energy in the atmosphere. If the moon energy is predominant, the left nostril has more flow. If they are in balance both nostrils are equally open and take in full capacity. Here however the left one takes in less air because its capacity is less

In my body, I would not be surprised if someone measured and found that the right nostril was bigger than the left but I know for a fact that generally during pranayama practice the right side infuses more breath energy. In my body, I have not seen anything which is equally balanced. In the astral world which I frequent, I do not see any such thing.

I have done kundalini yoga for years now raising kundalini at least once per day using a reliable *bhastrika* pranayama practice, thanks to Yogi Harbhajan Singh Sahib. Up to this day I never experienced a perfect ida and pingala in total equal balance, one is always more or less than the other even if it is to the slightest degree.

Rishi Singh Gherwal / Yogi Bhajan

I combed through the astral regions for Rishi Singh for many years. I never could locate him. Stranger is the fact that no astral yogi ever said that he knew where Rishi was located. During his last physical body Rishi was an agent for the British in India. Beverford who worked for OSI intelligence for the US military said that Rishi was hired by the British to find Rishi. He did this for years and the British never realized that they hired someone to find himself.

Rishi was a master of hiding both on the physical and astral planes. I could not find him. It is only recently within the past three years that I gained contact with him. That was because he wanted me to publish some translations.

I realized that he knew Yogi Bhajan because I once saw them talking in the astral regions about a year ago. Both were Sikh in terms of religious background.

Blocked Nostril / *Bhastrika* Pranayama

This morning breath infusion began with a completely blocked left nostril which meant that the sun energy was predominant. The moon energy was lacking in the atmosphere.

With *bhastrika* this is treated in a completely different way by ignoring this and doing the practice. After five minutes through my routine, the left nostril opened about 50%. Then after fifteen minutes, it was fully opened. Kundalini rose on both sides of the body.

With *bhastrika* the infused subtle energy spreads from one sector to the next, from one side to the next, from one zone to the next, until the system is filled. This makes it possible to ignore the blockage of a specific nostril and work on the infusement, letting that flow from one filled part to the next.

Due to years of practice, kundalini rises immediately as the practice begins. This is because of years of penetrating the various small microscopic channels. Now they remain open. As soon as the breath infusion starts, they accept charges of that force.

The charges no longer accumulate below the navel to gush into the pubic area and then to rush to muladhara to arouse kundalini. Instead the charge goes through the nadis directly. As such the entire trunk, neck, cheeks and temples have a cool frosty bliss energy shifting and moving continuously during the practice, surging forcibly in particular postures.

Accidental Kundalini Rising

Yesterday I built an outdoor deck. Due to distractions, I cut two supporting posts eight inches too short. This is after we sunk these post thirty inches into the ground in a sixteen-inch diameter hole with concrete.

We extracted the post and concrete. During the process while driving a cold chisel to crack the concrete, I bent over into the hole with my head hanging downwards. This was for about five minutes. When I stood up kundalini rose through the spine and came into the head.

Its journey through the central spinal passage, *sushumna* nadi, was accompanied by a tiny bliss feeling firing along the spine as it travelled upwards. This was like tiny slivers of glass shooting from the spine into the body. When it entered the head, there was supernatural perception which was an omniVision of seeing in all directions and seeing tiny microscopic globules of light.

When this happened, it occurred so quickly that I almost lost control of the physical body. I immediately applied the neck and mind locks while still in touch with the physical body while this consciousness absorption occured.

If I was fully absorbed into this state and did not track the physical form, it would have fell to the ground. The other persons who were present would have concluded that I fainted. These persons have no information of kundalini.

This is an example of how kundalini can rise suddenly without doing yoga to arouse it. This spontaneous rise of kundalini is not sufficient for a yogi. The ascetic should make kundalini rise at least once per day. This should be done prior to meditation.

Lahiri Mahasaya's Visit

I did a mystic procedure this morning which is the tight ball mystic action. This is when one does *bhastrika* or *kapalabhati*. With full internal focus, one draws the subtle body into a tight ball of energy. One infuses this tight ball until it explodes outwards.

This practice was shown by Lahiri Mahasaya who appeared this morning. He came from the same astral direction from which Yogeshwarananda usually hails.

This practice concerns going back to when the fetus of the present body was first formed as a cell structure in a roughly circular shape and also to the time about the third month of the mother's pregnancy when the subtle body is curled as a ball and the forming fetus is also curled with an arched spine. After this third month the spine of the fetus begins to straighten.

In this practice the energies of the subtle body are pulled to the navel area but with the spine arching around the navel until the whole system is a tightly-compressed ball. Then the breath is infused until it gets white hot in the subtle body. Then the yogi continues the breath infusion. After a time, the system explodes outwards.

This practice is part of the method for making sure that the subtle body sheds its tendency for coming back to get a physical body after the demise of the current one. Kundalini is the main force for reinforcing this need for an embryo. Hence if one can elevate the tendencies of the kundalini one can break this habit of repeated transmigration, of automatically recycling through physical existence.

I have not seen Lahiri Baba in the astral world for some years now. I was surprised that he appeared. Since he came from the same astral location where Yogesh usually comes, I assumed that he was there to give an instruction about my current practice.

That proved to be the fact.

Once the practice reaches an advance level and one is eligible to become a siddha, the advanced teachers, who are in the astral world with or without physical bodies, take note. One will come to assist with a certain practice. Then another will come, depending on the area of expertise.

In the astral world because of the vibrations which go out from the student's astral body, the great yogis see when someone practices at an advanced stage. Great yogis come to assist if the energy which emanates from a student requires correction.

The easiest way to find a great yogin is to practice sincerely and to be fully committed to a daily practice. That produces a vibration which is seen by advanced yogis in the astral domains.

Kundalini is not concerned about the observing self. It does not look out for the self. It does not plan to satisfy the spiritual needs of the self. It cannot be relied on to act in the ultimate interest of the self. Kundalini is a creature survival psychic intelligence. When one does postures, if one's attention becomes lax, kundalini may strike unawares. One will realize it after kundalini subsides and resumes normal bodily consciousness.

At the end of a breath infusion session never walk away in a mentally relaxed way. First wait with eyes closed being attentive to the energy movements. Leave the session only after you are confident that kundalini subsided.

This is a subtle observation. One will know it after some time of practicing and keeping the mind internalized. It feels as if one compressed energy and then that energy churns and churns about in a specific part of the subtle body. It goes from the infusion location to other areas. Then it seems that there is no more energy churning or spreading. When one makes that last observation, one will find that the lungs require more air. This is because the air which was infused was absorbed. The lungs are motivated to resume breathing again.

Most persons who get the opportunity to do breath infusion and who shy away from it are influenced by kundalini, which gives them the idea that it is a waste of time or that they should do nothing strenuous or extreme to make spiritual advancement.

The way to trick kundalini when it causes the system to stop absorbing air is to either assume another posture and then continue the rapid breathing or press the fingers down and do the rapid breathing. The fingers, if they are pressed, will cause the brain to feel as if the hands are working. Then the brain may order to the lungs operate. This will override the authority of the kundalini.

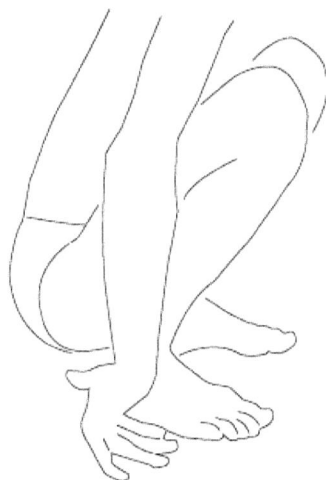

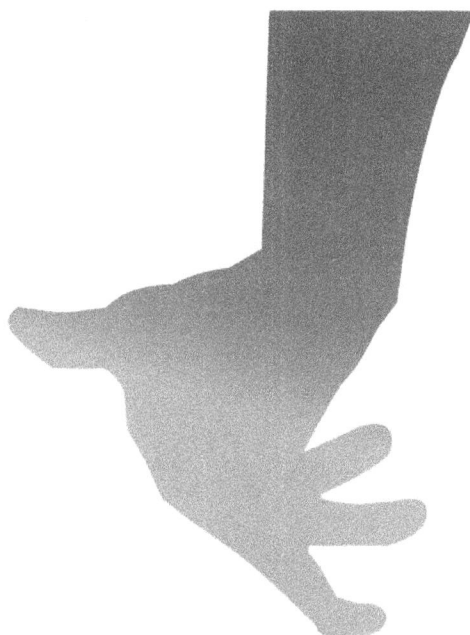

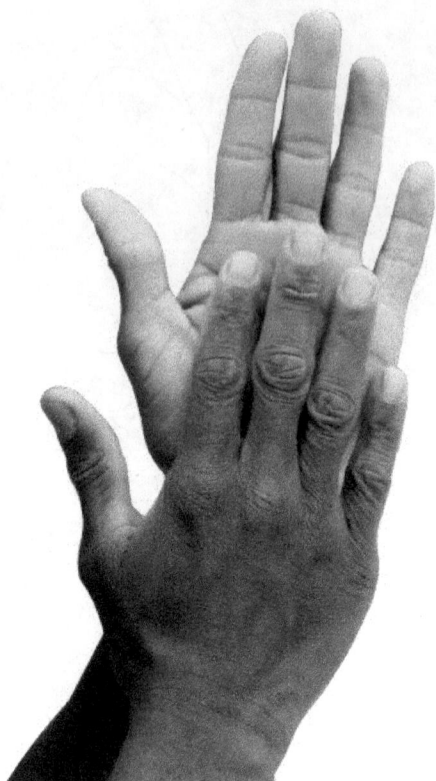

Rose Conjoint Chakra

There is the sex chakra on the spine itself, on the *sushumna* nadi passage in the subtle body. There is also the sex organ chakra. These two are close to each other. They work in unison on occasion.

The sex organ chakra monitors the formation of sexual fluids. For the mother, it directs many of the biological events which take place when an embryo is formed. That chakra is concerned with collecting hormones, setting a polarity charge to these hormones and then supervising how the charge is converted into nourishment or sexual pleasure.

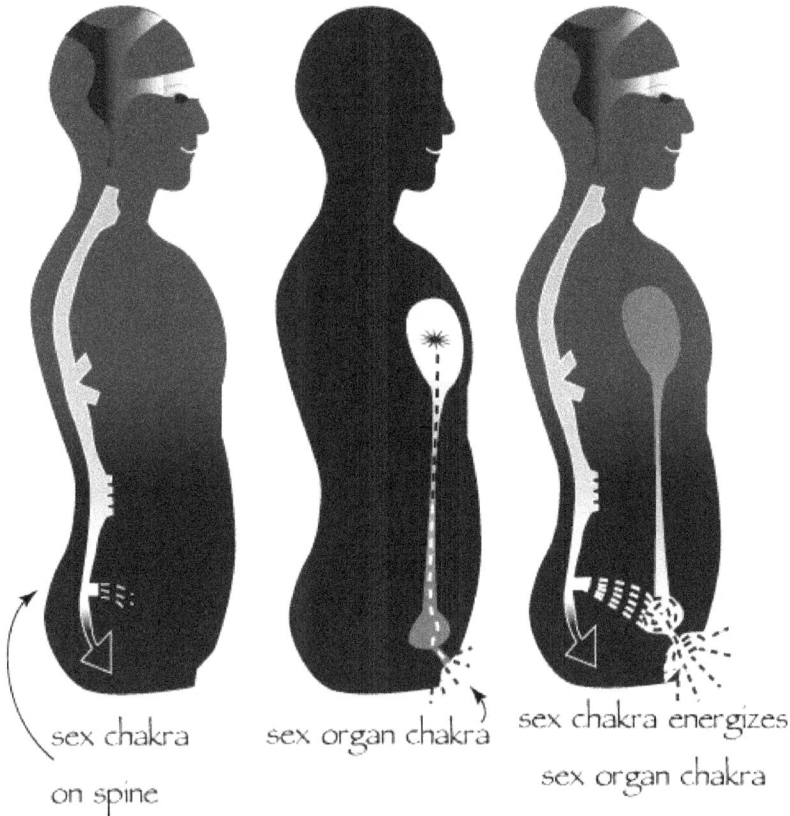

sex chakra on spine   sex organ chakra   sex chakra energizes sex organ chakra

Today during breath infusion, kundalini rose on several occasions. In this practice I restricted its ascent so that it did not go beyond the neck until the very last ten minutes of the session which lasted forty minutes. The reason for this deviation in kundalini arousal is an instruction from a yoga guru.

For some years, I worked on raising kundalini through the spine and into the head at least once per day. The object of that practice was to get kundalini to abandon its base residence, which is muladhara chakra, and move through the spine and enter the brain either to strike the third eye chakra or the crown chakra.

This is great but Yogeshwaranand does not think much of it. For him to assist me to become more advanced, he said that I should no longer use that as objective.

His idea is that the entire psyche, subtle body, must be infused with fresh energizing air, not just the *sushumna* nadi and the head of the subtle body

In compliance I worked on the sex/reproduction chakras. After infusing energy into the base chakra and its surrounding area (sacral region), I pulled negative subtle energy out of the thighs. After that I noticed that the sex organ and reproduction chakras were affected by the infusement.

Even physically the anus is close to the genitals. That is nature's design. When I looked at the two chakras it seemed that they were in a form of dark red rose. It was there with petals. It emitted a fragrance like a deep dark red rose which attracted one's attention by its scent discharge.

I directed the energy from the breath infusion to the red rose. It shattered into fragments. It faded. As I continued it disappeared as if it vaporized. I noticed that its scent was everywhere in the lower trunk and neck. It was diffused everywhere evenly and was no longer in the genital region.

The value of such practices is this:

Patanjali expressed a verse where he explained more or less that if someone wishes to transit to another species of life or another dimension, that person must develop the quality of life, which is on that level.

To live with siddhas, one must act like one and have a subtle body which is similar to one. Ideally this should be done before one is evicted from the physical body.

There will be that final astral projection, where one will find that one cannot again resume the social identity and functions which one is currently. At that time, one may go to a desired world but only if one has a vibrational energy which is compatible with that situation.

जात्यन्तरयन्त्रश्रयणाभ् प्रकृत्यानूयात्॥ २ ॥

jātyantara pariṇāmaḥ prakṛtyāpūrāt
jātyantara = jāti – category + antara – other, another; pariṇāmaḥ – transformation; prakṛiti – subtle material nature; āpūrāt – due to filling up or saturation.

The transformation from one category to another is by the saturation of the subtle physical nature. (Yoga Sutras 4.2)

Muladhara Chakra Attack

Breath infusion this morning was in sequence with practice for this period with more emphasis on the lower part of the trunk of the subtle body. This was to work on the lumbar region, the sacral bony area, with a complete attack on the muladhara chakra territory. This is not just the chakra in the traditional sense but the area where there is the circular bone ending with the coccyx area.

Usually this area is off-limits to yogis even to hatha yogis of the Nath sampradaya who are the best at attacking kundalini and getting it fully subdued.

After about five minutes of practice, Yogeshwarananda came, looked and departed. I practiced. I have a feeling that he checked to see if I did the lessons which at this time are to get the lower part of the subtle body cleansed of polluted breath energy. In the subtle body this is the removal of dark heavy astral force, replacing it with clear light-weight astral energy which when infused enough flashes as light (as in sunlight).

The lumbar area is inaccessible. It is remote but there are postures which make it easy to attack it. Overall, only people who do hard core hatha yoga kriyas and kundalini yoga will take the time to do this. Others are not concerned.

However, in the high end of the hatha yoga process one must be concerned with the dirtiest most profane areas of the psyche, because their condition have an effect on the status of the subtle body and on the outcome of one's life when one must at last leave the physical body and become a wanderer on the astral planes. At that time, after being evicted from the physical casing, the condition of any part of the subtle body which is not clarified, which is not sufficiently energized, will have a negative effect.

One can either hope and pray that one will attain a divine form or one can work now to guarantee the best hereafter condition for oneself. It is up to the individual. Much of this is based on whom one associates with. If one is with seekers who are in a religious discourse which says that God will give a divine form, there will be no impetus to strive for a yoga siddha form.

The attack on the sacral bone area, the circular area which is controlled by kundalini at its base chakra, was successful with light (as in sunlight) flashing in that area and with all the dark energy which is usually there, gone, vanished, banished. Of course, I must work on this for some months to make that condition permanent. The usual situation is that whatever one does to remove negative energy is undone shortly thereafter. In the next session of practice, one finds that the area resumes its previous undesirable condition. Repeated attacks will change that over time.

Yogesh came back after twenty minutes. He said that no one can help the student if he/she does not pass through the course of the lower level of higher yoga. The endeavor must be made. One must give it everything one has, all of one's determination and attention. One should withdraw one's interest in everything else and focus on the objective as defined by the yoga guru.

He said this:

The perfected yogis do not share. You work for it. You get it. You do not work for it. You remain in the neophyte stage. Why work for something else and then dictate how you will progress and what you should achieve. Dedicate yourself to your upliftment.

Later in the session, I did some thigh stretches and pulled every bit of stale astral energy out of the thighs. This is a way to evade ancestors. It is a cruel act but necessary anyway. Unless the yogi wants to beget children, if he aims for a yoga siddha form, he should avoid physical or astral sexual involvement.

For a yoga siddha form sexual intercourse is out, and not as a deprivation, not as a restriction, not as a suppression but only because a yoga siddha body does not have that interest and capability. It has gender but no sexual polarity, no libido sexual drive, no anxiety to consummate sexuality.

The thighs are the big helpers of sexual drive. If the yogi wants exemption from the world of sexual affairs, he must change the attitude of the energy in the thighs. It does not matter what they say or who they worship, if the thigh has the power for lusty energy, one will be involved on the level of sexual activities.

When I removed the polluted astral energy from the trunk of the subtle body, there was flickering of light in the lumbar region, in the lower trunk of the body. The buttocks area was light energy. Yogesh appeared. He directed some infusion in the head of the subtle body. One method was to infuse the lower back of the brain and the lower jaws.

A student showed up this morning. He did practice as I proceeded but I was not attentive to him. I was alert to Yogesh on the subtle side. This particular student knows that as I practice, he can follow the procedure. If I did something internally that he could not see I gave instructions physically.

The lower jaws are one area of the head that is neglected in meditation and so is the lower back of the head where the neck is connected under the brain. Some who meditate have no idea that there is a subtle body and that its condition should be monitored.

I was in a spiritual society where it was about the cleanliness of the physical body. The guru of the sect and the senior members would intimidate anyone who hesitated to bathe in a certain way before daylight. Their idea of cleanliness was an externally-clean physical body, marked with insignia which invoked memory of the deity, the teachers and information of the sect.

But for a yoga siddha form, that is unnecessary. The interest is the internal state of the subtle body. As they are so eager to intimidate anyone who does not take a bath and does not do this and do that for cleanliness of the physical form, so we are sensitive about the internal clarity of the subtle body. For that we use air not water.

- What of the internal condition of blood circulation with fresh oxygen?
- What of prompt evacuation of waste matter?
- What of the distribution of hormone energy and its lack of storage of the same for sexual purposes?
- Does the subtle body have heavy polluted astral energy?
- Can that be washed with water and marked with sacred clay?

Physical Body Value in Yoga

Breath infusion this morning was progressive in terms my current objective which is to remove impurities from the subtle body. This is not a physical practice and yet I do the practice with the physical body.

Due to the fact that the subtle form is interspaced into the physical one and that the physical system runs a parallel response mechanism to the subtle system, physical actions affect and are affected by the subtle.

The physical body is a special opportunity to keep the flimsy shifting subtle body in a stable condition so that one can observe subtle behavior and acquire methods for altering it. As great as the subtle body is, it craves pleasure. As it procures that, it imperils itself.

On the physical level one can regulate it by enforcing the *yama* behavioral restraints and *niyama* permitted attitudes. This eventually may condition the subtle body, causing its reform.

Of course, that is mostly external but even so it is a start in the quest to bring the subtle body to accountability. Any part of the psyche which can imperil the whole psyche should be brought to order to protect the self (psyche).

This morning after practice, I felt that perhaps I made progress to honor the stipulation in the Brahma Sutras which begin with this verse:

अथातो ब्रह्मजिज्ञासा

athāto brahmajijñāsā

That is an instruction, a challenge, that:

"Hey, you are in the human species, having moved through the ranks of evolution, you should stop and think. Look around. Gage the situation. Do not eat, sleep, sex and defend body and territory. Spend time inquiring to locate something substantial."

In yoga practice, if one reaches the stage where one transforms the inside of the subtle body so that it is no longer inclined for the eating, sleeping, sexing and defending business, then one moved on. In the *Yoga Sutras*, Patanjali said that even if one reaches that stage, it will continue for others.

द्रष्टृदृश्ययोः संयोगो हेयहेतुः ॥ १७ ॥

drastṛdṛśyayoḥ samyogo heyahetuḥ

drastṛ – the observer; dṛśyayoḥ – of what is perceived; samyogo – the indiscriminate association; heya – that which is to be avoided; hetuḥ – the cause.

The cause which is to be avoided is the indiscriminate association of the observer and what is perceived. (Yoga Sutras 2.17)

प्रकाशक्रियास्थितिशीलं भूतेन्द्रियात्मकं भोगापवर्गार्थं दृश्यम् ॥ १८ ॥

prakāśa kriyā sthiti śīlam bhūtendriyātmakam
bhogāpavargārtham dṛśyam

prakāśa – clear perception; kriyā – action; sthiti – stability; śīlam – form, disposition; bhūta – mundane elements; indriya – sense organs; ātmakam – self, nature; bhoga – experience; apavarga – liberation; artham – value or purpose; dṛśyam – what is perceived.

What is perceived is of the nature of the mundane elements and the sense organs and is formed in clear perception, action or stability. Its purpose is to give experience or to allow liberation. (Yoga Sutras 2.18)

विशेषाविशेषलिङ्गमात्रालिङ्गानि गुणपर्वाणि ॥ १९ ॥

viśeṣa aviśeṣa liṅgamātra aliṅgāni guṇaparvāṇi

viśeṣa – that which is specific; aviśeṣa – what is regular; liṅgamātra – a mark, that which is indicated; aliṅgāni – that which has no indication; guṇa – influences of material nature; parvāṇi – phases, stages, parts.

The phases of the influences of material nature are those which are specific, regular, indicated or not indicated. (Yoga Sutras 2.19)

द्रष्टा दृशिमात्रः शुद्धोऽपि प्रत्ययानुपश्यः ॥ २० ॥

drastā dṛśimātraḥ śuddhaḥ api pratyayānupaśyaḥ

draṣṭā – the perceiver; dṛśi – perception, consciousness; mātraḥ – measure or extent; śuddhaḥ – purity; api – but; pratyayaḥ – conviction or belief as mental content; anu – following along, patterning after; paśyaḥ – what is perceived.

The perceiver is the pure extent of its consciousness but its conviction is patterned by what it perceives. (Yoga Sutras 2.20)

तदर्थ एव दृश्यस्यात्मा ॥ २१ ॥

tadarthaḥ eva dṛśyasya ātmā

tad = tat – that; arthaḥ – purpose; eva – only; dṛśyasya – of what is seen; ātmā – individual spirit.

The individual spirit, who is involved in what is seen, exists here for that purpose only. (Yoga Sutras 2.21)

कृतार्थं प्रति नष्टमप्यनष्टं तदन्यसाधारणत्वात् ॥ २२ ॥

kṛtārthaṃ prati naṣṭam api

anaṣṭaṃ tadanya sādhāraṇatvāt

kṛt – fulfilled done; ārthaṃ – purpose; prati – toward; naṣṭam – destroyed, non-existent, non-effective; api – although, but; anaṣṭaṃ – not finished, still existing, effective; tat – that; anya – others; sādhāraṇatvāt – common, normal, universal.

It is not effective for one to whom its purpose is fulfilled, but it has a common effect on the others. (Yoga Sutras 2.22)

Liberation of one individual is liberation of one person. It is not liberation for others. The rest remain under the auspicious care of the most gracious mother, the physio-psychic nature.

Yoga Siddha / Thigh Alteration

Breath infusion, this morning, was a progression. A yogi is lucky when the progression is integral and progressive. There are times when a student makes no progress. Then he is advised by the teacher to practice and not be discouraged. When there is progression there is happiness about that. When progress is not there even when practicing, there is a discouraging energy which stuns some students.

My advice is simple:

Practice no matter what. Push past the discouragement. Practice because the yoga guru said to do so. All girls and boys, who are yogis, should accept Shiva as the supreme father or Krishna alternately. Taking assistance from the *Bhagavad Gita*, we should practice.

This morning I worked on the thighs. If they are not conquered before one leaves the body, one may as well set oneself to take another embryo, because the energy in the thighs have the authority to make even a yogi be receptive to the reproductive energy which translates into rebirth in a physical body somewhere somehow.

As nature designed it, the thighs support the sexual function which is to be used for reproduction and pleasure. It does not matter who the guru is. It does not matter what type of yoga one does. If the thighs are in servitude to the sexual chakra, consider that one will be reborn as an embryo.

This morning I pulled energy out of the thighs directly through the center of the subtle body and into the head. There was no routing through the pubic area to acquire a sexual polarity charge which will urge the body into a sexual contact, where it will pass sexual fluids regardless of whether that is enjoyed or not.

In the normal psyche, this thigh energy rises from the knees, and is accumulated where the thighs are linked into the lower trunk. It stays there and picks up a charge from the sexual organ chakra. The chakra then draws that sexually-charged energy into itself. It is infused with this energy which increases the sex drive.

For a yoga siddha subtle body however, that is undesirable. In the siddha situation, reproduction by sexual function does not exist. In fact, reproduction period, does not exist. The tendencies which concern reproduction are absent.

When the energy was pulled upward out of the thigh without it being routed through the sex organ chakra, it felt like tiny sliver needles firing upwards into the neck, chest and armpits with bliss slivers of energy bursting. This is felt during breath infusion practice, as the breath is the means in this case of extracting the energy.

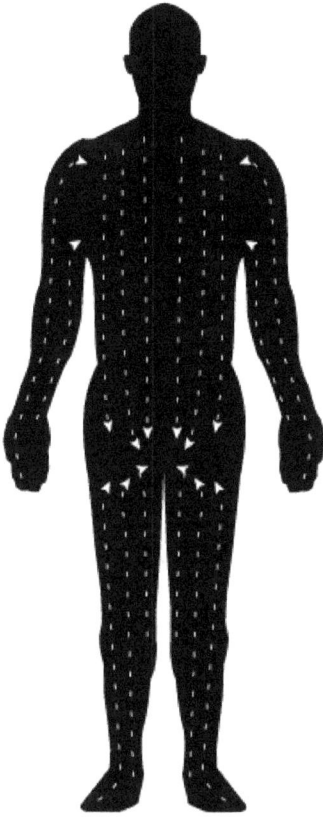

hormonal energy
travel to groin

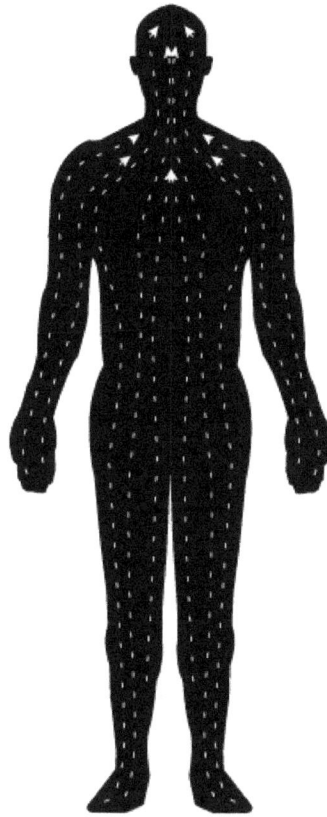

hormonal energy
travels upward only

Wayward Kundalini

Kundalini is wayward. It resists being controlled. Breath energy is wayward too. Keep the focus inside the body while practicing. Take time to practice *pratyahar* as explained in chapter one of the *Meditation Pictorial* book.

Getting proficient at the breathing takes practice. Once one is expert at it, one should focus on either the locks or the internalization of the attention and the ability to track how the energy is diffused when one holds air in or out after a sequence of breaths.

Even though it is a positive force, the infused fresh air will resist one's control. As one practices more and more one will get a grip on it. Locating muladhara chakra, tracking the sex energy in the organs, all of these aspects take practice to master.

The psyche will rebel once it understands that one is determined to be a serious yogi. There will be resistance even of the tiniest of cells in the physical body and even from the smallest subtle passages in the subtle form, but if one endeavors bit by bit, one will take territory and function more and more.

Changing the Subtle Body

Breath infusion practice this morning was productive with more improvement. I got the opportunity to note how changes are made in the subtle body to move it into being a yoga siddha form. Unless one achieves the required changes before death of the physical system, it is hardly likely that one can attain a siddha form after the body dies.

There is a chance that if one has a momentum of a change in the subtle body, it will continue after the physical form is lost and the subtle body will not be interested in procuring a physical form and will be attracted to a psychic level of existence where advanced yogis practice. But it is hardly likely because what usually happens is that once a physical body is lost, the subtle body immediately seeks to re-enter to participate in the earth's history. Even in the case of people who declare that they are liberated and that they are merged into the absolute, they too have subtle bodies which are earth bound and just as when they are living they had to evacuate that body, acquire prestige for it and do other things to it, so after leaving the physical form they have to deal with the subtle body's issues and habits.

If the subtle body is not dissolved out of existence now that I use the physical form it will not be dissolved merely because the physical system is no longer available. Death of the physical body does not change anything in the psychological format of a person. Simply closing the eyes to meditate and then feeling nothingness, does nothing to remove either the physical or subtle bodies or the responsibilities which are tagged to these in their respective dimensions.

During this breath infusion session there was burst of the infused energy in the chest and neck. This was like sparklets or fireworks which causes tiny sparks to go in all directions, glowing.

There was a down spiked kundalini which is the reverse of the normal kundalini. In a down kundalini it has its base in the neck. It fires downwards into the trunk of the subtle body with some spike energy darts. This is contrasted to up-kundalini where one feels spikes emanating from the spine and darting through the body upwards. At one point a small charge of infused energy glowed in the pubic area and then fired downwards through that area.

One event was when there was a firing of kundalini into the armpit, arms and forearms. This was a worm-shaped energy which was coiled like the small spring inside a ball-point pen. When it fired the spring energy which was white hot in color, stretched like when a child takes out a ball-point spring and pulls it so that it no longer retracts into a coil.

The infused energy burst into the nose. This happened while I did the breath infusion in lotus posture. I wiggled the lower part of the body back and forth. This served the purpose to cause the infused energy to penetrate blocked tiny nadis.

Why do these practices?

To change the nature and energy content of the subtle body.

Light Shattered like Windshield Glass

Breath infusion was a continuation in development from yesterday. Practice is not always consecutive and cohesive where the student derives a linear progression or even a rapid jump from one stage to another.

There were times when weeks of practice produced no ample progress. Still the student should push on with confidence in senior yogis and the process. A child at school cannot always feel that rush of progress, that satisfaction in learning. Still he is required to attend. In the end, it may add up and make sense as to why the parents insisted on his attending the classes.

Yesterday and for about four days prior, it was a situation of where the infused breath energy in the subtle body amassed in the neck instead of going through the neck into the head. After this occurred, light accumulated in the neck and acted like a blockage.

Light blocking light?

Light energy stopping other light energy or some other energy type? This happened, where the lower part of the subtle body was filled with more and more infused energy. Yesterday this happened. There was a change. The neck was no longer blocking the transfer of energy from the trunk of the subtle body into the head of it.

Today however the energy was stacked light rays which compressed in the neck and suddenly shattered. It was like crushed glass or crushed ice crystals, shattered into mini fragments. Then these moved through the psyche, through the trunk and head. It felt like a cool energy swashing around in the psyche.

During this session after a sequence of rapid breaths, I checked the energy distribution. Every so often I would either stretch to one side and then to the other corresponding side, or shift the head and neck back from right to left repeatedly. At some times, I would wiggle the body while keeping focused within to track any energy which would run through hidden or known nadi channels as a result of the wiggling action.

Here is a case where postures, which are physical actions, have subtle effects.

After the light in the neck shattered, light went everywhere evenly, in the head, in the torso. There was bliss energy everywhere as I looked and searched in the subtle body. I evaluated what happens when the pleasure energy which fires as sexual climax is spread in the system evenly but without the lusty feature of it, and without physical stimulation and companion involvement.

Using Subtle Body Lights

Breath infusion practice this morning was special with some new developments where the neck area acted as a constructive block to any energy ascending to the head. This was a new development because blocks are to be removed mostly in yoga or held in place for certain outcomes.

There are nadi blockages which are flushed in breath infusion practice. There are locks which when applied remove those blocks. A student yogi is sometimes baffled. In some cases, the student does not see the block. Thus, he cannot remove it and must continue with the impurities come what may.

While doing breath infusion, at about fifteen minutes into the practice, I noticed a scattered light through the neck which was produced by the breath infusion which pulled energy from the lower part of the trunk. This light was scattered through the neck not just in the *sushumna* central passage. As I did the rapid breathing, this light got thicker and thicker and more compacted. It sent shimmering rays of light. A little of this light escaped upwards into the base of the head.

There is an old saying in pranayama practice which is that prana will show the way. I let this light do whatever it would do. I kept infusing more and more air into the system using the *bhastrika* pranayama in various postures but with full attention inside the psyche and not permitting even one ray of attention to go outside the subtle body.

Prana or subtle energy which is infused in pranayama practice, will itself do things in the psyche, to aid the yogi in the quest for subtle body purification and pollution energy displacement.

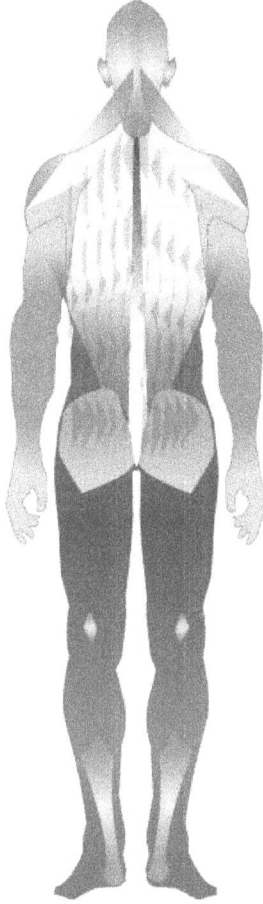

The key to regulate the passage of kundalini from base chakra to the head, seems to be the efficient application of the neck and belly locks. This gives space for kundalini to dispense in a controlled way. If one does not keep the locks tight after kundalini enters the head, the body may fall to the ground.

If one masters the neck lock, one can use it as a valve to only release so much of kundalini into the head at a time. In that way kundalini will not enter like a mad bull and ram the intellect which will put the witnessing self out of commission. The kundalini was originally given to the selves in a matching way. Look at this technical statement from *Bhagavad Gita*:

भभैलाँळो जीलरोके

जीलबूत् वनातन् ।

भन्छिठानीकिमाकण

प्रकृकतिाकन कळमकत ॥ १५.७॥

mamaivāṁśo jīvaloke

jīvabhūtaḥ sanātanaḥ

manaḥṣaṣṭhānīndriyāṇi

prakṛtisthāni karṣati (15.7)

mamaivāṁśaḥ = mama — my + eva — indeed + aṁśaḥ — partner; jăvaloke = jăva — individualized conditioned being + loke — in the world; jăvabhūtaḥ — individual soul; sanātanaḥ — eternal; manaḥ — mind; ṣaṣṭhānīndriyāṇi = saṣṭhāni — sixth + indriyāṇi — sense, detection device; prakṛtisthāni — mundane; karṣati — draws

My partner is in this world of individualized conditioned beings. He is an eternal individual soul but he draws to himself the mundane senses of which the mind is the sixth detection device. (Bhagavad Gita 15.7)

This is a vital verse to understand our existential predicament. It rids the nonsense about oneness and absoluteness. It is like seeing what happened when I was in the mother's womb where my mouth was filled with amniotic fluid.

Note the Sanskrit word *karṣati*.

In that primeval situation how did the entity get a matching energy from psychic nature which formed into a psyche which was experienced as a subtle body with senses?

What I hint here is that the kundalini is the exact match for the entity. It was attracted to the entity as a match, a perfect match but not to the head of the subtle body, or even to the coreSelf in the psyche. It was a match for the entire composite. This means that the kundalini is such that if it is focused on just one part of the system there may be problems.

Kundalini should be distributed through the psyche not just in the head of it. Of course, first one must identify kundalini, then control it and then distribute it.

Normally kundalini is a sex junkie. Initially in the practice, a yogi acts to be blissful with kundalini in the head. As he matures in practice that changes, he learns how to distribute it to each part of the psyche

Making of a Yoga Siddha Body

Breath infusion this morning was great. I worked on the trunk of the subtle body, disregarding raising the energy into the head of it. This practice however is not recommended for most students. Most should work daily to raise kundalini through the spine.

I describe an advanced process. It is of interest for the future for those who are not as advanced to practice it. Take note. Include it in future process.

I worked on infusing energy into the central spinal passage of the subtle body, *sushumna* nadi. But in this practice, it is done in the opposite way which is from the neck down to the base of the spine. This is reverse to the standard way which is from the base of the spine into the neck and brain.

In this practice the yogi looks down into the spine from the neck. When looking, he sees a spinal passage which is cleared so that there is no energy anywhere in it, like looking through a hollow cylinder. As soon as the yogi sees this cleared spine with no kundalini in it and no other type of energy in it, he does the breath infusion pushing air in through the neck down and pulling the air up through it. This causes an infusion into the spine.

Because there is no lusty charge in the energy, it does not act in the same way as before. The energy accumulates but without a lusty charge. It then gets more and more intense. It flashes through the channels which radiate from the spine. It does so in the reverse which is from the spine upwards in spikes.

The normal system is that the nadis come off the spine and go out mostly downwards like the nerves in the physical body but in this system the channels flip upwards.

When the subtle body of a yogi is fully reformed from the creature existence scene, the downward tendencies in the subtle body are reversed. The energy gets an upward draft applied which is the converse of the downward pull of gravity.

During this practice the infused energy radiated up through the shoulders. It felt like hot frosty micro crystals shimmering and coming in waves, one after the other.

This is part of a yogi changing the subtle body so that it can become a yoga siddha form. He can do this while he has a physical body or after he loses the physical body and is left out in the astral world with no way to awaken on this side.

Part 5

Vacuum Draw Kundalini

The primary method in kundalini yoga is the top pressure pump down system. Students must begin with that system which means that they infuse breath energy, force it into the system downwards through the navel area and then the groin area, and then pressure it to arc to kundalini at muladhara base chakra.

Once this happens kundalini must shift. If the locks are applied kundalini has no choice but to move upward through the central spine into the head. It may go into the head or it may rise through one or two chakras and then subside to its base position, all depending on the force of the charge which hits it.

This is like in rocket science where if the fuel tank is small, your rocket will only rise a few hundred feet or a few thousand feet. Then it will fall to the earth. If there is a large tank and if the ignition system works, the rocket will be sustained in its ascent because of the force of pressure which is emitted from the exhaust.

If when one infuses breath energy, that is compressed into the system and is pushed pass the navel, pass the groin area, when that strikes kundalini, if it has enough of a charge, kundalini will have no choice in the matter and will rise.

This is like in a hydraulic system, where someone pumps air or a fluid into a sealed system. Because of that downward pressure, the gas or liquid which is in the sealed system will rise through a pipe and gush out at the surface.

The more advanced method which is more difficult to install is a vacuum draw system. In that system instead of pumping air or fluid under tremendous pressure, one may lower a pipe and then extract the air in the system. In kundalini yoga that is possible as well but only after one advances by raising kundalini every day for some years.

The value of the more advanced system is that it eliminates the lust-charge from the kundalini energy, such that the student no longer has to exert during practice to remove the lust energy.

Sexless Kundalini

The kundalini as we are endowed with it by nature, is a sexually polarized lifeForce. In childhood, its sexuality is somewhat disabled. In infancy before puberty the body has gender but is sexually neutral. As soon as puberty develops, the body becomes sexually aroused. It develops sexual polarity. The neutrality is foreshadowed. The gender remains but it is polarized.

In kundalini yoga, the popular arousal is with a sexual charge. The energy which kundalini feeds on is the hormone energy in the body which is a combination of breath force and nutritional energy. However, kundalini uses this energy only after it is sexually charged.

This makes it necessary to deal with the sexual charge. After some practice, perhaps years of deliberately raising kundalini daily, causing it to course through the central spinal passage (*sushumna* nadi), a student can switch the focus to a system of pulling up kundalini, rather than forcing it to rise from muladhara chakra.

Of necessity because of the way the kundalini formed the fetus in the mother's uterus and because of the way kundalini designed everything, the student must work with it as it is, which is that it is a sexually charged condition. Later when this is mastered one may switch to the position of being sexually neutral. The same energy is used but it is used before it acquires a sex charge. Instead of the breath and nutritional energy going downwards first then being absorbed into kundalini or fused into it after it is sexually polarized, the student collects the energy and uses it in its neutral state, before it is influenced by the sexual apparatus.

This method works because kundalini is forced to move into the head of the subtle body without sexual enthusiasm. This is a lust-free kundalini, where the student has no requirement to remove the impurities and lower impetus of the lust force.

Ultimately this will lead to assuming a divine body in which penetration does not arise. There is satisfaction even without sexual expression but with gender awareness.

Today I did a *bhastrika* pranayama surcharge where the energy in the thighs were pulled through the trunk of the subtle body into the head. This is part of the neutralization process. The old method, the natural way, is for the energy of the thigh to feed the sexual chakra. This feed enriches that energy with a lust charge. Kundalini then takes this lust charge and uses it in sexual activities or the yogi may infuse it with breath energy in pranayama and fire it at kundalini to cause kundalini to move through the spine into the brain.

This new method bypasses that sexual charge system of the thigh energy. This keeps the energy free from the lust charge. A yogi does this practice to qualify for living with siddhas who have neutral energy subtle bodies.

Sometimes if one does *bhastrika* intensely and then one closes the eyes and compresses the eyelids tightly over the eyes, then press the fingers to the eyes, and do more rapid breathing, one will see a golden donut shape circle. It is intense. It may flash and disappear. After that a greenish round or odd shape pad will appear and then branches of light and a tiny star may also appear.

It is important to recognize minor activity at the third eye. One thing that helps with this is to blindfold the eyes and forehead with a dark cloth during meditation. This helps to detect the slightest activity at the third eye.

Kundalini's hitting the third eye, or coming into the head and then darting to the third eye will not necessarily give someone supernatural perception. It may. It may not. It depends on if one is focused through it or linked into it.

If, however, one does breath infusion daily, the third eye may be activated during any efficient session. That gives increase psychic perception especially increased supernatural vision. The trouble with that however is that one may not realize it or one may know of it and not have the skill to interpret it.

Fifty breaths in a sequence during a posture are a good lot. It could be less. The main thing is the absorption rate of the lungs.

Suppose I do ten breaths and the system absorbs that, it would be better than 20 breaths with only a 30% absorption. Absorption rate is the issue.

There is no sense in inhaling and exhaling if the lungs do not absorb the inhaled air. Usually after a number of breaths, and it varies from day to day, the lungs stop absorbing air.

One should be sensitive enough to know when the lungs no longer absorb the air. As soon as one feels that the accumulated air is distributed in the system, one should begin breathing again.

In a certain posture there comes a time when the air which is being absorbed is no longer absorbed. Then one should assume another posture until that zone is saturated.

Do not allow the mind to be unruly during practice. Do not allow the mind to pursue sensual objects externally through the eye or ear or any other sense. Do not allow the mind to chase thoughts from others except from the yoga gurus.

Between sequences of breathing in postures or in the same posture, the student should stop to let the system distribute the air which it stockpiled in the blood stream near the lungs. During that time, the student should be attentive to the way the system distributes the air. He should observe its effects on kundalini.

When kundalini makes a full ascent to the top of the head (brahmrandra), one is transposed into spiritual light. This is denoted by micro (super small) size balls of light, all compacted tightly together for miles and miles and miles in all directions.

It feels as if one is a microscopic ice-crystal in an ocean of other ice-crystals, where one cannot determine where one begins or ends.

When this happens, the yogi loses contact with the physical body and with the subtle body and even with the causal form. The yogi becomes aware of a sheer intense compacted golden light in every direction. The yogi cannot tell distinctly where he begins or ends. He feels a flawless all-pervading consciousness in all directions.

That is the brahman experience of the Upanishads and the Brahma Sutras. It is undifferentiated super consciousness.

After this experience, a yogi finds himself in the head of the subtle body in the default position of the coreSelf but with kundalini descending rapidly, like a snake quickly retracting into its hole. The yogi is then left with the memory of the experience.

When this experience is intense and when it last for say about thirty seconds or more, the yogi, once he returns to normal consciousness, feels as if a pleasure energy is in the physical body. This will last for a short time.

Doing Justice to Yoga Practice

Breath infusion session this morning was great. I felt that I met the requirements of the yoga gurus. I did a full session. How many times can a student say that he/she met the requirements? Is there anyone whom we try to please by doing yoga or is it just one's satisfaction?

Is there anyone who is more advanced, to whom one feels practice is an obligation?

Is one alone like a single island in an infinite sea?

Mostly the infused energy fired in the neck and lower head. The energy, instead of ascending *sushumna* nadi quickly and entering into the brain, diffused through the spinal bones in the neck into the flesh of the neck. This felt like shimmering warm frosty ice energy scattering out, vibrating whatever it penetrated. This happened repeatedly.

I accept this as a stage in the development of the practice of trying to make sure that every part of the subtle body is clarified, cleared of heavy astral energy, used energy which lingered there for weeks, months or years.

A wonderful practice during breath infusion is when one does a posture which is difficult. Because of the difficulty one is forced to note the stretch. This forced attention does wonders for reaching places in the subtle body (and the physical body) which usually one is unaware of mentally. Then one can check those areas to see if there is stale psychic energy, used polluted energy (carbon dioxide / ketones). One can extract that with breath infusion, replacing it with fresh energizing energy *(prana)*. This clears dark remote places.

This may be compared to cleaning parts of a residence which were not used for years and which remained dingy, dirty and cobwebbed. Postures are wonderful in this way. The breath infusion is like a vacuum cleaner/blower to extract or blast whatever was left due to neglect of kundalini. Kundalini makes sure that there is a fresh stockpile of energy for sexual purposes but it is not so concerned with what happens in the knee or even what happens in the rectal passage, which is so close to it. It pursues sexual pleasure. In so doing it neglects other vital sensations. One can tone the psyche by using postures and breath infusion simultaneously.

Today after practice, I felt that my yoga gurus were satisfied that I did justice to the practice. If kundalini is not aroused during a thorough session lasting for at least twenty minutes, that means that the infusion process is not done correctly or that the lungs did not absorb the air.

Be attentive to the locks. When one stops on an inhale or exhale, one should pull the belly under the rib cage. One should apply the neck lock with drawing the chin back to the throat while keeping the neck straight and not leaning the head forward.

The sex lock which is contracting the perineum should be applied. Do this by pulling the urinary muscles back and up.

The anus lock means that one retracts the circular anal muscle into the body. The mind lock means that the mind does not wander. It is not engaged in sensual pursuits outside the body. It is attentive to the practice.

If the lungs are filled with air but does not compressing that air into the blood stream, there is not much one can do except to keep practicing. Over time the lungs will change attitude.

There is a simple test, which is that when one stops a sequence and one inhales or exhales, how long does it take before one requires air. The period should be longer than usual. If the lungs compressed air into the alveoli, it will begin to distribute that air. It will not be urging for more air as it usually does. But as soon as the air is distributed one will feel the urge to release the locks and resume breathing.

As one becomes proficient, one will observe that after a sequence one can hold the breath in or out for a long period while observing from within how the accumulated energy is distributed through the system.

Yogi Evades Sex Tax

Breath infusion went well this morning. I recapped what Tibeti taught about pulling energy directly up through the subtle body and not worry about using the kundalini to assist in this.

Initially this is not possible and one must use the kundalini with this, if not for the basic reason that kundalini is the natural monitor. It created the fetus of the body mostly based on its creative powers. Once however, one batters kundalini in submission by raising it daily, things change. One can rule the psyche instead of being directed by kundalini.

I pulled energy from the knee upward. The thighs supplement the reproduction/sex pleasure operations mostly for generating progeny, but in the human species, we successfully evade generating progeny by using contraception, a technique of cheating nature which is not available in lower animal bodies.

Once one gets the specialized brain in the human species, one learns how to outsmart nature, so that instead of paying the tax of raising progeny after enjoying sex, we enjoy it while using a contraceptive method to avoid responsibility.

Who would stay in a country where there is tax such that for eating one glass of ice-cream, one has to work without wages for 18 years? That is what it amounts to in the modern society, where a male or female who has a child from a single intercourse is responsible for that infant for eighteen years. Of course, that is partially due to human laws. But what about in nature, where for instance parent birds must stay with eggs to hatched chicks. Do birds have a choice? If they do not, how does nature enforce that? Why are they compelled?

In a bird species for instance, after enjoying sex for just a short period of time, the female carries a fetus in the making. This is pushed out of her body in a shell. Then she sits on that egg for some time, giving it warmth for development. When it is born, she must feed it. In some bird species, the male involved helps the female with the chores of child care. In that way for a little sex pleasure, nature enforces the responsibility for progeny. In the human species however, we use contraceptive methods to avoid the liability and enjoy sexual pleasure.

For the human yogi however, he/she may see that nature may react to contraceptive methods. Who knows what nature may do in the future as a reaction to a contraceptive action? There are other lives. A yogi cannot be sure that he/she will control the layout of that future.

Who knows how providence will design that? In fact, what is the guarantee that the yogi's next body, if there is to be one, will be a human one? Can the yogi say for sure that in this life, he/she arranged to take the present body in exactly the way it was produced and operates at the present? Did the yogi plan the birth, growth, maturity, aging, terminal disease and death?

How many grey hairs did the yogi get?

Instead of using contraceptives and being uncertain about how nature will react to that, a yogi may quell the lusty energy in the body. Then there is rarely the need to use contraceptives because the driving force behind sexual polarity is diminished.

Once the kundalini is charged with sexual force from the genitals, it has to perform a certain amount of sexually polar activities. It has no choice. It must process the urges of energy. If one can change the subtle body so that it is divested of the sexual polarity, the package of sex responsibility will be absent. The yogi will be freed from the contract of having a physical body, which carries with it the obligation of sexual engagement for generating progeny.

Yogi Goes to Swarga Paradise World

This morning during breath infusion kundalini sparked here and there. One location was the spine behind the chest. Kundalini sparked like a hot cream in tubular form.

It fired in the neck where it was like a cool heat on both sides of the shoulders. It moved up continuously like lava creeping through the walls of a volcano.

I noted a message which was left in my psyche by Tibeti Yogi. He said that when the sex energy is distributed through the body continuously it stops accumulating in the sex organ area. The yogi experiences the subtle body as if it was in the Swarga heavenly planets. In those celestial places, the inhabitants drink a nectar which instantly rejuvenates the subtle body. This beverage influences the subtle body so that it has no intention for a physical embryo.

Even though the subtle body we use is long lasting, lasting for the duration of the sun planet at least, it has a need for a physical form. It becomes unsettled if it does not have that facility. The angelic beings in the Swarga heavenly world do not have that need. If a yogi can get his sex energy to be distributed evenly through the subtle body, he may go to the Swarga heavenly places after he is deprived of the physical body. There he will stay with the angelic people in a paradise world.

During practice there was a rise of kundalini energy in the neck. It felt like drifting cool cramps. These rose and rose and entered the cheeks where it felt like icicle rays shimmering.

Naad Reference

With breath infusion, one should sit to meditate immediately after. One should notice what the infusion did to the psyche. If one sits to meditate after the infusion, there should be some difference in the feelings of consciousness. If there is not the practice was inefficient. If there is a difference one should make a mental note and link the attention into that state of consciousness which the infusion caused.

Naad sound meditation is important because it can be used as the absolute reference when one is in meditation. For instance, if I meditate, then suddenly I may find myself looking at thoughts or images in the mind, these expressions in the mind may be of no spiritual value or may be disruptive of the practice. When I find myself in that undesirable state, I should have a reference which I can return to. Naad is one such anchor.

Another is the center of the eyebrows and yet another is the centralized axial position of the coreSelf, provided you know what and where that is.

Naad focus is for advanced practitioners who used it for years and who developed an affinity with it. With naad if you have no affinity, using it as a reference would not work because you will not hold the attention to it effortlessly.

Kundalini Subdued

Breath infusion this morning was a continuation of the practice of Tibeti for pulling the energy which usually goes to the groin area via the navel. As it is, this is the natural way for the energy to go down. Even gravity of planet earth endorses and supports this method. This causes the subtle body to be earth bound. It is continually under that influence which causes one to take one body after another in sequence on the earth plane.

This method attacks the system of transmigration at its roots which is that the kundalini gets energy from this which is surcharged by the digestion and reproduction influences. As the energy passes through the navel area, it is charged with the survival energy. As it goes further down and passes through the groin, it is charged with the reproduction mood for the purpose of investing in progeny to guarantee a passage back into the species of life one is in currently.

This method of Tibeti is in contrast to the traditional *up through the spine* method. In the up method which is the preliminary stage which one cannot avoid, the student must deal with sexually charged energy. The method is to infuse the energy, purify its intention and link it with kundalini for kundalini's ascent. If the energy gets linked to kundalini without the purification from the infusion charge, that will result in sexual expression.

Tibeti's method is to deal with the energy even before it is sexually charged. In other words, as the energy descends, it is not allowed to go lower. It is pulled to the frontal part of the subtle body. It does not go around the pubic loop nor to the kundalini at base chakra.

The energy is drawn up and is distributed without the survival and sexual charges which it is given at the navel and genitals. When it is done to proficiency, it affords the yogi a gender body which has no sexual polarity, which is a pre-stage for the yoga siddha form.

Classic Yoga:
Infused breath energy charges hormone
system and targets kundalini
which then ascends the spine
and enters the brain

air/food
intake

navel charge
survival

sex polarity charge
reproduction

infused breath
attacks kundalini

Reverse gravity method:
air/food energy never reaches kundalini.
It is pulled up by breath infusion pulling
force and is then distributed without being surcharged
for survival and reproduction.
Kundalini is deprived of its main food source.

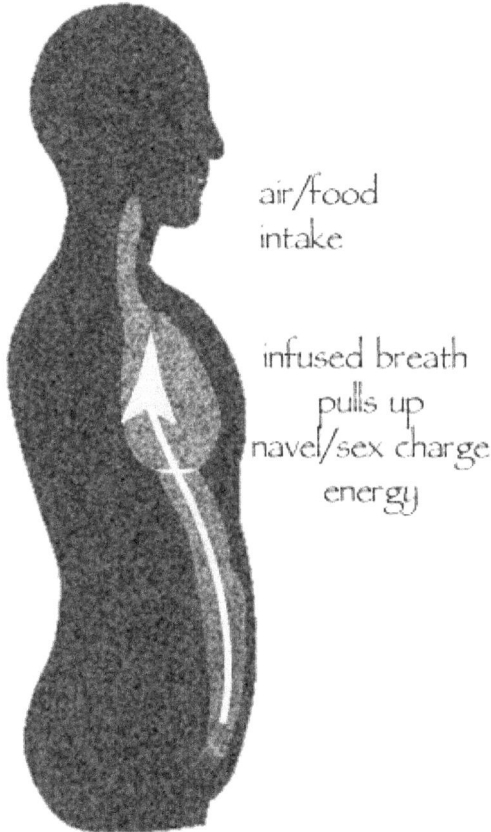

air/food
intake

infused breath
pulls up
navel/sex charge
energy

Radical Elimination of Kundalini

If one is to get a yoga siddha form, the energy distribution system of the astral body must be changed. A yoga siddha form is the same astral form transformed.

It is reduced to consuming energy, converting that into power and living in an environment. Everything we do is reduced to that. We are power consumers. The psyche is an engine system.

Who should design the subtle body so that one can go to a divine world?
- Can it be done by chanting Sanskrit mantras?
- Can it be done by focusing affection on a deity?
- Can it be done by prayer?
- Can it be done by singing?
- Can it be done by sitting to meditate?

Whatever method produced the effects desired, the changes needed, that process is the approved one.

Mastership of standard kundalini

distribution system. Energy is first conditioned

by navel and groin area then it is purified

by breath infusion treatment. It is then through

the sushumna nadi into the subtle head

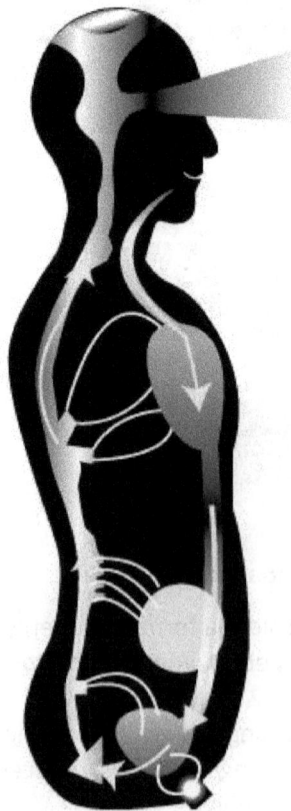

unconditioned energy with no kundalini
supervision, no navel/groin conditioning
with sexual neutrality

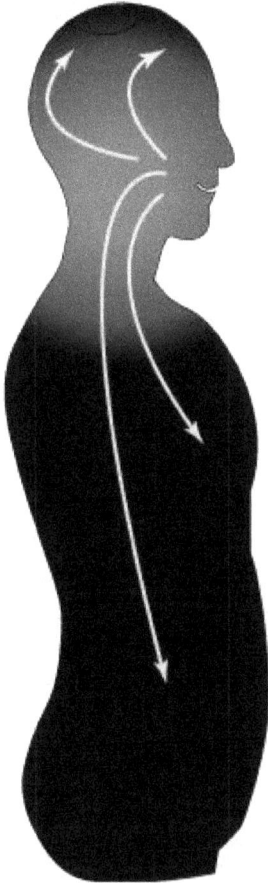

Kundalini's Game Plan

Highlight of this morning's breath infusion was the full pull of the energy which usually descends. The situation is that. The design of the subtle body, when kundalini does its involuntary operation is that it absorbs energy for the purpose of begetting other bodies. In the process of doing so it conserves a portion of that energy for sense enjoyment and for sensual enthusiasm in acquiring for nutrients.

This maxes out in predatory species like eagles and lions. The human beings are also part of this system of procuring food, extracting nutrients, feeding sensory pursuits, reproducing and enjoying in whatever little time there is in the breathing spaces nature allows.

The divine beings live in a different way. Their system is nonexistence on the physical plane. To get information on their situation one must hear and read of the invaders, the aliens who cross the threshold and move into our world. These persons are Krishna, Shiva, even Jesus Christ and Buddha.

The system is that kundalini gulps energy. It uses that to support its sensory prowess. Through that it hunts for more nutrients for its survival. The next step is to conserve this energy so that there is spare time. Who wants to hunt day and night with no respite?

When kundalini can, it absorbs more than enough energy. It concentrates and conserves the excess. As soon as the energy enters, it takes the downward route, through the gut into the sexual apparatus. There it is enjoyed in sexual intercourse and it is used to beget other bodies, which is kundalini's investment in its future, its social security plan.

If there is no investment in the future, kundalini will have nowhere to live. Its instinct is correct in this regard. It should store energy for the future.

In the process however kundalini becomes addicted to the sex vice. It gets this idea that once it invested a little by procreating just a little, the rest of the energy can be used to furnish sex pleasure.

To disrupt this system of kundalini, one must deprive it of nutrients. One must scrap its system if one wants to transit to the divine world.

The passage of nutrients for kundalini which is from the nose and mouth down to the base chakra via the navel and groin area, and then to the head through the spine is the first passage to master. However, that will not get the yogi to the divine world. It will however get one to the higher astral regions.

Brahma's Place

I read of Brahma, a deity who reproduced mind-born sons. Without sexual intercourse, by himself without sexuality, he produced entities in bodies. Is that possible? Can someone reproduce without sexuality being expressed, without polarity?

Can there be reproduction without sexual union?

I read in the *Mahabharata* that when at the heavenly place of the Brahma deity, King *Mahabhisha* saw the Goddess *Ganga*, the king's subtle body was sexual aroused. He wanted union just as a male in this human world would naturally desire. The goddess's flimsy and skimpy semi-transparent clothing flared by a celestial breeze. *Mahabhisha's* sexuality could not tolerate the exposure.

Other astral beings at the place saw what happened and looked away. The goddess for her part appreciated *Mahabhisha's* reaction. She was attracted to him. Brahma told the pair of lovers that they must descend to the human world to consummate the attraction. It could not happen in his zone. Sexual intercourse does not occur there.

The goddess for her part did not mind being physical on earth. What had she to lose? She is a goddess any which way. She cannot stay on earth no matter what incidences cause her to descend to the lower plane.

Kundalini Routing System

In Tibeti's process the sexual energy is drawn from the sexual area upwards. When it is dissipated, the yogi attacks the navel region. At last he attacks the lung-chest area and removes that charge. This can be achieved by *kapalabhati* or *bhastrika* rapid breathing.

Mahayogins like Milarepa did austerities with a motive to retaliate offenses of relatives. When this happens and the person reaches the top chakra, he/she reaches there from a contaminated stage.

Either by direction of a guru or by being inspired, he must return to the lower chakras to discover the impure motivating energies. He must remove them. While he does that, he gets bliss energy satisfaction which frees him from negativity.

Some ascetics go to the base chakra. They uproot it because it carries in it, certain strands of survival energy which are impure and which would cause more transmigrations in the physical world in a hunt for survival opportunities.

The higher type is a descent either through *sushumna* nadi or through a special tube which is in the center of the neck (not in the center of the spine). The yogi goes down through that and gets into the causal body *(karana sharira)*.

If he goes through the *sushumna* nadi, then when he gets to the heart chakra on the spine, he must remain there for a time. He waits to be transformed into a subtler state. He finds himself in a cosmic space which is the causal body.

If he goes through the neck, he immediately finds himself in the causal body. This body is not a chakra. It is neither the heart chakra on the spine nor the expression of the heart chakra in the frontal chest area. It is in a subtler dimension.

There, the yogi is motiveless. In that place, motive is in bija form only, micro-seed, unexpressed form. Nothing there is expressed. Nothing exhibits polarity.

The yogi does this to get some idea of what he was before he became whatever he is currently, which is basically nothing in terms of what we perceive in the subtle and gross physical worlds.

When kundalini falls from being in the head, either at the crown, brow or at the intellect or at the base of the brain, it does not usually stay at any of the chakras on the spine. It usually descends quickly to the base and stays there until it is recharged and aroused again.

It is near impossible to hold kundalini at the heart chakra when it falls. If kundalini remains in the head, the yogi can descend while kundalini ascends. In other words, kundalini is in the head and the coreSelf goes down through the light which kundalini maintains in its passage while it is in the head.

If a yogi tries to go down with kundalini or to descend when kundalini recedes, what usually happens is that the observing self is left in blank darkness because the descent of kundalini is due to it being deenergized. Its natural state is to be at muladhara chakra and to rise to the sex, navel or heart chakra and then return to the base.

Kundalini is deprived of its favorite food which is sex hormones. But in back kundalini one must feed kundalini the sex hormones and then trick it to make it go up. This is because its habit is to eat the sex hormones and then enjoy the explosion of the energy and hormones as sexual climax in the genitals.

In this process mentioned above what happens is that you pull up the sex hormones from the frontal part of the body. Then pull up the navel formation juices. Dry the reservoir of this energy and kundalini will have no access to it.

Bhastrika or kapalabhati rapid breathing is used to evaporate the navel secretions and the sex hormones so that they do not pool in the sex kanda bulb, so that kundalini has no access to them and is thus deprived. That puts an end to its control of the psyche. The yogi becomes a siddha.

kundalini system beginning
at 1 base chakra

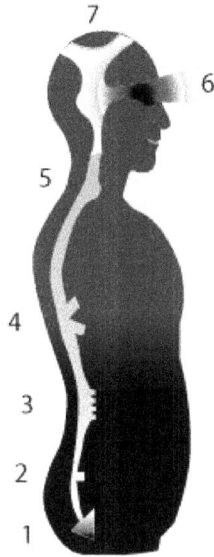

regular kundalini attack
using standard route through navel 1,
looping through pubic area 2
then finally to the kundalini base chakra 3

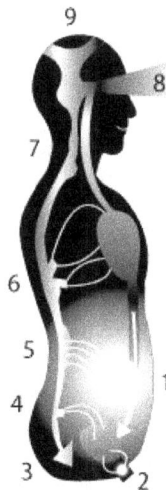

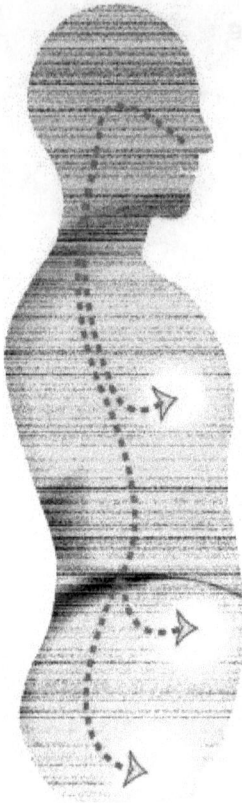

There is no back kundalini,
no shushumna system.
There is the sex area, navel area and
heart-chest areas which are
energized directly from the
center part of the subtle body
where there is a gap space

The full effect of raising kundalini last for one hour for the most in my psyche. There is always a residual effect but it varies from day to day. Over time, years, I find that the kundalini may stay up to the heart chakra.

To be honest if I do meditation without doing breath infusion, the meditation is static and is not of the same quality as when it is done after the infusion. Therefore, I always do infusion prior and have maintained this habit for some years.

There is a residual effect but it is not like when meditation occurs immediately after the infusion. In my system kundalini would descend to the base chakra. Its radiance would spread far if the sushumna passage and the nadis are not blocked again. However, these block at the slightest deviation from spiritual focus. They block immediately if I associate with anyone who does not have as advance a practice as my own.

Initially when I took this body, my subtle body became saturated with a low level of energy. This was due to being in a family which had no interest in yoga. The mother and father of the body had the usual mundane focus. The subtle body once it got under their influence in the father's body and in the mother's uterus, changed for the worse and became just as dense as the parents' energy.

During childhood however there were flashes of intuition. The third eye was open. After I became a family man, that ceased until I established this pranayama practice, which I did in the past life. Unless I can isolate myself from physical association and from even psychic contact with non-yogis, the *sushumna* and its nadis will be blocked again.

If the student does the hatha yoga austerities prior, the heart (physical organ) will be smaller and the impure substances in its tissues will be extracted. But without the hatha yoga austerities, I do not see how one can succeed.

Keep the neck straight during breath infusion. The head should not droop. The chin is pulled back tight to throat. This chin pull is primary.

Do not for a second let the mind drift outside the body. In fact, if you feel anything you should drop to your knees while keeping the eyes closed. If for a second the attention lifts to go outside of the psyche, kundalini may strike and the body will fall to the ground.

Raising Kundalini Posture

The posture below is reliable for raising kundalini. In that posture the perineum and the anus locks are automatically applied. The backward neck lock is applied. The chest is taut.

Yogi Bhajan's hand grip

These features cause any built-up energy from the rapid breathing to be intensified and focused down in the body into the base chakra.

If enough energy accumulates, as soon as one releases this posture and stands up or in any way straightens the spine, kundalini is likely to cross through the *small of the back*. If it does so, depending on the amount of energy, it will either travel through some chakras or penetrate all the chakras on the spine and enter into the head.

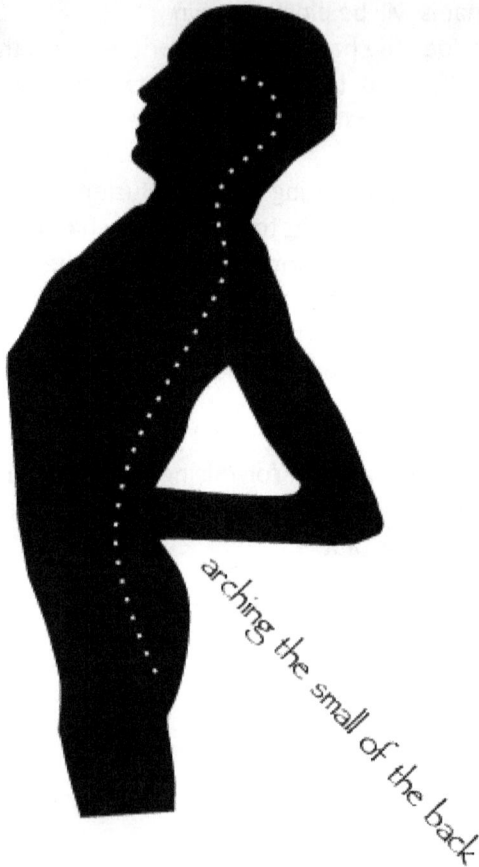

arching the small of the back

If it does not have a full charge, it will partially ascend the spine. That may or may not be felt by the student. If it is felt it will be an electric sensation or a shimmering energy sensation.

If it enters the head, if the student does not have the locks in place and is not attentive to know that kundalini moved, it will hit the student unawares. This means that it will hit the intellect unawares. This may result in one of these states of consciousness:

- complete blackout
- feeling of intense bliss pleasure in the head

- feeling of being in intense golden light in all directions being present in the spiritual brahman level of consciousness
- feeling of trying to control a vast energy reservoir which overpowers the observing self with intentions of overpowering the consciousness and then feeling this energy subside.

Any student who stands after assuming a squatting posture, while doing breath infusion runs the risk of having the body fall to the ground. Why? Because when the intellect organ is hit by kundalini in this way, the intellect loses control of the physical body. With that loss the observing self can do nothing because that self does not control the body except indirectly through the intellect. However, it will last for a few seconds; for the most, fifteen to thirty seconds.

When this student becomes aware again, he will remember nothing of the experience or will remember being in a shimmering golden light in all directions, or being in intense spiritual bliss energy. Or he will remember diminishing alertness and then remember nothing. Or he may have a headache or dizzy feeling or may be disoriented, not knowing his name or number. The danger in this practice is one, which is that the physical body may fall and be damaged.

This movement from squatting to standing should not be done unless one is supervised by an advanced yogi. If one squats and does breath infusion, one should not stand from it. One should go down while keeping the spine straight. while applying a tight neck lock by not bending the head forward but by pulling the chin back tightly into the neck.

If one does breath infusion while squatting and kundalini is not aroused in a noticeable way it means that the infusion was insufficient.

Why is this?

This means that the lungs did not absorb the fresh air. The air went in and out of the lungs but the fresh air was not absorbed.

How to change this?

Practice, practice, practice, while being attentive within the psyche, keeping the mind in the psyche during the practice.

Kundalini is an intelligence. It is an instinct unto itself. It has no intentions of giving control to the observing self. It will not under any circumstance allow any limited spirit-person to get control. That person must fight with kundalini to gain control over its operations. The factor which prohibits advancement is the individual kundalini. The enemy of the self is the kundalini of the very same self.

There is no point running here or there for combatants. There is an enemy and a very powerful one too, one which has the power within the psyche. The self, the glorious self, does not have the power. It only wishes to have it. For achieving it, it must fight to finish with kundalini.

Do as Instructed

Sometimes in yoga practice, the student must do as instructed:

During practice this morning an energy was left in my psyche by Yogeshwarananda. He left when I did a posture and was disinclined for the rooster pose (*kukkutasana*).

Yogesh insisted that I do it and the full lotus during each session. I do not recommend this to anyone with an inflexible body.

Painful Posture / User Friendly

Breath infusion this morning was efficient. I worked to pass the energy through a channel in the subtle body. This is a down curve channel as in the diagram below. This gives direct access to the lower part of the trunk. I did some intense practice reaching remote places like the toes, feet, fingers and forearms. The value of difficult asanas during breath infusion is that one can mentally reach distant areas and pull stale energy, replacing that with fresh energy.

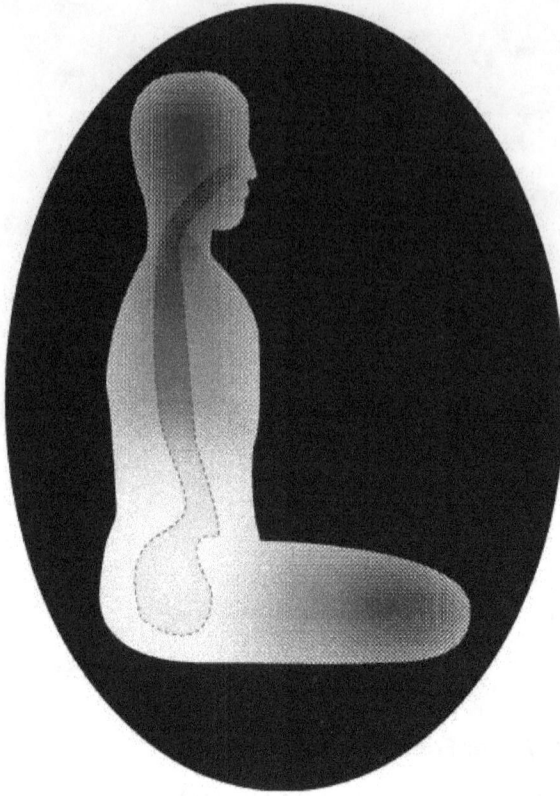

Pain from difficult stretches is the friend of the hatha yogi. Pain shows blocked nadis and areas which were hidden by the disobedient kundalini. Once these areas are exposed by the pains during stretches, the yogi can attack them to extract subtle toxins which accumulate there and cause those nadi passages to be blocked.

While usually people run away from pain, the hatha yogi welcomes it. He uses it as a discovery tool. One can target the thighs, knees, legs, ankles, feet, toes and other mentally inaccessible areas very easily when doing asana postures. I penetrated the thigh bones, knees, and even the bones of the feet. I extracted polluted subtle energy (apana) from these places. I infuse in fresh breath force in displacement.

This does wonders for the meditation afterwards, as then no part of the psyche lags behind at a low level. The entire subtle body shifts into a higher dimension, not just the spine and head.

I worked on some stub kundalinis in various parts of the spine. These are areas which during the session, I suddenly discovered a buildup of the infused force to a gold hot or white hot consistency. It felt like a cylinder about two inches long about one quarter of an inch wide, glowing and glowing and glowing as I infused breath.

Management of Sex Energy

Breath infusion practice this morning was guided by Tibeti Yogi in the matter of what happens once the kundalini is pulled from its base chakra. The location of the chakra remains. It is regarded as a location, cleared and energized by the yogi.

There is also the matter of what to do with sex energy which still accumulates. That is used by kundalini as it is primary interest in the matter of survival and pleasure. What will be done with that energy once kundalini is reformed from the use of it and is withdrawn from that interest?

The yogi must dissipate such energy on a regular basis following in the example of what the kundalini did itself, which was to use that energy in sexuality, then to withdraw the usage and then to use it again just as soon as it would accumulate. This pans out in regular lifestyle, as having sex to the max and then getting tired and depressed from it, eating, taking rest and then letting it accumulate again, and then repeating the behavior.

The yogi should descend to the pubic area and repeatedly lift the energy without allowing it to bridge to the base chakra where kundalini may consume it for sex indulgence.

For sex indulgence when the sexual charge is stimulated by sexual exposure and foreplay, the sex energy compels kundalini to jump from the base to the sex organ chakra (not sex chakra on the spine). When kundalini jumps, the action begins as sexual excitement. This quickly builds into a crescendo climax of experience, where there is an explosion of irresistible overpowering pleasure feelings. In that case instead of ascending the spine, kundalini arcs to the sex organ chakra. In a mad rush to max out sex pleasure which is a bliss experience, it invades the sexual organ territory.

In the other way where the sex energy leaves the sex area and fuses into kundalini, kundalini becomes nervous. It tries to run from the base area. If the yogi knows how, kundalini may go through the spine into the brain and give spiritual pleasure *(brahmananda)*.

But this practice of Tibeti is neither of these processes. Here the sexual energy is lifted from the sexual area directly. When it is dissipated, the yogi attacks the navel area. He takes that energy. At last, he attacks the chest area. This is achieved by effective practice of *kapalabhati* or *bhastrika* rapid breathing.

Without Meditation

This morning breath infusion was efficient. I got help from Tibeti Yogi. He appeared in a horizontal cylinder. His head peeked out. He showed a passage which is a rectangular slit. It runs from the chest of the subtle body down to the pubic area. He said that at a certain time, the subtle body will have this slit which is a breath channel.

I vigorously breathe through it. It is an efficient method. However, I was unable to review its effects in meditation because I had some visitors during this session, two persons, one of whom videotaped the session.

Sex Charge Removal

During breath infusion this morning, I contacted Yogeshwaranand. It was a slight contract which lasted three minutes. It seemed that he was in a trance but peeked to see how my practice progressed. He said nothing.

Later during the practice, Yogi Bhajan appeared. He gave encouragement about being urdhva reta in terms of middle of the body lift. This is different to the practice of urdhva reta with spinal energy flow upwards. The traditional practice is to have semen flowing upwards through the spine, not directly but to have that sexual charge mix with the kundalini at the base chakra and then rise through the spine into the head. Or to have the kundalini attract the sex chakra on the spine so that it retracts interest in the sex organs, and have the energy there forge a passage through the spine.

This other practice which I did is more in line with what was described in some Taoist books where there is a central channel through which the sex energy charge is pulled through the center of the trunk.

Yogi Bhajan added two other aspects which are that one should pull the energy which accumulated at the navel and which will go downwards. There is a practice where one pulls the energy which goes to the navel but which has not flowed to the sex area.

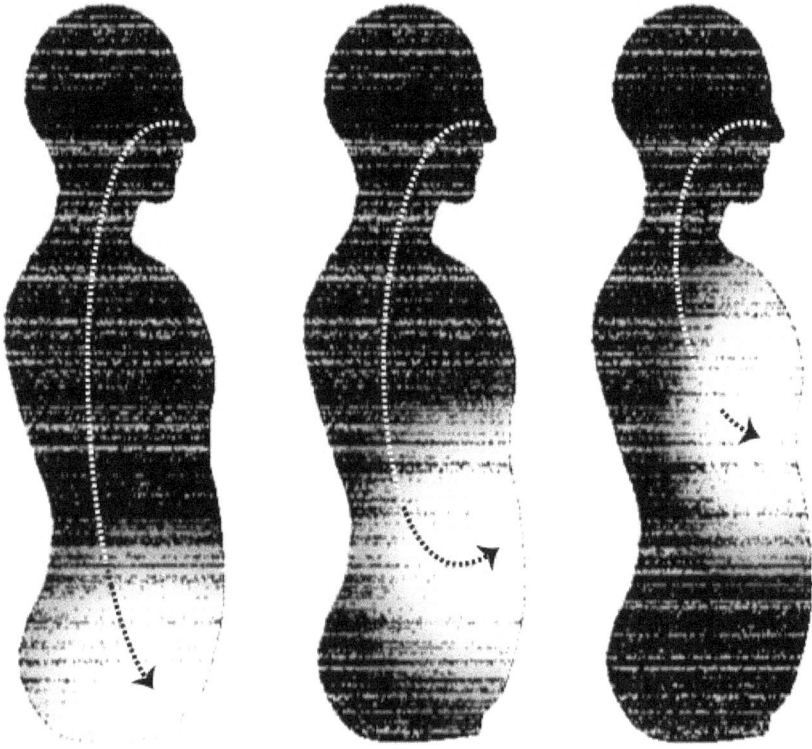

arrowhead shows infusion focus

the infused energy with any sexual charge or food energy charge
is lifted through the center of the trunk

These two processes and the ones with pulling from the sexual reservoir of energy up through the middle of the body, are the complete process.

To this the yogi must first master the traditional practice of getting the sexual charge to go through the spine with kundalini taking it up through the chakras until it gets into the head. When one does this daily in practice for at least six years, then perhaps one can do it.

Pain Focus

The way the psyche is designed by nature, the awareness concentrates itself at sensations and pain. If for instance one's arm is caught in a door, the pain from the pinching action will put one's attention to that area of the body.

This means that nature has a system of getting one's attention. In the case of sex desire, nature pulls the attention, except that sex pleasure is so desirable as to encourage nature to do more of it.

To be a human being and to be honest about it, we must first understand that nature constructs most of this scene. We simply tag along, like children being pulled through the street by the force of their dependence on the mother who walks along as they hold the end of her skirt and are dragged home.

Can anyone focus on his arm and create pain? Can one reverse the relationship with nature, where one puts the attention somewhere and then nature is compelled to come wherever that attention is placed?

I use postures to cause the attention to go to certain areas. I learnt from nature that when there is a pain somewhere, the attention is drawn there under compulsion. I use that procedure of using the postures and doing the infusion in those postures while keeping the attention at the place of tension or pain in the posture. First, I use postures with the breath infusion. Then I get the attention to go to specific areas.

There is a posture which I discovered. I put my body on all fours, and then I slap my feet so that my toes hit the ground while I do the rapid breathing. This hitting of the toes causes the attention to go to the toes. When that happens, the attention is also at the base chakra which is connected to the toes. In that way I attack the muladhara chakra.

Efficient Practice

Breath infusion practice this morning yielded some success in terms of stuffing fresh subtle energy tightly into the trunk of the body. That is an accomplishment because the system is sometimes resistant to this compaction process. Unless this stuffing is efficiently done, a whole session of breath infusion can add up to nothing. This is very similar to hydraulics. In a cylinder if the seals are not tight there will be inefficient conservation of energy.

If the breath infusion is sloppy, one cannot expect the legendary results achieved by yogis like Gorakshnath. One must tighten the practice, the way persons like Milarepa did. Then things will happen.

Yogi Bhajan

In 1971, I saw a poster with a photo. It advertised Yogi Bhajan, a kundalini yoga master. This was in Kansas City, Missouri, USA.

Kundalini Arousal

I pioneered some aspects of my practice but the greater percentage of it, is from superiors. Perhaps I have some value in this regard due to the willingness to record and share experiences.

There are millions of people who are engaged in sexual indulgence. They arouse kundalini by sexual exposure and foreplay which causes kundalini to energize the genitals and give pleasure. Kundalini is aroused by many people on a daily basis. Some even have sex more frequently.

We must understand what kundalini is in normal experience. We should recognize kundalini in regular activities like sex, and other types of excitement.

In order to awaken the kundalini with breath infusion such as *kapalbhati*, one can do so immediately, if sufficient breath is infused in the system and if one manages to get that infused energy to go to the groin area. Kundalini's arousal has little to do with purity. It has to do with infusion of energy into the psychic system of the person.

To arouse kundalini during sexual intercourse, no purity is required. Hence, why should it be required for other purposes. Purity has nothing to do with it. When I first did rapid breathing way back in 1971, kundalini was aroused. Since then I raise kundalini daily, because it always subsides into the base chakra.

It is true however, that when the body is purified to a certain degree by the daily rising of kundalini, there will be higher perception, more psychic sensitivity for that yogi.

The reason why kundalini rises in sex has to do with the fact that hormone energy is stored in the sex organs. If someone has surgery and those organs are removed, that person will no longer have sexual pleasure through that body, even though kundalini is still present.

The nadis are important but we use kundalini to purify them. For this usage kundalini must be aroused. Otherwise it will be at the base chakra and will not move an inch from there except in conventional stimulation like in sex indulgence.

Once the yogi gets the charge from the infused breath to kundalini, it is aroused. It ponders movement and intention. If it is a small charge, it will go back to sleep. If it is a large charge, it will come out of its hole to find the one who was crazy enough to arouse it.

In sex desire a similar thing happens. One hustles to find a sex partner. When kundalini had enough by a climax, it recedes, the organs flop and lose their charge. One develops a disinterest.

When kundalini is aroused with a large enough charge, the yogi applies locks to keep it confined and to force it to travel in a certain way. This is like when at a rodeo, they confine a hasty bull. The creature cannot jump into the arena. It is kept in a steel pen and is released at a certain time. When it gets into the ring and charges and when it is just about to kill the rider, they send people to distract it. Those persons force the animal into an entrance where it is corralled. Once we arouse kundalini with the infusion, we use locks to channel it.

When kundalini is forced, it goes through certain polluted blocked nadis and because it is forceful it blasts its way through and cleans the nadis. This is felt as a pleasant or intense sensation.

Over time as one keeps raising it day after day, one discovers the nadis and guides kundalini to cleanse them. In this way kundalini, an untamed force, the original lifeForce energy in physical nature, is harnessed and made to assist for the liberation of the self.

Kumblak

Antar kumbhak means holding the breath in the body as contrasted to breathing out and then holding and not breathing in.

With the *kapalabhati/bhastrika* practice, one stores fresh invigorating subtle energy. There is a stockpile. The yogi stops in a posture, holds the breath in for a time until he feels he should compress more air. This is kumbhak, but it is different because it is applied not to restrain the system from expelling air and not to stop the system from getting air.

When one senses that the system consumed the fresh air which was infused, one begins the breathing again in the same or in a different posture. You begin to breathe again rapidly because the system absorbed what one compressed into the lungs. It distributed that.

It is a system based on what happens in the body due to infusion of air. The practice of kumbhak when done haphazardly cannot produce the right results because it is not coordinated with anything specifically. Rapid breathing itself does not require any mixing with another pranayama or breathing method. By itself it will raise kundalini.

Navel Attack / Infusion

Breath Infusion this morning was done under guidance of Yogi Bhajan. Currently he monitors the practice. Yogeshwarananda and Tibeti Yogi were nowhere in sight.

Yogi Bhajan had me focus on a loop attack of the frontal navel chakra. This is not the navel chakra on the spine. This is its outcrop expression chakra which works at the navel in the front of the body. The attack on this chakra is an effort to suspend the kundalini's grip on the psyche for the purposes of survival.

Kundalini's Intelligence

Kundalini's perpetual intentions are clear:
- Get a body.
- Survive in it.
- Prepare to be deprived of it, by generating more bodies.
- Enjoy sexual pleasures in the adult stages of the body.
- Survive! Survive! Survive!

With these intentions, kundalini conducts itself to acquire a body, to make one survive for as long as nature will allow. It contributes socially to procure the next body. At the heart of this concern however is pleasure, particularly sex pleasure. For the work it has to do in procuring bodies, the kundalini must get some benefit. No one wants to work day after day for nothing. The benefit is the sex pleasure.

Along with the kundalini there is the intellect psychic mechanism. This system is slightly different but it comes under the influence of kundalini because it lacks emotional intelligence. It is a rational meter. It is a psychic organ for analysis. Kundalini for its part is not rational. It does not have to be. For that matter its emotional intelligence is a superior information system. For this reason, the intellect becomes subordinate to kundalini.

The two principles strike a bargain where kundalini says to the intellect organ, "Follow me. I know this. You are imperceptive. If you serve me as a kind friend, I will get whatever pleasure you need. Make no effort to supersede me. Rationality has no place in this. This is based on gut feelings, vulgarity. I will sense the pleasures. You assist me by scheming how we would achieve it. Without me you are nothing for all the logic you have."

Sometimes there is this conversation where the intellect talks to the kundalini about the coreSelf. It says, "We should serve the coreSelf. We are nothing without it. What do you think?"

Then the kundalini will reply like this, "Serve that? The thing is nothing. It depends on us. It cannot do a thing without us. It has no identity without us? Serve it? No! It should serve us. If it refuses, we bring it to its knees by terminating its means of experience. Then it will become morose because it wants the pleasures which I provide and the analytical process which you display. We are a force to reckon with. If it does not cooperate with us, we should bring it to its knees by blackmailing it. We can starve it into submission by depriving it of services?"

Navel Chakra Attack

The loop around attack on the frontal navel chakra is the method of breath infusing that location from behind. The standard method is to infuse that from above but when one demolished the resistance of that chakra and removed its blocking energies, one should attack it from behind.

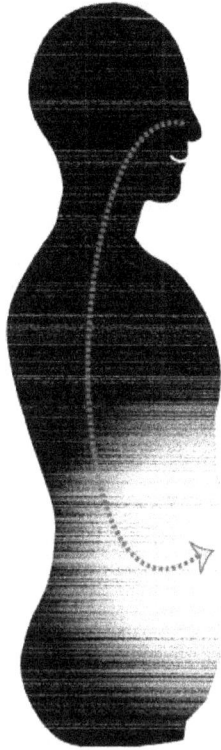

During breath infusion one should focus on the air going to that chakra from behind. To cause it to become fragmented so that it breaks into pieces and then is dissipated, one should constantly compress air into it. This removes any trace of kundalini's method of procuring a new physical body after the present one is finished.

Part 6

Yoga Siddha Form Created by Yogi

Breath Infusion this morning was guided by Yogi Bhajan. He showed a process which is used after one mastered raising kundalini through the spine. This is done by yogis who use some effective breath infusion to raise kundalini.

There is an argument about which *pranayama* to use. That is a silly conversation because the answer is that any type which gives the person the result of raising kundalini daily in a definite noticeable way within the psyche, is the right process.

In this case I use *bhastrika* or *kapalabhati*. Both are effective. Both are the same practice with *bhastrika* being a more advanced type of *kapalabhati*. *Bhastrika* is when there is emphasis on the inhale and exhale while *kapalabhati*, the easier of the two, is emphasis on the exhale which is done rather forcibly with the inhale as a reflexive action.

Yogi Bhajan said that when during each session the disciple can raise kundalini without fail for a minimum of once per day, that person should do this for about six years minimum. Then he may ask the teacher for further instruction.

The key feature of a successful session of breath infusion is the raising of kundalini with the sensation which indicates that it happened definitely. Depending on the student's progress and on his karmic destiny, the teacher may instruct the student to develop a family or he may give instruction on how to gut out the subtle body and smash the rule of kundalini.

If the student has a family, kundalini is left to act as it would through sexual indulgence and whatever else there is to do for bringing ancestors across the existential border. This type of student should, have a family. During those activities he should practice a minimum of once per day but should always ponder about being a full-time yogi. Later after family responsibilities are completed, when children grow into adults, that yogi should seriously think of seeing the guru for the advance course.

What is this advanced course?

It is to begin working on creating for oneself a yoga siddha body. One thing to know is that the student will not be awarded this. He has to create this by endeavor in yoga practice.

When kundalini raises, one feels an electric sensation which may be super-pleasant or bliss feelings. These frequently occur in the spine or head, but it can occur elsewhere in the body.

In sexual pleasure experiences, kundalini (the same lifeForce) fires itself into the genital area. One feels an irresistible pleasure when this occurs. When the same kundalini fires without sexual interest, another bliss aspect occurs.

New Kundalini Formed

This morning as directed by Yogi Bhajan who entered my individual psyche, I worked on infusing energy into the sex kanda. This is a little bulb in the subtle body in the pubic area. This bulb holds subtle sexual fluids.

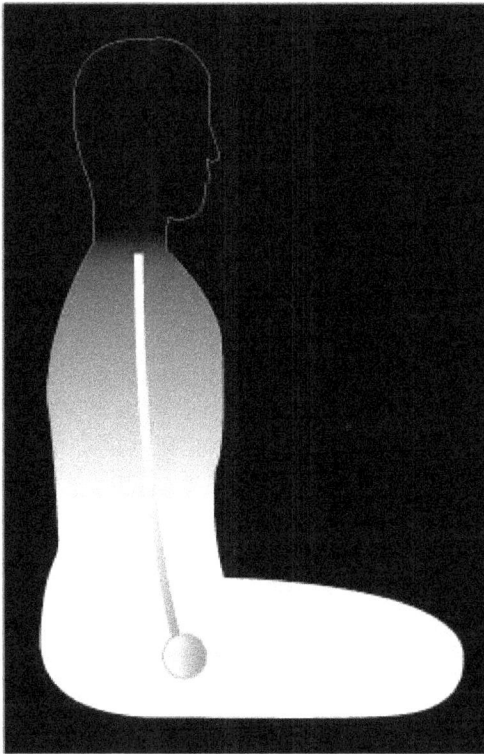

In preliminary kundalini yoga, the student sends infused energy from the lung into the navel. It is compressed further into the groin area. There it mixes with the sexual energy. It becomes charged. Due to accumulation of this charge, it arcs to the base chakra and arouses kundalini.

When this first happens, kundalini becomes aroused and unsettled. Like a snake which is alarmed, it shakes itself. It resettles like a snake which is aroused by a rat which it can easily kill. Because the snake is drowsy and is not hungry, it ignores the rat.

In this way during practice, kundalini is aroused. A little tingle, a sensation, is felt. Students may not understand that when this happens it means that kundalini was aroused but it resumed its sluggish condition at the base chakra.

As the infusion continues, a higher more forceful charge accumulates. If it is large enough, kundalini awakens in a big way and rises up the spine. Sometimes it reaches the neck. Then it subsides. Sometimes it will enter the head and mystic events will be experienced.

This is like when the rat inadvertently makes a squeaking noise which arouses the snake. Except that this time, the reptile becomes alert, feels hungry and strikes to kill the rodent and consume it happily.

Kundalini may arise, take the energy and digest it in a matter of seconds. The result of which is that kundalini moves up the spine into the head in a jiffy.

In the preliminary process breath energy is compressed and forms a charge in the groin area. This arcs to the kundalini at the base chakra. The charge caused kundalini to move up the spine into the head.

The practice which Yogi Bhajan showed this morning is a different procedure. This is the practice used when the yogi pulled kundalini as a stub under the back of the brain.

When that happens, the yogi can operate to evaporate the sexual energy so that in his or her psyche it does not accumulate. To do this the infused energy must go directly to the sex kanda without being routed through the navel. In addition, instead of arcing to the base chakra, that charged sexual energy is pulled and dissipated into the center of the subtle body.

This creates a different kundalini force which affects all parts of the trunk. This practice is part of the process of redesigning the subtle body so that one can be compatible with the perfected yogis, the siddhas.

When this was done there was a kundalini formed in the center of the subtle body. It burst in the form of lightning and struck through the chest into the neck but it did not go into the brain. The areas of the chest and armpits absorbed that generated kundalini.

Talking with a Deceased Yoga Guru

Breath Infusion this morning was guided by Yogi Bhajan. In a discussion I asked him why he did not leave books with detailed descriptions of the kriyas. These are subtle processes. There is no way the average student can know these methods.

He said this,

"Some yogis write. Some do not. There is no other reason. I will empower you to write. I am dead and gone. During the time when I had the body, I was occupied with disciples, especially when I first went to USA.

"With disciples there is no time to focus on personal sadhana. The teacher spends so much time managing that he does not think of the necessity for composing books. There was an effort but it fizzed out. Some disciples planned to publish the information but we did some diagrams only. It was workshop after workshop, intensives and so on. We lost the focus.

"That is the result of having many disciples and becoming popular. The focus changes. Every teacher cannot be methodical at writing as you are. Anyway, you can write for me. Thanks in advance."

I replied, "You do not know that I will write it. I could be dead tomorrow. In the mean time I will note anything. Students will not know these tiddly widdly details. They are not that sensitive. If it is mentioned, if it is shown, and if they practice, they may have an insight during practice, not otherwise."
He replied,

"That may or may not be true but irrespective, I will let you worry about it. I am no longer there as the teacher. You do not advertise yourself as

the teacher, because no one has cursed you to be a lineage guru. You are lucky in that way. You have time to write. For this, your teachers depend on you.

"A student who is advanced and who is not assigned as the accursed lineage guru, is the right person to be persistent with personal sadhana and a record of notes. That is you"

Yogi Admires King Tongue

This evening I had an occasion to consider the rulership of the tongue. In the kingdom of the body, the tongue rules supreme. It does so to such an extent that it does not care what harm it brings to the body in its quest for a variety of eatables.

Some eatables are horrible but since the tongue wants to have them, it commands the entire body to do whatever is necessarily to procure those foods even if they poison the body or ruin vital organs.

For the sake of the tongue, the Europeans created colonial territories and enslaved other human beings. This was for sugar which the tongue demanded. Even if a person is aware of a particular fault in a certain food, still if the tongue wants that substance, the person is impulsively forced to eat it, even if it means harm to the entire body. Like this as a supreme monarch the tongue rules with much cruelty.

How admirable it is to see this King Tongue running the show and being so merciless on the entire body. It is wonderful. A yogi can envy King Tongue since a yogi wishes to have more control over the body.

One thing that is admirable about King Tongue is that he never gives in. It has no mercy. It makes sure that it completes the satisfaction for various eatables at any cost. It is a wonderful ruler, which can be admired by a student yogi.

Yoga Siddha Body Creation

Breath infusion this morning was great. I managed to comply with Tibeti Yogi's request for getting the bottom of the subtle trunk cleared of polluted energy. Instead of being dense and heavy there, it was light and transparent.

The preliminary and necessary first step in infusion is to compress air from the lungs to the navel and then push further to the groin, then accumulate a charge which arcs to the base chakra.

However, this more advanced practice is when the navel and groin area are reformed sufficiently so that there is no blocking of the infused energy in these areas. To do this successfully one should be proficient at the downward thrust through the navel.

In this practice the air is pushed into the groin targeting the organs which generate reproductive fluids. Whatever is digested goes downwards to form reproductive fluids. These hormones are used to generate more bodies in the species. They give sex pleasure to potential parents.

In this practice the air is thrust from the lungs to the reproductive organs. It then diffuses that energy and more infusion causes that diffused energy to be pulled up into the brain. This is a direct method as compared to the other method which is to cause the sexually charge energy to hit muladhara base chakra and then to move up the spine with the kundalini consuming that sexual charge.

As one masters this direct practice from the throat to the reproductive organs in slanted direction, it switches.

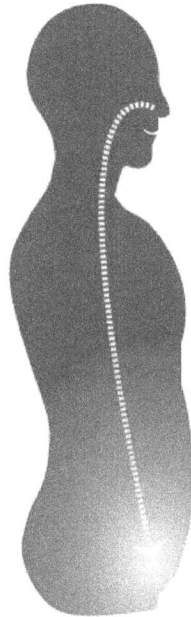

One sees that there is a clear space between the brain and the reproductive area.

In the Taoist system it is said there is a cauldron in the reproductive area. This is called a kanda in yoga wording. The yogi by breath infusion causes the stored energy in the reproductive area to vaporize on the subtle plane, then it is pulled into the head of the subtle body.

Kundalini fired several times during practice, mostly in the trunk of the subtle body. It did once and very noticeably fired from the chest through the neck and into the face, into each cheek. This felt like tingling ice crystals in the cheeks. This is different to when kundalini fires through the spine and then moves through the neck into the head.

What is the value of such practice?

It has to do with getting every part of the subtle body to have clarified high quality energy. That is the secret to creating a yoga siddha form to replace the pleasure-seeking subtle form.

Yoga siddha bodies are not awarded by the yoga guru or the deity. The yogi must endeavor with the subtle form as it is. He must change the quality of energy which saturates it.

Kundalini Black out / White out:

Each person is given a kundalini when that particular limited spiritual entity enters this physical creation from the causal level of existence. The kundalini is spontaneously endowed. It is matched to the particular coreSelf. As a compliment, it has the exact amount of energy which is required by that self for operations in the physical and psychic creation.

It is an electro-psychic system of energy. If, however, a part of it malfunctions, there will be upsets.

When kundalini rises suddenly with full force and enters the spine, it will usually courses though the spine, penetrates the neck and then enters the brain. This occurs on two planes simultaneously. It happens physically and also in the subtle body.

If a forceful high charge of kundalini energy hits the psychic organs in the head of the subtle body, the entity will experience a black out or a white out. A black-out is when the entity feels a loss of consciousness after a blank space in awareness. This may be a grey or dark space or just a blank colorless space. A white out is when the entity feels or senses a bright or shimmering light or a golden effulgence and then loses objective awareness for some seconds, after which objectivity is resumed.

Kundalini does not directly hit the coreSelf. It does not directly hit the sense of identity, which is known as ahamkara (sense of I-ness) in Sanskrit. Kundalini hits the analytical orb or intellect organ, *jnana-dipah (jnana-*

chakshu). If it hits that organ with too much force, the entity loses objective consciousness because it so happens that a spiritual person, the self, is dependent on the intellect for objectivity.

Why does it happen that the kundalini is not matched perfectly to the intellect, so that kundalini cannot overpower it? The answer to this question is simply that the kundalini is matched to the individual psyche as a whole and not just to one component.

The full power of kundalini should not reach the intellect but if it does, there will be a black out or a white out. Then the psyche will be reset. Things will resume as normal after some seconds usually. As soon as the kundalini force drops back in its surge the intellect will be reset. The person will be conscious but will know that something was amiss since there was a gap in the continuity of objective consciousness.

If when doing the exercises, one does the locks efficiently, there will be no black out or white out, because the locks will control the flow of kundalini to limit how much of its power flows to the intellect. Thus, the orb will become infused but not to the extent of being put out of commission as the chief perception organ.

In this respect, just recently Rishi Singh Gherwal gave clarification on this issue. He said the following.

Kundalini is matched to the psyche. It is the total power required to operate the individual psyche. What is the psyche? Is it just the individual self alone? Is it the self plus other psychic components?

A yogi should be sure to make kundalini become distributed throughout the entire psyche, not just a part of it, not just the head.

Due to sexual pleasure, there is this stubborn idea that one should climax energy for pleasure. This idea must be removed, so that the entire psyche has well-being and not just one part of it like the sexual organs or the head.

The locks restrict the flow of kundalini. When these restrictions are mastered the yogi can regulate kundalini's flow so that it does not over-power the intellect.

Later with more advancement, one does not rely on the locks in this way but instead uses the locks to cause kundalini to go to other parts of the psyche. That gives the result of even distribution of the infused energy through the psyche. Since kundalini is a match to the entire psyche, there is no black out or white out. Instead there may be light-outs in the head and light-ins in the other parts of the body.

Everything hinges on a steady practice. One advances in that way. The subtle body must evolve for certain things to become evidence.

The main reason for black outs and white outs is the location of the intellect and its relationship to the self. The self is surrounded by an energy field which is the sense of identity (ahamkara). This is mistakenly called the false ego by many people who have no idea that there are psychic organs in the subtle body. In proximity to the sense of identity is the intellect or analytical orb.

Kundalini hits the orb. If it hits it with too much power the orb goes out of commission because it has an energy absorbing limit. Then the self experiences a white out or black out.

As soon as kundalini subsides, the orb is reset. The person resumes the normal state of awareness. This happens because the orb has a sensor system which causes it to resume operation as soon as kundalini drops to a certain level.

A question arises as to why the coreSelf suffers a consciousness black out if the intellect is hit, the answer to that is that the coreSelf cannot perceive anything in physical existence without the orb. If you remove the intellect, the core will become like nothing, as if it did not exist, at least until the orb is reconnected.

These psychic actions are way beyond the power of the self, unless it can become proficient in the Patanjali samadhis. People think that the self is infinite, that it has absolute autonomy. Actually, these assessments of the self should be reviewed.

The psyche is not one homogenous whole. It is one psyche for sure but within it there is diversity, both in the physical system and astral body. This means that the states experienced when kundalini enters the brain or the subtle head, will not be the same as when it enters other parts of the psyche which has different components.

For example, if kundalini rises into the toes of the right foot for instance there will never be a black out or white out because there is no psyche component in that part of the body which does the service to the psyche which is rendered by the intellect which is in the head.

The coreSelf is more indirectly connected to the toes, than it is to the head. Thinking occurs in the head not in the toe. For this reason, when kundalini penetrates the toe it will feel just as it would be if kundalini enters any other part of the body which has similar components to those in the toes.

Both the brain in the physical system and the mind in the astral body have completely different organs as compared to the rest of the body. The grey matter found in the brain is found in small bits elsewhere in the spine only. If the psyche was homogenous, all one and the same in every part, there would be no variation.

The tingling sensation is the typical feeling when kundalini goes into other parts of the body, like the tendons, muscles and other types of flesh even most of the organs in the chest of the body. There may also be visions of light of varying colors when this occurs.

Yogi Bhajan Instructs the Author

During practice this morning I had two yoga gurus present during the breath infusion. These were Yogeshwarananda and Yogi Bhajan. It appears that Yogesh told Yogi Bhajan to check my practice.

Yogi Bhajan was of the view that my *bhastrika* pranayama practice is not tight enough. Tight here means not as efficient in distilling the stale energy out of the subtle body and installing fresh energy.

After a short while Yogesh went away. Yogi Bhajan instructed me. He advised for a longer session of practice and more infusion into the psyche during each posture. In one posture he gave a count of thirty to be said mentally while breathing without the breathing being counted. He wanted a count of one hundred and fifty. That longer count I did not reach because after about sixty, the lungs were not absorbing air even though the breathing was being done. The lungs are rebellious on occasion and do not cooperate.

When this happens, one should stop the rapid breathing on an inhale, hold the locks and then resume the breathing either in a different posture or in the same posture.

Sometimes there are arguments among yoga gurus. One yoga guru will tell the other, 'This is my disciple. Please go away. Find your own *chelas* (students). Why do you bother my son? Do you not have children? Get a wife if you want a family. Stay away from him."

Then sometimes it is like this. "Do not say that he is my disciple. I do not have retarded people in the boarding school. My disciples are top class. We have no fallen people in our sect. Take him with you. He looks as if he is your son. His left eye is defective and so is yours. Like father like son."

In that away yoga gurus will joke over a common disciple who they both instruct in particular kriyas.

I usually assume a tight lotus in the meditation which is immediately after breath infusion practice. This morning during the session, Yogi Bhajan instructed for a tight lotus with an erect spine to do *bhastrika* at the end. This allows the yogi to focus on the spine and brain. However, it is best to do the *bhastrika* in other postures first and then at the end do this sitting in tight lotus if one can assume that posture.

Trunk Infusion Kundalini

During breath infusion there was hardly any firing of kundalini spark energy into the head of the subtle body. Most of it was in the trunk. This was due to the influence of Tibeti Yogi and some demands made by Yogeshwarananda.

I can verify now that working on the trunk of the body is not a waste of time. It does cause desirable effects in meditation in the head of the subtle form. The reason for this is as follows.

The system of the subtle head which is usually called the mind of the person and the trunk which usually concerns the kundalini and the emotions of the person, are intimately related to such a degree that if the trunk of the subtle body is polluted, progress made in clearing the head will be foreshowed by the pollution in the trunk.

There is a continuous exchange of energy and influence of the two areas. Thus, if one is neglected the other will have the effects of that neglect. In fact, the way the psyche is designed, a person will pay attention to the head mostly because the head is where the thinking, planning component is located. By necessity one must be attentive to that in a world where wheeling and dealing are a must.

In the first part of kundalini yoga, the student is concerned with getting kundalini into the head. That is the general objective. Later after that is mastered so that kundalini rises into the head in a definite way each day during practice, the student should give priority to causing kundalini to spread through the trunk of the body, to be aroused there.

I caused kundalini to spark in the end of the thigh bone which is at the knee. This is an important area. At first one must conquer the pubic area. Then one can attack where the thigh is connected into the pubic area. Then one can move into the middle of the thigh. Then at last to where the thigh connects with the knee.

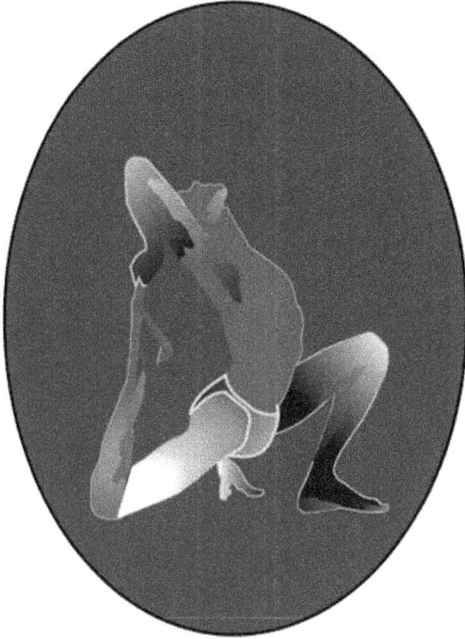

Confiscating kundalini's hold on the sexuality of the body is a must for anyone who wants to become a siddha. It is a joke to think that one can reach siddha status without complete conquest of the sexuality of the subtle body.

Sleep

The matter of sleep is important in yoga practice. The student should be sure to be free from anxieties which cause insomnia. Insufficient sleep puts the person in a regretful relationship with the kundalini? One should get the proper rest. Do justice to the physical and psychic systems, otherwise the yoga practice will not be as desired.

One of the five chitta vrittis (cittavrittis) listed by Patanjali is sleep. It is one of the aspects which a yogi is required to control. The way to control it is to breath energize the psyche and give the system its quota of sleep.

Intensity-Energy from Yogi Bhajan

Breath infusion was thorough this morning. Each day one should check the results of the practice. Each day with a sloppy practice is to be regretted. At first Yogeshwaranand was there but he signaled that I should take instructions from Yogi Bhajan. The issue was the intensity of practice. It seems that Yogeshwarananda is disgusted with my practice. He thinks that it is not intense enough.

This is the situation. Anyway, Yogi Bhajan is cool-headed. He gave some practice-impetus which I took. This is energy from him to cause the infusion to be tighter, more compressed and directed.

When one is dealing with a yoga guru one must endure insults. On occasion when I teach someone, I insult the person. Then he goes away. I may not see him again ever. Such is this process. For me however an insult from a yoga guru is welcomed.

If a parent insults the child, the offence does not alter the fact of their biological connection. You cannot erase the birth record because your mother insulted you or your father intimidated you. With yoga gurus, insult is acceptable. They are the fathers. There is no shame in such insults. It does not matter if they are right or wrong.

Yogesh left with disgust. Then Yogi Bhajan graciously gave an intensity energy. As soon as I got it, I realized that he gave this energy before in 1972.The reason why I lost the energy is still up in the air but one part of it was that after that I went to see Arthur Beverford in Ojai, California. Both Beverford and myself recently returned to the United States from the Philippines.

Beverford learnt yoga from Rishi Singh Gherwal but Rishi did not show him *bhastrika*. Beverford learnt deep breathing and nadi shodana. Since he was primarily a martial arts expert, Beverford regarded yoga as a secondary discipline. Except for Sir Paul Castagna, I was the only yoga disciple Beverford had. In Ojai at his place, I showed Beverford what I learnt from Yogi Bhajan but he was not privy to it. He issued discouragement energy. That caused my practice intensity to decrease. At the time I did not notice this. Because of Beverford's unfamiliarity with *bhastrika* pranayama, my practice suffered.

Yogeshwarananda was disgusted with my practice. When I got things in order, he resumed instructions. In the mean time I have his energy in my psyche. That will inspire.

Tibeti Yogi vanished. He went to the causal plane. He is done with the subtle level.

There was a student this morning who practiced as I went through my procedure. Teaching a student is not the same as doing practice by yourself but with this student it is the same because he is there to follow without my paying attention to his needs.

Usually in the presence of students I abandon my personal practice and study the psyche of the student. I give directions which are tailored to that person. In any case, I did explain to this student something about wiggling the body to the left and right. This is done in many postures, especially in postures like lotus or when the bottom of the trunk of the body is in contact with a surface.

This allows any charged energy in the trunk to be released. The student did not understand what I said. I explained that this is not the same as getting kundalini to pass through the central spinal passage into the brain. In this practice, the brain is not involved. This has to do with the trunk and getting kundalini to release itself into the trunk in various parts through various nadis which one becomes aware of when this happens.

Kundalini is a criminal element. It is a wayward energy. It wants to express itself for sex climax and for other addictive pleasures; otherwise it is reluctant to express itself in the trunk of the body. The yogi should make kundalini express itself in the trunk.

Initially the student should get kundalini to go through the *sushumna* central passage but when that reaches a level where one can do that at each practice session, then it is high time that one cause kundalini to be expressed in the dark parts of the trunk.

standard kundalini   inTrunk kundalini
                              without sushumna nadi

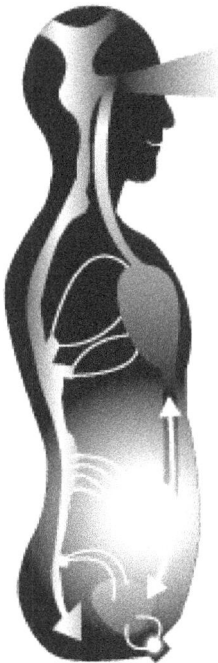

Sex and a Yogi

To recognize that there is a subtle interplay with persons with whom one has deliberate or casual flirtation, is itself an advancement. It is an increase in psychic perception. It shows great sensitivity in this regard. By that alone, half the battle is won.

However, some warriors, who won half the battle, went on and were killed by the enemy. Therefore, one should be on guard.

The intellect analytical orb, translates, mixes and even distorts what happens on the psychic plane. It does this in conjunction with the kundalini which is after gratification and which breaches morality so that it can get happiness from sensual indulgence.

Many types of sensual indulgence are censored in human society. If the kundalini needs these forbidden pleasures, it will indulge on the psychic side where it can evade social restrictions.

The only way to stop this is to change the habits of kundalini by changing its energy intake. It acts in a certain way, expresses a certain behavior, and desires sensual satisfaction because of the energy it consumes.

So long as one is exposed in an environment one must deal with the activated and newly created effect energy *(karma)* which arises. There is no escape from this. One can do yoga but still if one is exposed this will happen. Ideally, yoga should be done in isolation. Originally yoga ashrams had strict sexual segregation. There were only a handful of females, mostly the relatives of the yoga guru.

The point is that if one must be in a sexually charged environment to make a livelihood one must endure what that environment permits. If one is in an environment where people use sexually suggestive clothing and where flirting is the lifestyle, those hazards must be tolerated. There is no easy way to escape.

Response of Lungs

Students should be concerned to be breathing intensely because that is how the diaphragm and the intercostal muscles are toned. However, one should not think that a good breathing rate with an aggressive drawing in of and discharge of air, means that the lungs respond.

The response of the lungs operates through a different system of nerve instructions in the body, such that one may do the breathing in the correct way and the lungs may not absorb the fresh air nor discharge polluted air.

Tingling sensations anywhere in the body should be noted, as these are usually the nadis. Eventually there will be visual perception of the nadis and/or pranaVision which is vision through micro particles of energy, like how a fly sees through compounded eyes.

Take note of this and then meditate in the head of the subtle body.

The preferred time to take note of nadis is during breath infusion. One can note many nadis if one is attentive within during practice, and does not have a skeptic's restrictive way of perceiving what is in the psyche.

Details of Practice

This morning's breath infusion was productive. I bridged the instructions of two yoga gurus, being Tibeti and Yogeshwarananda. Yogesh gave the top end instruction which can be followed after completing Tibeti's process to proficiency during a session. It takes a huff and a puff to reach this stage.

People who speak about the happiness in meditation and about the good spiritual life are obviously on a utopian stretch of the imagination. They are not making progress in the way I am. For me this is an uphill battle every step of the way.

Just to awaken in the morning is a hassle. It consists of balking from the body and mind. I did this practice since 1972 when I learnt *bhastrika* pranayama from Yogi Bhajan. Still today so many years after, it is an uphill climb pretty much every morning. But while I fight with the devil of stupor and sleep, most people slumber away.

The physical body has cells which need to rest and recuperate on a daily basis. Those cells have no interest in spiritual life. Rising early at about 4 am is not their preference. Then there is the subtle body which likes to roam the astral planes early in the morning. It desires to finish its activities there before it is transferred into the physical body and is forced to confirm to the rigors of being a physical being. In an animal form it has others rigors to deal with, but it can piss anywhere, shit anywhere, eat anywhere, have sex without being married and without having to pay child support, wander here and there and not have to confirm with a civilized lifestyle. But in the human body the subtle body is hindered by rules of behavior. Thus, it becomes necessary to escape in astral projections so that periodically one can get rid of the inhibitions which are enforced in the human society.

The subtle body needs rest too. Sometimes it floats inside or outside of the physical form. It sleeps like that just the way fish floats in water and sleeps. Is the self, the glorious, spiritual self, the godSelf, concerned with this? The coreSelf is content for certain psyche mechanisms to do involuntary work by thinking and feeling.

I satisfied Tibeti's requirement for getting the used energy which lingered in the lower trunk and thighs, removed. This was done by doing rapid breathing *(bhastrika pranayama)* in various postures.

This is not about sitting and observing breath. This is about aggressively and rapidly extracting carbon dioxide from the body and replacing that with fresh air, even from the feet, legs and thighs.

I must aggressively fill the system with energizing energy on the subtle side, and new fresh air on the physical level, to effectively do the breath infusion. Once this is done, there is daylight in the dark psyche. Then I can sit to meditate and make progress.

During the night in the astral world, someone asked about the process which I use but it is no mystery. It is the aggressive breath practice listed as *kapalabhati* or *bhastrika*. I do this in various postures in order to reach various parts of the psyche and to extract stale energy, replacing it with fresh air energy.

I do not run my mind up and down the chakras. I do not follow breath in meditation. After breath infusion when I sit to mediate, I am done with breath. I give breath its quota of practice during breath infusion. Then I leave that aside and practice *samyama (dharana → dhyana → samadhi).* That leaves out *pratyahar* sensual energy withdrawal except that breath infusion is so effective that it accomplishes the *pratyahar* practice. When I do a thorough *bhastrika* session, I achieve *pratyahar* without having to practice sense retraction. When I sit to meditate, I can do *samyama*, which is the three higher states of yoga as one sequential practice.

I worked on the lower trunk and the head of the subtle body. There was an energy link between the two areas. Just before this happened when I worked on the head, I began to perceive Yogeshwaranand. It is encouraging when he is seen because it means that I reached the level of existence where he resides.

When the infusement of the trunk and the infusion into the head made contact with each other, there was a flow which is shown in the diagram. This morning a student came to practice. I am not concerned with students. As I write this my body is sixty-one years of age. I must deal with upcoming death. If you are on a highway and your car will crash in ten seconds, why would you be concerned with others?

Gone are the days when I was eager to assist students. That is finished. Whatever I wrote, that is the gift to students. Do not try to be my student. A dead teacher is useless. My time is up. My crisis is about being deprived of a physical body.

I do not want death to catch me teaching students. I want to be attentive to my practice and teachers when death happens.

Once in 1973, Arthur Beverford, a disciple of Rishi Singh Gherwal, showed the anuloma viloma alternate breathing technique for forcing the breath to alter its course and move down to the base chakra with stress on forcing it mentally to do so by holding a special count ratio of inhalation, retention, exhalation and holding breath out. That is the only system which worked in my system to do this but it had to be done for at least one hour to really penetrate. And as soon as I stopped doing it, the breath resumed its passage above the navel. It did not awaken kundalini in a distinct way but only gave it very subtle prodding which it simply ignored.

The other thing is that if someone does this, I must know of how long it takes before kundalini rises in a distinct non-vague way. What is the experience when kundalini rises? If kundalini does not rise during each practice, it is an incomplete practice.

In the practice I used which I got from Yogi Bhajan; kundalini rises without fail at each practice. This guarantees that it does not remain sleeping and acting involuntarily at muladhara chakra. Best of all, it guarantees that it courses through the nadis and keeps them open and clear. Otherwise they stay clogged.

Mouth may be open during these actions and a sound may emit from it due to action at the throat (epiglottis) but it is mostly a nose inhale and exhale. It is sometimes done with mouth closed and with tongue rolled up and back, but it can be done with mouth open, even though the breathing is primarily through the nose.

On occasion there are mouth exhales. Rarely are there mouth inhales.

Bhastrika and *kapalabhati* are aggressive practices. Yogi Bhajan called it *breath of fire*. Some yogis do it slowly with little aggressiveness but when he first came from India, Yogi Bhajan taught the aggressive type combined with various postures.

In India some yogis are seen doing it only in the *sukhasana* or *padmasana* (easy pose or lotus posture). It is done in other postures. In each posture one puts the mind where the posture focuses. In this way one gradually learns how to target and infuse specific areas of the subtle body. One does not take it for granted that the energy scatters everywhere. This process is a combination of *asanas* and *pranayama* as one practice.

There is a technical difference between *bhastrika* and kapalabhati. A beginner should do *kapalabhati* and should begin *bhastrika* only when *kapalabhati* developed into a reflexive habit. *Kapalabhati* is rapid voluminous breathing with stress on the exhale. This means the focus of the mind on the breath action is on the exhale. It is done with emphasis forcibly.

In *bhastrika* the student has the extra task of doing both the exhale and inhale with force. *Bhastrika* should not be done until *kapalabhati* is reflexive. The mind should be kept within the psyche which is to say within the boundaries of the subtle body. It should not be allowed to wander outside the subtle body. In addition, any pose in which one stands up should be done with great care in terms of observing and restricting kundalini.

Kundalini has a way about it, where sometimes during the practice, it rises suddenly without warning. If one is not expert at detecting its movement, one will be caught off-guard. Inner attentiveness is required.

To develop this, I gave chapter one in the *Meditation Pictorial* book. It has the diagrams and instructions needed to develop the mind lock *pratyahar* practice. This is the practice which equips the student to deal with kundalini when it arises and moves through the spine into the head.

Astral Yoga Teachers

I am an agent. The real yogis are Krishna, Brahma and Shiva. These are the people who are ultimately at the head of the lineages of genuine yogis. This means that I am dispensable. My importance is there because of agency, because I was sent to share methods.

I am not indispensable. If one agent disappears, they will send another.

Reaching me on the astral planes later after I am evicted from this physical body residence which I am now use, is a crazy idea. An agent may be sent home in which case the service will continue coming through another employee.

No yoga gurus gave instructions for me to maintain disciples later or to return and tend disciples. I have no plan for this.

In assuming this body, I did as requested. Now the work is done. I should leave quietly and be with siddhas on the other side. It is not that they gave that as a boon. I must purify myself to achieve that. If I am attentive to anything else, I will indirectly hurt myself.

Have no fear! I came because someone else wanted to assist you. That someone else, Krishna, Brahma or Shiva, still has interest in you. They will see to it that you get the technique required for progress.

Control of Kundalini

Kundalini constructed the physical body while the embryo was formed in the mother's system. This was a physical and psychic construction. Even though we assume physical bodies, it is the same subtle form with transformation and adaptations according to the birth environment. This is conducted by Kundalini.

Where is the coreSelf in this existential situation?

It is present as the ego which is itself under the influence of the kundalini.

Can it be released from this?

Yogesh told me that a yogi must assume many activities of kundalini. Then he can break out. If the kundalini keeps taking someone back to another physical body after each birth, there is no hope.

Saying I am absolute or that I have the absolute nature, believing firmly in this, will be of no value if one does not get kundalini under control.

The Yogi Who Became a Servant

Something happened during meditation that caused me to think that I should develop stub kundalini.

normal kundalini stem   stub kundalini as subtle body brain stem
spine connected to brain   no connection to spinal passage

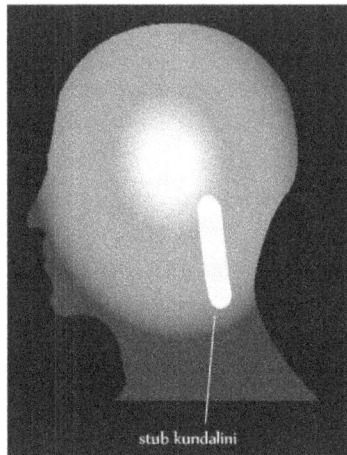

stub kundalini

This is Yogeshwarananda's unusual idea about getting rid of kundalini shakti. To get the bubble body which is used by Siddha Swami Nityananda one must get rid of kundalini.

The problem with this idea is that it sounds far-fetched. The other problem with it is that if you get rid of kundalini, then who will run the show for you, for the coreSelf. Right now, the kundalini does the hard work in the body, even the janitorial tasks like collecting impurities, processing chemicals and evacuating waste.

A king has leisure in the castle but only if he is served fittingly by servants. Once they become free, he is deprived of services. They develop a *Bill of Rights*. They demand incomes which he cannot afford.

They desire to sleep on the royal bed; something that is an affront to the king's dignity. Imagine yourself as God, as the Absolute, would you handle the trash, meaning pass stools from the body. Would you manage the plumbing meaning operate the kidneys? Would you pump the urine from the bladder?

You are Oneness. You are everything. Now you must partition yourself to do menial tasks. That is what faces a yogi if he/she thinks of getting rid of kundalini.

In the story of King Puranjan, he did nothing but enjoy in the city of Bhogavati, the Place of Excitement. That is how a king, a God, or a coreSelf should live. Now what to do when the yoga guru says that you should do the work of the servants, that you should dismiss them and do the duties yourself.

Instead of becoming God, his advice caused you to be a servant.

Does it make sense?

Do you think it is possible to pull kundalini from its spinal spread, to have it be a stub object in the head?

Obligations

Right now, I am under a spell due to an obligation which formed in this life during its childhood. I went to a kindergarten school. There was a single teacher, a lady. She was a good teacher. Subsequently she gave her students the basic in A, B, C and 1, 2, 3. Now I do service to that lady. I am under a spell doing it, the spell called the consequential reactions. This is explained in the *Anu Gita Explained*. Do not cheat yourself by not reading that book. It is a small book but it is potent. It is the clearest explanation of how consequences form and return.

It is essential to see these influences and to understand how they operate. This does not mean that a yogi can suppress or avoid them. Arjuna, even in the presence of the Person God, of Krishna, could not be released from social obligations, even ugly ones. If one understands them one can better negotiate or absolve them and then proceed with spiritual practice.

The questions are:
- Why should I serve this person?
- Why am I compelled to be with these folks?

Navel Clearance

Burning of stomach muscles or even of the navel regions during breath infusion is a boon for a student. I recall when I went through that with excitement and great appreciation for that stage. Those were the days when I worked intensely to change the genetic tendencies this body derived from the parents.

The burning sensation is valuable to the student yogi. It means that the energizing energy accumulates just above the navel where it can be compressed downwards. This is a physical and psychic pressure applied mentally by the yogi. This causes the knot or bandhas at the navel to burst. The energy passes the navel and targets the groin, which is another holding place for it which the yogi must conquer.

When people who never did breath infusion, speak about doing things with their chakras, I usually wonder. If the navel is not penetrated, visualization of chakra purification is child's play. Kundalini could care less about their practice if they have not conquered the navel by destroying its blockage.

This does not mean that there is no breath below the navel but it means that there is no fresh breath energy below the navel. It is not permitted to go there because the navel chakra in the front of the body (not the one on the spine) stands guard to protect kundalini so that it does not have to do what the self needs to do for spiritual elevation.

Yogi Severs the Umbilical Cord Finally

This morning breath infusion was great. When I finally rose this morning, it was one hour later than I should have. In any case, I did practice in the astral world. When I tried to remember what I did, it was like I practiced in a faraway galaxy and lost the memory on my way back here.

I remembered that I made a major breakthrough because of the influence of Tibeti Yogi and Yogeshwarananda. I was with Tibeti Yogi in some faraway place, where when one gets there, one forgets the existence on earth.

I tried to stretch back to that place but it was too far, totally out of reach. The memory of the practice, I did, was gone, like when you are on a ship and you drop a diamond ring overboard. You realize that there is no hope for finding it ever. It is there somewhere in the deep but you cannot claim it ever.

The information was stored in another level of the subtle body in a memory apparatus on that psychic plane. Intuitively, I knew it was vital, something having to do with the gut transformation.

When I rose, this missing memory haunted me because if I could not remember that mystic action. When I got out to do the breath infusion with various postures, I got a telepathic message from Tibeti. It said that the memory would resume while doing the session. It did.

As I did it there was that last bit of disappointment about losing the memory. Then that energy left my psyche. I did the procedure by intuition. Tibeti sent a message saying that the name of the kriya is either *destruction of the food brain* or *severance of the umbilical cord*. Apparently in China, the Taoist gurus called it *severance of the umbilical cord*, while some Hatha Yoga gurus from the Nath sampradaya considered it to be *destruction of the food brain*.

In terms of the umbilical cord, tradition has it that it was severed by the midwife or physician when the blood from the mother's system stopped flowing into the infant. But that is the physical tradition. The Taoist gurus are of the view that the cord is still connected not to that specific mother but to the mothering energy of the earth goddess, Quan Ying. Everyone suckles energy from Quan Ying, but at some point in the future, each person should cease this parasitic behavior.

A Taoist yogi reaches a stage where he cuts the umbilical cord from within the psyche. Then he either starves or becomes liberated in another body, a divine form, where he is born or where he appears in a divine world which is different to this earth goddess domain.

Yogis like Milarepa did austerities and then ripped the cord away from the goddess in a brutal way. Buddha did this during his gruesome starvation austerities. It can be done in less violent ways or one can also continue practicing and after many births, trillions of practices, the cord eventually falls away from the goddess. One develops the divine body.

One is not God. One must exist in someone else's environment. It is a matter of getting permission to transfer from here to someone else's place. One is not original, one takes energy from somebody, some deity.

The destruction-of-the-food-brain system is done in hatha yoga practice. This is hatha yoga not yoga postures which are asanas which are an elementary part of hatha yoga. Hatha yoga is really ashtanga yoga. In that system the yogi practices in the way of the Indian tradition which is to aim for a yoga siddha body. In that system the subtle body is pressured on and on, using pranayama practice. It is transmuted, changed.

Like for instance Swami Nityananda Baba, Muktananda's guru, used a bubble body which is the same subtle body we use but completely gutted out, changed to an unrecognizable form. It has a bloated head and bloated balloon like trunk and nothing else, no feet, no hands. That is a special stage of development which is even beyond a yoga siddha body. It concerns the masters of brahma yoga.

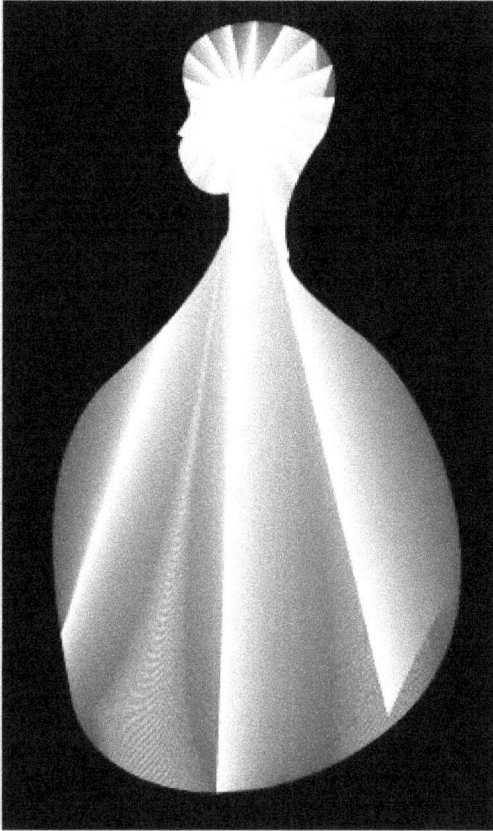

In any case for the *destruction of the food brain* there are two methods. One is the method which Swami Rama advocated and swore by, which is mastery of agnisara kriya practice. This is the one I do not recommend except if you were born with a body from a yogi family from India, a family which carries special physical genes which designed the body to have a special type of yogi gut.

The other is the way for modern students which is to do the breath infusion so much and for so long, then eventually it tunnels through the gut area and eliminates the resistance in the front navel chakra.

This front navel chakra is not the navel chakra on the spine. This is not about imagining that energy goes up and down the chakras on the spine. It is not a visualization practice. This is infusing breath into the body and forcing it down from the lungs into the navel area. It accumulates there. The yogi forces it through the pelvic area.

After years of practice, finally the break through occurred in the subtle body. The physical body is still the same with the same configuration it had genetically which it assumed from the current ancestral line.

The main thing is to thrust the air through the navel and then let it attack the muladhara chakra directly. But if you do this and you did not clear the navel region, you will not get the full effect.

The honest way is to work on the navel for years if necessary until it is flushed. The impurities are removed because of the constant thrusting of the breath energy which passed through that area, goes down to the groin and then loops around to the kundalini base chakra and up the spine into the head.

regular kundalini attack
using standard route through navel,
looping through pubic area
then finally to the kundalini base chakra

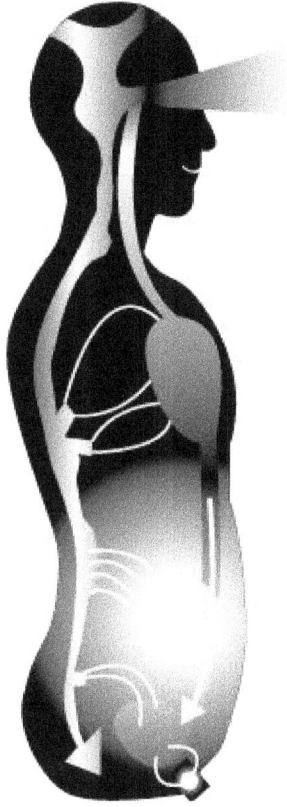

direct attack on kundalini
after front navel chakra is
eliminated in subtle body
navel and pubic area are not involved

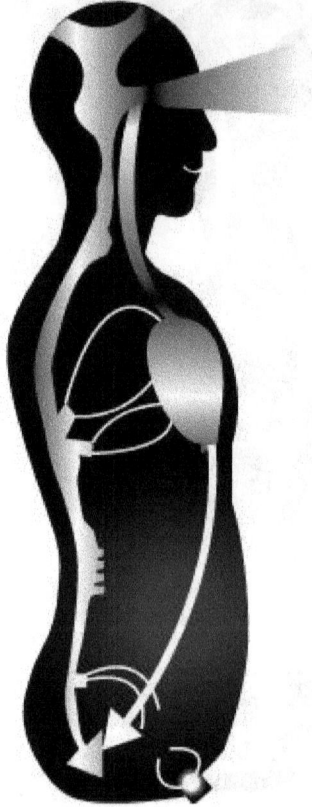

It is not so much the breath infusion method used but the actual contact of the infused breath energy with the will power attentive energy of the yogi. There has to be such a tight contact between the two that the yogi manhandles the infused energy and directs it. Mantras are permitted but they are not effective if the will power does not manhandle to get the achievements.

Patanjali and Chapter Two of *Bhagavad Gita*

Breath infusion this morning was good. I was enthusiastic, trying to comply with Tibeti Yogi's instruction for bringing the intellect organ into the lower trunk of the body, to meet kundalini.

This practice requires intense concentration. One must do it while doing rapid breathing in various postures while one focuses fully. I use a full head blindfold while doing these exercises. This discourages the eyes from causing the intellect to wander.

During practice, Tibeti Yogi sent a message telling me that the second Sutra of Patanjali described the intellect yoga process Krishna explained to Arjuna in chapter two of *Bhagavad Gita*. He did not give details or particular verses.

Actually, I knew all along that chapter two of the Gita was it, in the sense that the kriya practice is in that chapter. I explained this in my book Kriya Yoga *Bhagavad Gita*. Of course, that book was inspired by Babaji, so the credit for the discovery is his.

I never considered the connection to the *yogah cittavritti nirodhah* statement of Patanjali. However, it makes sense because the stopping of the *vrittis* of *chitta* really means shutting down one psychic organ which is the intellect. That is what Krishna discussed in chapter two with Arjuna. Krishna named the process intellect yoga *(buddhiyoga)*.

Tibeti Yogi sent another message which was that the system does that anyway, especially in sex indulgence.

He spoke of moving the intellect into the lower trunk. In sexual indulgence the intellect is relocated in the genitals, especially during sexual climax. Thus, the idea of moving the intellect down while doing breath infusion may sound strange and unnatural but really the system does that during sex instinct. If there is damage to the lower part of the body, one is forced by the pain of it, to shift one's attention down. A woman carrying a fetus must shift her attention there.

Yoga is about Practice

This morning's breath infusion was great. I had a student this morning. I lectured about the necessity of practice. Yoga is not a cult. It is not about gurus nor asking questions of gurus. It is about learning. It is a course like when a child is educated in kindergarten and gradually over time reaches graduate level at a university.

Yoga is more about learning and practice, and then it is about teachers. A million teachers of the best qualification cannot help a student who is unwilling to practice in the course of the particular subject.

Practice is the way to advance in yoga. Teachers surely help but their assistance is mostly utilized if there is practice side by side. If the student sits with the teacher and does not do the lessons recommended, that sitting will not get the education into the head of the student.

Carbon Dioxide Extraction

This past weekend, I checked a student's breath infusion practice. This person did the practice for three years. In any case, his practice is good except that he does not compress the infused breath. I suggested that he should focus on that.

The lungs may not do what is required in breath infusion. Normally, the lungs are under the control of the lifeForce mechanism which means that they operate for bare survival. In such a system there is little need for infused breath. The system cares for itself by taking whatever breath it deems to be necessary.

For yoga this must change. The student may do *bhastrika* or *kapalabhati* practice which sounds very regular and efficient and still the lungs may not efficiently process the air.

Merely taking air into the lungs in no way guarantees that the system absorbs it. One must compress the air into the blood stream. Do not be in illusion thinking that because you breathe fresh air, the lungs took it and compressed it into the system.

Each student must check inside during practice, to be sure that the system not only takes air into the lungs but absorbs that air, compresses it and sends it down so that it does not go out of the lungs on the next exhale. The student should check to see if more and more carbon dioxide is extracted from the system and is vented from the body on the exhales.

The compressed inhaled breath should be pushed down mentally so that it goes below the navel and is pushed further into the groin area, and is pushed further yet into the sacral region at the base chakra and is then forced upward with kundalini through the spine. While this takes place whatever polluted air is trapped in front of the compressed air should be pushed out of the body and not allowed to escape into other parts of the psyche.

Flush the old air from the cells. Remove as much carbon dioxide as possible. Cause the lungs to change their way of operation. Kundalini designed this system for survival but it has no standing in spiritual life. It will not change by mere wishing. It will change under pressure of a consistent practice.

That must be done. In addition to that one should search in the psyche and find places where carbon dioxide is hoarded in cells. Because of being addicted, some cells retain carbon dioxide.

For instance, for a very strong and robust body, one must have carbon dioxide. For a firm erection in males, one must use that energy. The organs involved in certain activities which require that will hoard that energy and keep that energy from being removed from the body. By increased psychic perception, one can locate where this happens. One can pull that energy from those places in the psyche.

Yoga Objectives

Yogah cittavritti nirodhah means that a proficiency in yoga practice is denoted by the ability to stop the mento-emotional force from operating impulsively. The convention is that the intellect operates on its own as it is goaded by the sensual inputs and memory.

When a yogi shuts down this automatic system and implements absolute control over the mental and emotional fluctuations, he/she is said to have accomplished yoga.

This includes the kundalini because it is the main psychic system which goads the intellect to visualize. Kundalini is independent and wants to maintain its autonomy over the psyche. Thus, the self must come to terms with it, to make it submissive to the long-ranged interest of the psyche.

Kundalini or the lifeForce psycho-physical mechanism and intellect are in a conspiracy to keep the self under their joint control,

Yogah cittavritti nirodhah is the statement about shattering the authority of the intellect so that even the kundalini cannot execute impulsive actions.

Of course, we enjoy some of these actions, so it is not easy to restrict something if one gets a pleasure from it.

inPsyche Projection

During breath infusion this morning I got an instruction from Tibeti yogi about using the intellect which has the head of the subtle body as its default location. I was to move into the sacral cage. When this is done it feels as if one moved one's head so that it sits in the sacral cage.

It is hardly likely that one would come up with such a kriya on one's own because the convention is to stay away from that area. At least the intellect stays away from that area which is the exclusive territory of the kundalini force.

However, once a yogi breaks the choke-hold of the senses on the mind, he/she can do this. One is born under captivity, where one is kept entertained by the sensual data which is fed from the senses to the intellect. One becomes addicted to this sensory display in the head of the subtle body (brain of the physical form).

Even after practicing yoga for years, where people pretend that they are sensually detached, they remain sensually attached in secret because the intellect is not concerned with one's aspirations.

To outright rip the intellect from the senses, is a cruel act for anyone, a self-inflicting punishment but it is worth doing if one is serious and wants to be an advanced yogi. One should have no fear thinking that all sensory pleasure will come to an end. After all what goes up must come down. Or stated in this case, if you were hooked sensually before, even if you break away, you may surely become addicted in a deeper way in the future.

When I did that practice of pulling the intellect into the sacral cage, I found that the pubis bone and its astral part became evident. Tibeti sent a message saying that this is the co-ordinate of the third eye. When the subtle head is pulled into the sacral cage, the third eye touches the pubis bone. This is a very important bone because it is the centralize situation of the sexual pleasure force.

This practice is the real astral projection but within the psyche of the yogi rather than a prowling adventure in the astral realms.

Use of Mystic Power in Patanjali

I learnt the application of the Patanjali process mostly from Yogeshwarananda of Gangotri but I was tutored by him on the astral planes. There was a restriction which he placed which was that siddhis were to be reinvested into yoga practice and not be used for any other purpose.

This may be compared to having a business and using the profits to expand the business and not using any proceeds for anything else. In that case, the use of siddhis is prohibited except for reinvestment of the skills in more practice and in developing more psychic sensitivity to see the way to advance more in self-realization.

Part of his requirement was that a mystic power should never be displayed to anyone. As soon as one realizes or recognizes that one has a siddhi one is supposed to conceal it and never reveal it to anyone.

Yogeshwarananda felt that if it was shown, one would be forced circumstantially on the plea of others for its use and demonstration. That, he said, deters advanced practice, since one becomes involved socially again. The big part of his instruction is that if the student does not comply with this, Yogesh's association will not be forthcoming.

I will give an example of a how this application of siddhi mystic perfection is applied to practice instead of being revealed to others. Let us say for instance that I felt that I was the target of a thought of someone. I get an intuition that someone will call me to postpone a payment of a fifty-dollar loan which he took from me.

Five minutes after this, the phone rang. It was that person. He apologized for not repaying. He wanted the time extended so that he could pay it in two months. I told him that he could repay it as proposed.

In this case a simple siddhi, telepathy, was observed. I could have said to that person that I had a hunch that he would call and I suspected that he would require an extension for payment of the loan.

If I did this, he would be alerted that somehow, I read his mind. He may inform others. This in turn may cause others to approach me.

Someone may remark, "Since you read minds can you tell me what someone else thinks about me. I wish to know if he favors me. Please read his mind. I know you can do that."

According to the training from Yogeshwar, a siddhi like telepathy should not be exposed to anyone. It should be invested in yoga practice only.

The student can invest that into reading his subconscious impressions, his own pre-conscious activities, and causal states. He can use that to read his mind before his mind formulates an idea or thought. Then he can be more in compliance with sutra two of the *Yoga Sutras* for *chittavritti nirodhah*, stopping impressions in the mind in their seed form before they burst as thoughts and ideas. He can know what they are in their seed form, just as an experienced farmer may look at seeds of wild plants and know their potential for growth into specific types of vegetation.

Yogeshwarananda made vital contributions to the yoga process. He published books. Some are:

- *First Steps to Higher Yoga*
- *Science of Divine Light*

The other prohibition is the yama and niyamas which Patanjali himself gave as being the *mahavrata*, great commitment. Patanjali said that they should not be violated in any time or place.

It is the only place in the sutras where he lays down this harsh stipulation on the practitioners of the *ashtanga* yoga. In India, if someone makes a *vrata*, it means that he made a vow but if it is a mahavrata it is serious. For instance, if one takes a vow to fast on Shivaratri and one is an ordinary temple goer, that is a *vrata* but if one takes a vow to become a sannyasi who will be single for the rest of his life, that is a *mahavrata*.

Patanjali gave rules which prohibit the demonstration of siddhis and their usage.

Another thing that relates to this is that he gave the means of having these siddhis. Yoga practice is only one of the means. Yet even though yoga is only one of the means, drugs (herbs) being another, true yoga is such that if a siddhi develops it cannot be used whimsically.

I will give an example. This is something I learnt recently when I translated of the *Anu Gita* of the *Mahabharata*. In that story, after the battle when the Pandavas had a good time ruling without opposition, Arjuna asked Lord Krishna to show the Universal Form and again go over the details of the *Bhagavad Gita*. Surprisingly Krishna refused to exhibit the form. Krishna addressed Arjuna as a no-good person. But the point is that Krishna said he revealed the form under special yogic state. He refused to exhibit it again. That was a *siddhi* of Krishna. Still he did not exhibit it on request, even upon request of Arjuna, his declared friend.

Part 7

Conspiracy in Yoga Practice

This morning's breath infusion was with emphasis on the lower brain area of kundalini. This is a switch in kriya method because of the influence over my practice of Tibeti Yogi. Yogeshwarananda came on the subtle side of existence. He was happy because I took Tibeti's instructions seriously.

Yogesh said,

"Complete first steps of yoga. Master prana. Then ask the teacher for help. What can he do if the preliminary steps are done in a half-hearted manner?

"Do not cry for assistance when you do not do as instructed. There is an ashtanga eight-tiered process. Use that."

The fact that after forty years of practice I now use this process of Tibeti shows that unless one gets help from higher yogis, one cannot practice the higher stages. One will be stalled and will not progress as desired. I used to target the upper brain which is the head of the subtle body. That is not enough. One must target the lower brain and the bastion of kundalini which is the sacral area.

There is a conspiracy by the kundalini. There is one carried out by the intellect. Besides these two very different agendas, there is the joint conspiracy of the kundalini and the intellect. Considering this, what chance does the coreSelf have to gain dominance in the psyche?

The intellect's conspiracy is to keep the coreSelf involved in sensual presentations which are essentially photos of the physical objects. Some are taken with the eye camera, some with touch sensor, some with the taste receptor, some with the audio diaphram and some with a nasal alert. The intellect's conspiracy involves keeping the coreSelf spell bound with the pictures which preoccupy the coreSelf in the mind.

Kundalini runs another conspiracy all of its own, which is to lure the coreSelf down into the lower parts of the body. The chief attraction for this is sex pleasure but there are other traps.

Since they are involved in separate conspiracies, the two adjuncts have no interest either in each other or in the coreSelf. The kundalini wants dominance over the psyche and so does the intellect. Sometimes they work together but only because they have a common target which is the coreSelf.

When they work together it is because that is the only way to intimidate the core. Besides that, they work against each other.

Tibeti yogi said that so long as one is partially disposed to the intellect, one cannot understand what kundalini does and one will never fully curb it. It is also true that some entities favor the kundalini. For them they cannot curb the kundalini ever.

One requires detachment from both adjuncts.

During practice this morning the brain of the kundalini which is the space in the hollow of the sacral bones, was targeted. It got to where this area showed a clear space with the dulling energy of it dissipated, melted away, replaced by fresh energy.

Bucking the Horse Kriya

This morning Tibeti Yogi showed a kriya which he said is called *bucking the horse*. He did not appear in his astral body but sent this instruction by a teleportation message.

This bucking-the-horse originated from a system in Mongolia where boys were taught to ride horse and to gain complete control of the horse by forcing it to buck while riding and never letting go. This fools the horse into thinking that it can never upset the rider. Hence the animal never attempts to throw the rider at any stage.

The rider, a boy in training, has to spur the horse in such a harsh way that the horse bucks while the rider holds and is not thrown from the back of the animal. Many Mongolian boys either became permanently crippled or died outright when trying to do this ruthless practice. According to Tibeti Yogi it was a system which was taught in Mongolia before the days of Genghis Khan. It became a ritual performance while the Khan ruled much of Mongolia.

During the night on the astral side of existence, I saw Arthur Beverford. Later I was with some members of his family in the Philippines. Mostly they did things astrally as if the astral world is this physical existence. Just as in dreams we usually do things as if the dream existence is physical, a person who is deceased usually continues acting in the way of physical existence even after being transferred fully to the astral planes. This is called physical conditioning which carries a momentum force which does not permit the person to make progress with psychic realization in the interim period between losing a body and assuming a new embryo.

Tibeti Yogi told a story in that transmission about a time when in Tibet, there were people coming from Inner Mongolia. He said that these people were crude. They lived under very harsh conditions of sparse vegetation and long dreary winters. They were nomadic, following herd animals which moved to get fodder. Somehow, some lamas who were deceased took bodies among the Mongolians. When their instinct for spiritual practice surfaced, they travelled to Tibet.

Once, a head lama, made a rule that any Mongolian who applied for being a monk should first master the *bucking the horse* kriya before he would be taught anything else in the practice of kriyas.

What is this mystic procedure?

It is the process of focusing on the sacral cage which is the bastion of kundalini. According to that lama when a person had a tough life, where he/she ekes out an existence in the physical world the hard way, that person becomes very physical, which means that kundalini is housed in the sacral skeletal cage like a mad king who is housed up in a fortress and who plans on living there forever.

These Mongolian applicants had to buck the horse within their psyches the way they bucked the horses on the cold Mongolian steppes.

The real meaning of the bucking-the-horse kriya however is that the yogi gets to understand that he was a total idiot when he followed those gurus who said that rising kundalini into the head was the culmination of the practice. The truth is that there are two brains. One is in the head of the subtle body. It is called the intellect. This is a psychic technology in the subtle body.

But there is another unknown brain in the system which is the sacral cage.

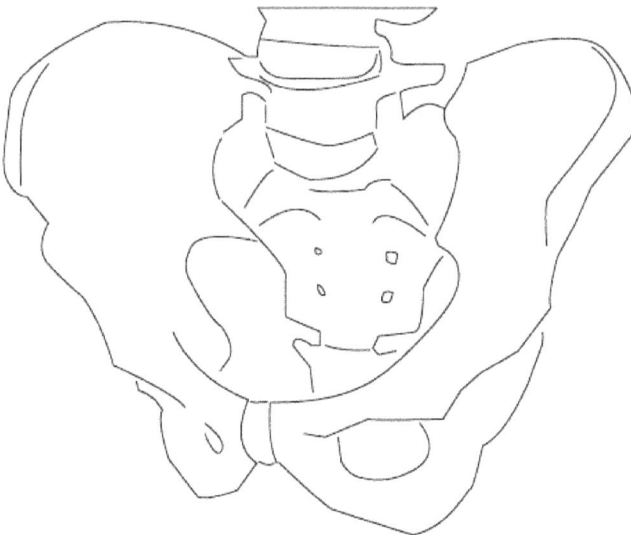

This place belongs to the kundalini. It is where that system carries out its ghastly calculations making the ultimate bombs for the end of the world. The evil genius in the psyche is kundalini. Therefore, focusing on the brain or head of the subtle body will not upset this evil ruler.

If one wants to get the best of this evil tyrant one must attack his bastion directly. It is located as the sacral region, a place in the body like no other, a place which is hemmed in on all sides and which is impregnable.

Tibeti Yogi said that it is in fear of the kundalini that the coreSelf runs into the head to develop occult powers but he said that such powers are a joke to kundalini. Those powers do not help in demolishing the walls of the fortress of kundalini.

Tibeti Yogi said this,

"A yogi who does not break this fort of kundalini, who does not attack it outright and take possession of it, is a failure. The matter is that simple. Do not mislead people by telling them something else. What has it to do with religion or philosophy? Attacked and crushed the fort outright.

"When a senior lama used to tell the Mongolian applicants to do this kriya, we Tibetans wondered about it. We felt that it was for the Mongolians. Actually, it was for everybody but we did not understand.

"It took me five lives of practice after that occurred to get insight into the fact that I should do this. I was misled by some senior lamas who thought they were masters of kundalini. The joke of it. You are a master of kundalini and you never attacked it outright. What king declares himself as a master of territories which he never even walked upon? How can he control a population which has never followed one edict from his royal mouth?"

Kundalini as Cause of Behavior

I use a breath infusion practice which is known as *kapalabhati* and *bhastrika* pranayama. This allows me to infuse physical and subtle energy into the kundalini system.

When this is done sufficiently, kundalini gets surcharged. It moves in this way or that way from the base chakra. It acts in completely different ways. Doors of perception to the subtle and super-subtle existence opens.

Kundalini behaves differently when it is surcharged in this way, which proves that it is the driving force behind my survival behavior on lower levels. One discovery I made is that meditation only goes so deep when kundalini is not first infused.

It may be of use if one can realize that what we call kundalini is being experienced by us in terms of our particular social behaviors and personal habits. That may break the mystique of it.

Kundalini is involved in sex pleasure and in other forms of pleasure which are routine for anyone using a mammal's body. Kundalini is the factor which brings about puberty and sexual maturity. It is the influence which scales down life's activities in old age.

Some of its behavior work in our favor. Some do not. How can one compel it or induce it not to behave unfavorably?

Yoga when it is *ashtanga* yoga begins with *yama* and *niyama* which are behavioral restrictions and approvals. Yoga therefore, begins with an attempt to control kundalini's expressions.

When one has sexual intercourse the door of sex pleasure perception becomes wide open. Then it shuts as soon as the orgasmic energy subsides. This sex pleasure is another feature of kundalini perception capability.

When kundalini comes into the head it pushes the subtle body into a higher dimension in which that body has supernatural perception. The reason why people have a kundalini experience and do not have supernatural perception along with that, is this. They cannot use the supernatural perception even when it is available because they are oriented to physical perception and lack subtle focus. The subtle body has the potential for higher level perceptions and psychic perceptions, supernatural insight, but it must be energized by some means before it can experience these.

Subtle Sex Bulb Problem (July 7, 2010)

Yogeshwarananda's Kriya: July 7, 2010
Kundalini Swipe-Back to Crown Chakra

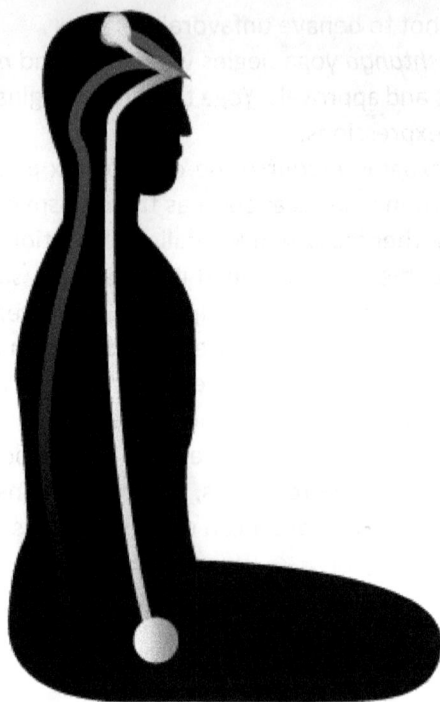

Practice:
Raise Kundalini from sexual energy kanda in the subtle body.
Do not raise it from the base chakra.
Do bhastrika rapid breathing for at least 50 counts.
Hold energy at brow chakra while drawing it back to crown.
Energy may try to disappate at brow chakra.
Mentally prevent it from doing so.
Be sure to hold the coreSelf in naad sound during this experience.
Naad is the anchor zone.

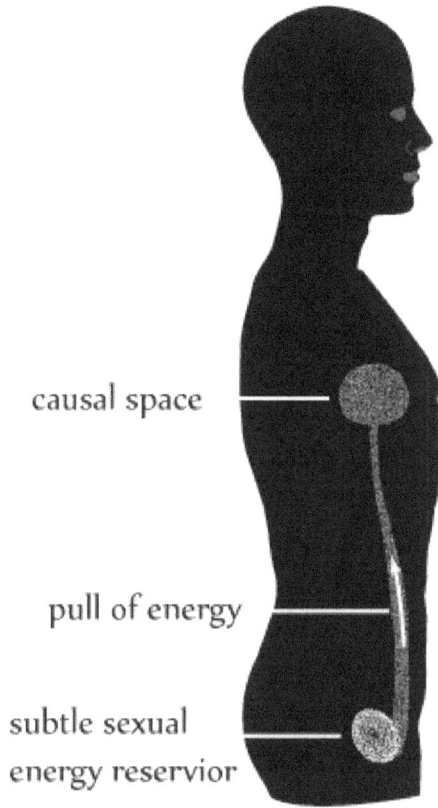

causal space

pull of energy

subtle sexual
energy reservior

Bliss aspect of kundalini

This morning's meditation was a struggle. During the night there were several unwanted astral encounters, like being lost in the hoodlum part of a city. Finally, the night was over. It was 3 am. Time to consider sitting up to meditate, which I did. But there was a weariness of bones and tendons due to working physically yesterday.

There were the muddled memories of the astral encounters. I decided to be firm, to sit up and meditate. I did this. I connected with naad sound. Some astral interference reached me, however.

At about 5 am I had sufficient resolve to do breath infusion. Yesterday it rained I could not go outdoors, subsequently the air was not as energizing as it was today.

Air in a building even fresh air, is not as energizing as air outdoors, except perhaps in freezing temperatures. The air outside was good. kundalini was aroused many times with the bliss aspect within the trunk of the body as compared to its raising and entering the brain and having a bliss aspect there.

During the session I noted that the bliss aspect was present with each movement of kundalini here or there. Then I was touched by someone. It was Tibeti Yogi. He smiled. I do not know where he resides or in what dimension. I depend on his visits. He said this,

> *"Everything is spoilt by sexual indulgence. The psyche is perverted by it. Those who are bewildered by it cannot understand. The bliss aspect should be in every part of the subtle body. What has it to do with sexual organs? These organs have no monopoly on it. Spiritual body! Spiritual body! That is it!"*

Then he disappeared.

When I sat to meditate after the session, there was mental disturbance from persons who tried to reach me. Regrettably, I haggled with this energy for ten minutes, Suddenly I heard naad. It was as if naad had pity for me. It made the connection. I keyed into it. Sometime after there were astral encounters again. This time it was due to mental contact with the astral forms of others. These forms were like transparencies, flashing in and out of perception.

After thirty minutes, I got up to complete some duties. So much for a flawed meditation session.

It has to do with what cold air does to the body if the body is unable to heat it up quickly enough. In normal breathing, due to the slow intake of air, the body can warm it, but in rapid breathing, with volumes of air coming into the system over a short period of time, the body may not be able to warm such volumes of freezing air quickly. The result of this will be that the body may develop influenza.

In the winter months, it is best to be in a warm place and allow a certain amount of cold fresh air to be mixed with the heated air, so that the body does not have to deal with the coldness.

Some cold air from the frigid regions of the earth has dormant viruses. As soon as these pathogens enter the body through air intake, their dormancy expires. They invade the body. Thus, if one does rapid breathing, one will ingest many pathogens. These may cause influenza while for normal breathing, only a limited number of these germs will enter the body.

The point is that in the winter one should be careful and not be fanatical or superstitious about *pranayama* practice. Be health conscious. Do it in a way where nature does not attack you as a result in another way. Cold viruses may be dormant in cold air coming from the frigid regions of the earth but as soon as these enter the body, they come alive.

Breath Infusion Advanced Stages

Two methods of breath infusion which should be understood are the compression of fresh air into the system and the extraction of stale air from cells which hoard that negative energy. The preliminary method to master is the compression of fresh air. The advanced one is that of first infusing fresh air and then going to hidden places in the psyche to extract hidden stale air from cells which hoard it.

A student should first master the pumping of fresh air. This system causes a buildup of pressure in the lower front of the trunk of the body. When this accumulation of fresh air becomes saturated, it hits the kundalini lifeForce at the base of the sacral region. This prompts kundalini to move. By applying locks like the anus lock, the stomach lock and the sex lock, the student forces kundalini to go upwards, even though it is mindful to go down.

When by daily practice a yogi did this compression of fresh air for some years, he focuses on going to the hard-to-reach areas to extract stale air which is hoarded by cells in the extremities of the body, in places like the thighs, legs and feet, even in the hips and genitals.

Pushing air in the system does not remove every bit of used air which certain cells hoard. A special effort must be made to remove that remnant pollution. Certain cells will hold polluted air no matter what. The student must confront these energies and switch them for fresh air. One should peer in the body for any movements, energy shifts or changes which are signs that kundalini will strike the intellect in the head of the subtle body.

If kundalini strikes that psychic organ unawares, there will be one or two effects. One effect is a complete black out, with no recall of it. The other more preferred effect, which advanced students get, is an awareness of being in shimmering intense golden light *(brahmananda),* and then finding oneself out of it but again aware of the physical/subtle body.

This intense golden light may be experienced as bliss energy without perception of light, like an intense sex experience but in the head not in the genitals. In the case of a black out, kundalini is armed with polluted energy. It strikes with that dulling or retardative force. In the case of the intense bliss energy or golden light, kundalini is armed with energizing energy. It strikes just the same but propels the self into higher zones.

In either case that of dull consciousness and that of enlightened awareness (golden light or intense bliss energy); the yogi may lose control of the physical body if he did not apply the locks effectively.

Why?

Because control of the body is indirect. One cannot directly control a physical body. As a core spirit, one cannot directly make contact with that energy. One does so through adjuncts. If an adjunct cannot contact the body, guess what?

In a foundry, men handle molten metal but how?

Was there ever a case of a foundry man holding a piece of white-hot iron?

Is it that he does so only with gloves and tongs?

The student should peer in the body during the breath infusion. As soon as he senses a movement of energy or sensation, he should apply the muscular and mental locks and assume a squatting or sitting position. This will protect from having the body fall to the ground if the kundalini strikes the intellect.

When one infuses fresh air, it accumulates a charge. This is forced into the body from the front side. This hits the perineum area. That jumps to the base chakra. If one does the locks, this will cause kundalini to go upwards but it will go upwards with the polluted used energy which is being pushed by the newly infused energy. If this used energy continues to rise, it will eventually enter the head. That will cause the intellect organ to crash which will be experienced as a black out.

There is a way to stop this stale energy from doing this. It can be extracted from the body through the lungs but that expertise comes after long practice. It does not happen overnight, nor by wishful thinking. One must practice daily. Then the lungs will change operation. This will happen.

Stated simply, the lung system is genetically designed not to extract all old energy in the cells. One must change the attitude of the lungs but this will take time. Nature has its way of doing things. To adjust that, one must endeavor for a time.

kundalini strikes buddhi organ   kundalini enters head
with dark dulling energy   with only infused fresh energy

compressed stale energy
attacks kundalini

compressed dark energy
moves up and away from kundalini
going to lungs for discharge out of body

Bliss effect of breath infusion practice

Initially the bliss effect of breath infusion practice comes only when kundalini rises through the spine into the head. Some students feel the energy and then blank out and have no experience.

By consistent practice, over time, one learns how to motivate kundalini to rise during each session. A determined student should practice aggressively so that there is at least a small rise of kundalini if not all the way into the head, at least up the spine above the navel area.

The bliss effect is special since if one can experience it daily, it may free the student from having to pursue for happiness in other ways. If you have a balanced diet, it is likely that you will not chase every food smell which reaches your nostrils.

Once you master the arousal of kundalini into the head, the next effort is to cause kundalini to rise in the trunk of the body and in the extremities, in every other place except the head.

The problem with this is that it does not give the intense pleasure bliss experience as when kundalini comes into the head. This is because usually for there to be a bliss experience, the kundalini has to be appreciated by the intellect which is in the head.

Sexual climax is a type of bliss experience. In Sanskrit it is called *prajananda* = *praja* (progeny) + *ananda* (bliss), -- which means the blissful experience one acquires when one attempts to beget progeny.

In yoga however the objective is *brahmananda* {*brahma* (spiritual reality) + *ananda* (bliss)}, which is the pleasure derived from linking into the exclusive spiritual plane of existence.

However, we can learn something from sex experience, which is that it is appreciated best when the intellect in the head of the subtle body comes down to meet the sexually-expressed kundalini in the genital regions and the auxiliary sexual equipment like the lips and breasts.

If a sexual experience occurs and the intellect is not involved, there is no intense bliss experience. From this observation one can decide to bring the intellect to where energy is aroused during breath infusion practice. If this is done there will be bliss experiences in other parts of the subtle body besides the head.

Tibeti Yogi and Yogesh gave the information I shared above.

Ashwini Mudra Effects

Query: Will ashwini mudra stop kundalini from going downwards?

Ashwini mudra would help if there is a corresponding psychic check in the same way. Just to do it physically will not confirm that it occurs in the subtle body. A physical action may not have a corresponding psychic movement. Without that, there will not be the desired effects.

Yogi Who Will Win

The rewiring of the brain must be done by the yogi. This is because the brain was designed by the kundalini lifeForce based on the instincts which were carried from previous lives and which were absorbed from the parents and others in the social environment.

The coreSelf is unable to control the formation of the fetus once that process begins. It does have some input into this formation but much of its desires are altered in the process by the kundalini under which the process of fetus development takes place.

This means that once I enter into the emotions of my father's psyche, and is transferred into my mother's psyche, I no longer have control over the formation of the body in my mother's uterus. Everything there is done under the influence of kundalini.

For details of this please see my book:

sex you!

Kundalini wired the brain to proceed with animal instinct, to accelerate that and to be the best at this in the creature survival bid in the physical world. The game is on. It began millions of years prior. Kundalini, yours or mine, is in a race to the finish. I intend to win. And so, do you. But I do not intent to lose. Neither do you.

Breath Infusion Lapse

I made an observation during the infusion session this afternoon. This was that for a student, it is sufficient if he/she can get the infused breath energy to reach the bottom of the trunk of the body. That itself is an accomplishment.

Beginners usually master infusion to the navel. Those who go further are able to push the energy down pass the navel into the pubic area. Others cause it to arch across from the pubic area to the base of the spine. And yet others gain mastery in causing it to arc to the base and then go upwards.

This however will not give one a yoga siddha body. But those preliminary accomplishments are an achievement because usually the kundalini encourages the entity to not fuss with breath infusion since by doing so one may luck out in physical achievements, lose one's status in the physical world and become a nobody. How will one get a college degree, a decent job and a fair shake at a comfortable retirement, if one loses ambition?

If one wants to be a champion athlete, one should try to increase the body's tolerance for carbon dioxide (*apana* – Sanskrit). When this is increased one can excel at sports. But for gaining a yoga siddha form, this will be counterproductive.

People who excel at keeping the physical body fit for strenuous sports achieve that but they will not get a yoga siddha form in that way. For a yoga siddha body, one should efficiently remove the carbon dioxide, extracting it from the body, so that a negligible amount is in it. But such a yogi may not get status in the physical world.

If one does breath infusion twice per day, and then one stops doing this for a week, when one resumes the practice one will notice that one must exert harder and for a longer time to refill the system with the infused energy.

I experienced this today. For the last week my practice was sporadic. This afternoon I got the opportunity to reestablish the routine. I noticed that the thighs were back to their old way with much carbon dioxide energy.

It took some time to get that energy extracted into the blood stream, back to the lungs, expelled and replaced with fresh air. But a student who is not that expert should be sure that at least he/she accomplished some infusion to whatever extent possible and should not let the system regress to its old habits which are to keep much of the carbon dioxide packed into the cells as possible.

It is the physical and subtle so long as there is a physical body. The systems are paired so long as the physical body is present. When the physical body is done, there is only the subtle side to respond to.

The value of having a physical body is that one can indirectly observe what happens in the subtle form by a gross means of observation which is much easier than keeping track of the subtle actions directly.

Unless one developes keen psychic perception, the motions and inner workings of the subtle form cannot be observed. Hence the necessity to have a physical body to begin yoga practice in earnest. Ultimately however one must abandon this physical help and use only the psychic energies, the subtle stuffs.

When they are together either of the bodies try to mimic the other. For instance, in a wet dream when someone is sexual with someone else in the astral domains, the physical body may mimic the subtle one by secreting sexual fluids. Conversely, when there is physical sexual activity, the subtle body will secrete subtle sexual fluids. The bodies are directly related. Hence one can observe the condition of one of the bodies by knowing the condition of the other.

In the advanced practice, however, these mirror effects, should be abandoned by the yogi. He/she should track what happens in one system, in the subtle situation, because after one is deprived of the physical form, one will be left only with the subtle body.

The yogi breathes normally when he is not doing the exercises but he feels the residual effect of the last infusion session. Due to the reduction in the carbon dioxide his motivational basis for living changes over time.

In the life of the Pandavas we see this change in their attitude at the end, where they lost interest in everything competitive. Yudhishthira suddenly abandoned interest in political and social management. People were shocked since if someone came to him to complain about an injustice or criminal activity, he did not response. People were disappointed. This means that he lost interest in physical existence, even his interest in the good side, even his interest in correcting wrongs and doing good for society.

Kundalini and Sex Climax

In sexual orgasm, the kundalini links with the sexual energy in a highly charged sparked condition. When this happens the intellect links with that already linked energy. That is experienced as sex pleasure. If the intellect does not link into it, it is a sexual experience without the intense pleasure.

This means three components are involved in sexual orgasm which are sex hormone energy, kundalini lifeForce and involuntary intellect focus.

When kundalini is experienced in the head of the subtle body, these same energies are involved. The difference then is one of location.

In sex experience the primary location is the genitals. From there the energy spreads to different areas of the psyche. In the kundalini spinal arousal experience, the primary location is the spine and head. From there it may spread to other areas.

In terms of travel, in sex experience there is the accumulated sexual hormones which produce a charged condition of energy. This energy is then stimulated which increases its charged condition. This charged force, attracts the kundalini which arcs to the genitals. This linkage causes an intense charge which is experienced as sexual climax. During the increase in energy but before sexual climax, the intellect comes from the head of the subtle body. It fuses into the aroused sexual force. That is interpreted as sexual pleasure.

In terms of travel for kundalini arousal up the spine into the head, kundalini becomes supercharged in one way or the other. When it does this at the base chakra, it pulls to itself the hormone energy which is in the system. This energy flashes through the spine. It enters the head where it darts itself to the intellect. When it fuses with the intellect that is experienced as spiritual bliss energy. This causes opening of brow and crown chakra. The person experiences various levels of higher consciousness.

Remarks on Patanjali *Yoga Sutras*

Patanjali gave the syllabus for yoga, something which is standard regardless of the teacher for meditation. If a system does not fit into Patanjali's syllabus, it cannot give the proper results from meditation.

The main aspect I feel, is the last 4 stages of *pratyahar*, *dharana*, *dhyana* and *samadhi*.

Patanjali puts the last three stages as a sequential practice named *samyama*.

That suggests that the stages move one into the other spontaneously, so that if one does *dharana*, it may evolve into *dhyana* which may evolve further into *samadhi*.

Now there is one more important thing which is *kaivalya* or *kevalam*, where Patanjali described that in two stages. The elementary one is when the observing self is segregated from its psychic perception equipment. Due to that split, the equipment become purified. Then the final stage of *kaivalya* is when the observing self reunites with the purified perception equipment.

Adjuncts Control by Self

The two adjuncts in the psyche which are the most important to redesign are the kundalini lifeForce in the lower trunk of the subtle body and the intellect orb in the head of the subtle form.

If these adjuncts are reformed the profile of the living being would be changed for the better. As they are designed by nature, these adjuncts work in the interest of nature while using the coreSelf as a power supply. The core is not the only source of power. Nature itself produces power to run the psychic organs but that power is not enough. Initially it lacks directiveness. The power from the pin-point infinitesimal coreSelf has value in that it is directive energy. Physical nature is also power. It has an instinct of its own but it operates only after it is activated by the directive power of the self.

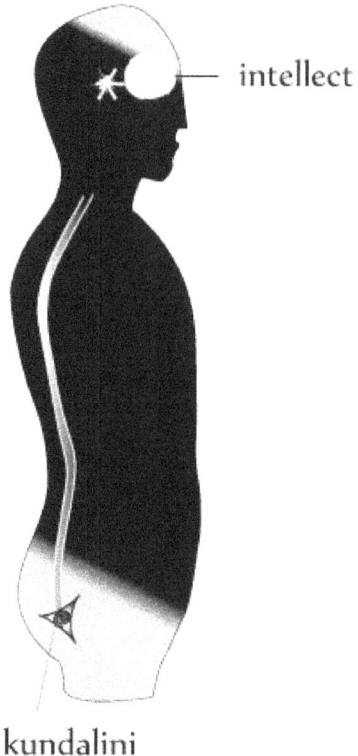

intellect

kundalini

The coreSelf, individual spirit, provides the initial directive power and then physical nature, keeps the operations going. Until a yogi can redesign the two adjuncts, the intellect and the kundalini, he/she cannot successfully overcome physical nature. Talking about it, does absolutely nothing to control these psychic powers. Mantras are merely entertainment to these powers. A direct assault on their territory and a confiscation of their primal rights by whichever means is required.

The coreSelf is supposed to control the adjuncts and still it uses mantras, visualizations and other indirect methods as if it is afraid to command the adjuncts. This is just like a mother with an unruly toddler.

The plain truth is that the coreSelf woke up in the physical world. It discovered itself as a captive of the physical energy. That is how it all started. It did not start with the self in control as many sympathetic philosophers proposed.

If one is born a slave, telling oneself that one was originally free will not help the situation. It may make one feel better in terms of self-esteem.

Kundalini / Intellect: Pleasure Potency

In doing the practice which was introduced by Tibeti Yogi, which is the system of infusing the extremities of the subtle body beginning with penetration into the fleshy part of the thigh, I got from him another key technique:

This is the system of bringing the intellect organ into the lower parts of the body to meet with the aroused kundalini in those lower areas. Actually, this is not a new system because the natural way is for the intellect to descend into the body for sexual pleasures.

Tibeti's process causes the intellect to come to the lower trunk to experience the small kundalini spreads which occur there during breath infusion.

My guess is that this frees the student yogi from the need for sexual pleasure, in that the intellect which is a pleasure-starved organ gets its needed quota of such pleasure when it comes into the trunk of the body during the rises of kundalini in the lower extremities.

When kundalini goes into the head, it immediately looks for and links itself to the intellect but when the kundalini sparks in the trunk of the body or into the thighs and arms, the intellect organ is not linked to kundalini. As a result, the kundalini spread-energy is not interpreted in the psyche as a pleasure energy.

Tibeti Yogi left some information in the astral planes which states this:

"Due to attachment to the pleasure potency, a student must strive to overcome that in a practical way, in the way of actually using the pleasure energy. But for the use of it the intellect must be involved since in the psyche interpretation takes place through the intellect. If the intellect reports that certain potency is not pleasure energy, the psyche will regard that potency as being pleasure-less. Therefore, when one reaches the stage just before creating the yoga siddha body, one should trick the system by bringing the intellect to wherever the kundalini energy will burst outside the head of the subtle body. This is done by internally focusing the attention on that area.

"To draw the intellect down into the body in this way, make no effort to relocate the intellect. Instead do a consistent practice, while having confidence that at a certain stage the intellect will become curious. Be confident that it will descend into the trunk. This will happen after sufficient practice.

"Just as by its own interest in sex pleasure the intellect descends into the body to enjoy sex pleasure, it will descend for a small kundalini burst even when the sex organs are not involved.

Kundalini Spread

Distribution of kundalini energy in the head facilitates increased psychic perception and gives the person the happiness that is sought after in aspects of animal life, features like sex indulgence. Not to be taken lightly, not to be brushed aside by the yogi as just a side feature of life, sex indulgence stands its ground and subdues even the greatest of the renunciants, the swamis and monks, who dare to ignore it or feel that they are beyond it.

The need for sexual relationships is paramount in nature. No limited being can brush it aside permanently. Those ascetics who feel that they can eliminate sexual needs and escape into whatever obscurity pleases their silly little minds, all return into manifestation sooner or later and willingly give themselves over to it again.

To shatter the power of this sex potency, it should be consumed as fast as it accumulates. After practicing to raise kundalini for a time and becoming expert in the skill of making it ascend the spine into the brain, the student yogi should scatter it so that it spreads throughout the psyche.

In a spiritual body, all parts of the forms are capable of the same sense expression. The fingernail of it can see. The eye of it can act as a fingernail. Such a form is all-responsive in every part.

To head in that direction, one may begin to make the subtle body all-responsive. This is realized over time by the practice of distributing the kundalini energy equally through the body. How to do that?

Use the sexual potency in its link to kundalini and cause the joint force to spread through the body first through the trunk before kundalini goes into the head of the subtle from.

To achieve this one must master postures and breath infusion methods which cause the nadis in the subtle body to be receptive to the joint kundalini and sex energy force. It should be more than the *sushumna* nadi. All the nadis should be accepting of the joint force, not just the *sushumna* central channel in the spine. The energy should go in all directions, not just into the head where it stimulates the intellect organ, which is the main pleasure receptor of the psyche.

The whole system of the subtle body should be infused not only the head of it, the thing we call the mind. The psyche is more than just the subtle head or mind. The entire psyche needs be regarded not just the mind part of it.

Pleasure /Kundalini Outburst

This morning during meditation, I observed the bliss aspect which arises from the aroused kundalini force. This is a report on why kundalini has an intense bliss aspect when it comes into the head and a very mild bliss aspect when it spreads elsewhere in the body. Some meditators say that the bliss aspect is homogeneous but rare was that my experience.

Let us get down to basics by reviewing regular life. In regular life we find that things are not equal. For instance, a sweet beverage is not the same as a sour one. A mint is not the same as a toffee. Each has specific aspects which we experience and which caused them to be categorized.

Even in the body, modern researchers show that even in terms of tasting, it is not equally received in the body. A particular part of the tongue handles salt tastes, another part sweet taste. Each has specialized cells. Nature is involved in specialization and distinction.

In this research I checked on the fact that when the kundalini rises into the head, it has an intense bliss aspect which is usually not felt anywhere else in the body, unless that other part of the body is connected to the brain area when it is felt. This is supported by nature's normal operation, say in sex indulgence. We find that naturally only in sex indulgence is there that intense pleasure experience. Why is this so? Why not have a sex experience at the fingertip alone intensely. Why not stimulate the elbow and experience a climax there? Strangely there are a few individuals in the world whose bodies may do that, as in the case of fetishes.

In this research I found that the missing ingredient is the intellect. In other words, whenever kundalini energy is aroused anywhere in the body, if the intellect organ is not in direct contact with that energy, there will be a sensation, but there will be no intensity of that energy. The same is true about sexual indulgence, except that in sexual indulgence, the kundalini forcibly pulls the intellect from the head of the body into the genital region. However, as soon as the energy is expended, the intellect returns to the head, usually in a depressed mood.

When doing the breath infusion there may be a rise of kundalini, say in one arm or say in the left side of the trunk. It will be there and will be noticed as a special sensation but it will not have the intensity because the intellect is not directly involved in it.

This means that in the present configuration, the psyche cannot experience intense pleasure unless the intellect organ and the kundalini experience that pleasure together.

A person can, for instance be happy in the head without sexual excitement. But if we add sexual excitement to happiness, it is a different experience with noticeable intensity. A person can also be happy in the genitals in the sense of a genital arousal but if there is no mental involvement, it is not as intense. The conclusion is that unless the two adjuncts are involved, there will be no intensity of pleasure or feelings. The intellect organ and the kundalini lifeForce must be brought together for a conjoint pleasure intense feeling.

Take the example of ice-cream. Why is it that ice-cream is tastier than the same substance if it is not frozen? Is there a difference in ice-cream which is frozen and ice-cream which is a liquid at room temperature? Why is it that when we add the concept of cold, of freezing, it has a different taste and texture? Freezing is not something physical which you can hold. To sense it one must have a physical substance which conveys it to the sense of touch. It is subjective in that sense. Yet, it has an impact of what is objective like the liquid of ice-cream.

The intellect which is a concept has an impact on the lifeForce to such an extent that the pleasure aspect of that lifeForce is intensified when the intellect is present. The sweetened milk yields more pleasure when the cold is fused to it, even though no one has ever seen cold except indirectly by its effects.

During breath infusion this morning, I had several small kundalini outbursts in the lower trunk of the body. I observed these and found that the missing element was the intellect. Since the intellect was not fused into the energy outburst of kundalini, there was no intensity even though there was an observable and definite spread of the energy. This spread was like a mild pleasant electric current spreading in some parts of the body.

Hitting harder

The head lock is the mind lock which begins with mastery of third eye focus. One should practice third eye focus as described in chapter one of the *Meditation Pictorial* book.

This gives one a grip on the intellectual faculty, so that during meditation and during the rise of kundalini, one can better channel energy in the head as well as energy which seeps into or forcibly penetrates the head.

Kundalini power and its accessory hormone boost system should be distributed through the body but the instinct is that it should be conserved in the pubic area for sexual expression. Once a yogi masters the practice of raising kundalini, that reservoir of sexual energy will rush into the head but it should be distributed into the head and elsewhere. It is too much for the head alone even though initially in the breath infusion practice, one can only direct it into the head. If the yogi keep practicing progress will occur over time. He will gain a better intuition about this.

Astral Sex / Surya Namaskar

Retention of sexual fluids without the distribution of those hormones through the body is a faulty practice.

In kriya practice the retention of fluids may be compared to when an army keeps an ammunition dump under the main barracks where most of the soldiers, sleep. This is dangerous, because it may explode when the soldiers are present.

In kriya yoga, the idea is that if the dump has to be under the barracks, and that seems to be the law of nature in this case, then at least we will distribute any ammunition which is acquired.

It seems that by a law of nature, anytime the ammunition dump is empty, it immediately fills again. In kriya yoga the energy is continuously distributed. It is not focused to accumulate.

Nature designed the psyche so that the accumulated sexual fluids are in the pubic area. If it remains there and accumulates, then even a celibate monk who has everything to lose will find that he is forced to indulge sexual. If this can happen to a monk and it happened to some celibate religious leaders, we can understand its power in the life of other individuals who do not have as much to lose.

If you think that by hording sexual fluids you will get enlightenment, then please reconsider. Sex fluids can help if somehow one can get that energy to arouse kundalini in an upward direction?

There were many sannyasi and monks who had dreams of having sex with partners. Then sometime after it happened on the physical level. In kriya yoga we do not consider such occurrence to be mere dreams or mere imagination but we consider it to be an actual occurrence. There is a story about Arjuna in the *Mahabharata*, where he left his body in *samadhi* in the Himalayas and went to the Swarga heavenly places. There an angelic woman, who was like a demigoddess as compared to earthly celebrities, invited him for sexual affairs. Arjuna took the invitation so seriously that he refused to go to the woman's room because he felt that she was like an aunt or mother to him.

Arjuna did not consider a dreamy experience to be merely dream or figment of imagination. In kriya yoga we follow this example of Arjuna and regard sexual breaches in the astral world.

What is the difference if I meet a woman in the astral world for sex and if I meet that woman in the physical world? One may see a difference, perhaps because in the physical world there is the possibility of pregnancy while in the astral world pregnancy will not occur. This type of thinking is terribly flawed.

In fact, astral sex is more hazardous than physical sex, because at least with physical sex if there are no contraceptive methods one may be tagged with the responsibility for a child and that is reformatory, because it makes one understand that association is present with liability.But in the astral world, since there will be no children from the intercourse, how will one understand the responsibility involved?

Sex is a natural part of the psyche, even for the animals? Sex is there for reproduction, at least in the lower animals. How did one get the human body one now possess without taking help from sex?

Yogis in the World and of It

So long as we are eager to enjoy the physical world through a physical body, we will not consolidate yoga practice in the psychic sense. One may do postures perfectly, teach these to others and be the model of what a certain posture should be, but if one does not complete *pratyahar* sensual energy withdrawal, one will not advance psychologically in yoga practice.

If one buys into the idea of being in the world and not being of it, one will not be successful either. If someone wants the world, that is what he will get. His success in yoga will be trivial or he will use yoga to boost his success in the world. There are many wealthy people who do yoga. Many are masters of being in the world and being not of it, along with their deluxe lifestyles.

If one wants to switch the focus to yoga, one should withdraw as much as possible from the world. Do not try to walk on two rails at the same time. You may split in two and not benefit from either.

Make a gradual shift of focus, moving away from the worldly perspective to that of the psychic one which is conducive to higher yoga. Over time, as one anchors more and more in the abstract subtle existence, one should scale down the physical desires.

Different Breath Infusion Process

I reviewed the flushing of dense astral energy in the thighs, legs and feet. I noticed that the approach to this is different. I did this for some time now. I did it the way Tibeti Yogi stipulated. His method has a change in approach which is a vacuum draw of the energy in the thighs.

In breath infusion as taught by Yogi Bhajan, the system is mostly to push the air in, to compress it in and drive out the pollution energy. This is a good process. I used it for years. I can swear by its effects.

When it comes to the thighs, legs and feet, the process is changed so that there is a vacuum draw rather than a compressing effect. This means that while doing the infusion, one draws out the dense energy from the thighs. Instead of pushing energy and compressing energy into the thighs one should mentally connect and draw out the polluted energy, while doing thigh stretches simultaneously with the rapid breathing. I notice that as one extracts that, the infused energy rushes in to take the space which the dense pollution occupied.

This is an example of why one must stick with yoga gurus and not think that one can do this because one is potentially a Buddha. One must be assisted by senior yogis.

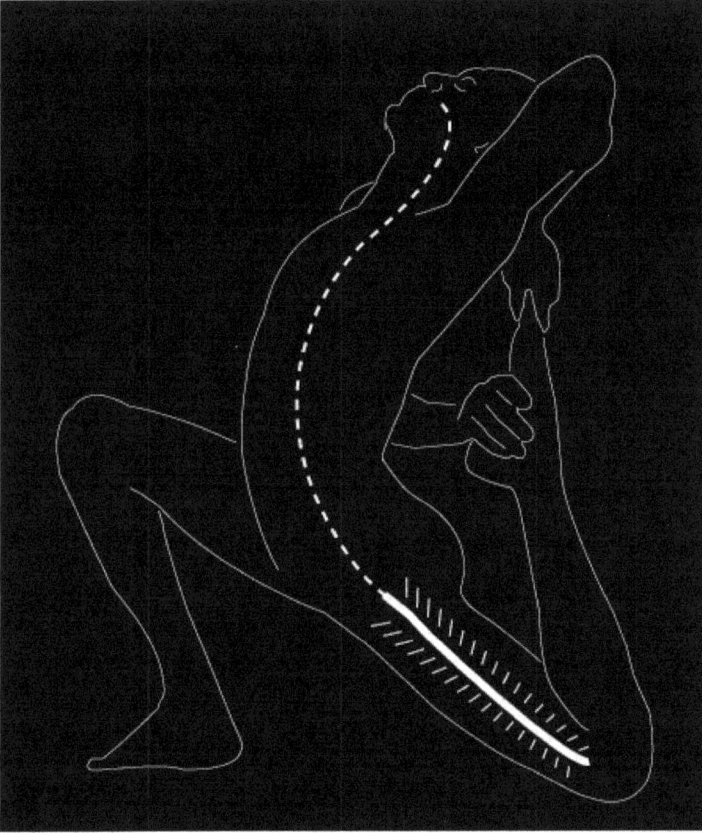

While in a thigh stretch, with eyes closed, and mind focused through the thigh, especially at any tendons and muscles which are felt at the time, one should do the breath infusion. While doing this the mind's focus should be in the thigh. If it is not there or if one cannot focus there, one should increase the tension in the posture. This increase should cause the mind to go to the tensed stretched area.

Once this contact is made mentally with the thigh, and with the rapid breathing continuing, one should feel as if the energy in the thigh comes into the torso. This happens mentally as one does the rapid breathing. It is as if the dense energy in the thigh leaves the thigh by floating up or by being pulled out by a vacuum draw force. As this happens fresh energy which was infused into the torso, earlier on in the exercise session, will rush into the thigh to occupy the areas which the dense energy inhabited before.

There is a track or subtle passage in the thigh bone, which connects into the leg bone and then has an outlet downwards through the feet into the earth. This practice is not involved in using that route to the earth. This practice recognizes that there is dense energy around the thigh bone in the flesh area of the thigh. That dense energy which is in the flesh of the thigh cannot be removed by downward pressure. It cannot go down because at the knee it is constricted. To flush it one must lift the dense energy.

A yogi will know that he did it correctly when during practice of infusing the trunk he feels that he reached the bottom of the pubic area and the infused energy spreads across the bottom. This is seen sometimes as white or yellow-white lines of force running along the pubic floor in the subtle body.

The charge is the result of successful infusion of the air into the blood stream of the physical body and into the nadi channels of the subtle one. A long breath infusion session does not necessarily mean that the body is charged. It depends on the conditions of the lungs and their resistance or acceptance of the air. One person may do breath infusion for half hour and another for five minutes. The one who does so for five minutes may infuse as much energy as the other.

Many human bodies keep a reserve of carbon dioxide. These forms do not allow the person to change the ratio of fresh air to carbon dioxide in the blood stream. Some students have this problem. It requires months of practice to tip the balance for increased proportion of fresh air.

Some lungs absorb very little air. Even if the air is presented, a lung may refuse to absorb it. A student should work with his/her body to increase the absorption rate.

Locks

The locks are ways of channeling, directing and compressing the infused energy. It is a method of disciplining the energy so that it goes in certain directions. For instance, some people hear of these locks, then sit and apply them during meditation or during certain postures. But in the *bhastrika* system one applies a lock to control the infused energy, either to release it in a certain direction, to prevent it from going in a certain direction or to restrict it and use it as a valve. Once the energy is infused, the situation is one of how and where to direct it. That is where the locks have meaning.

Initially the important locks are the mind lock, neck lock, navel lock, sex lock and anus lock. These are the five major locks. There are many other minor locks which come into focus as one advances.

In the beginning the anus lock is the most important. Why?

It is because nature created a microscopic vent at the base of the spine. Kundalini vents itself through this orifice. In fact, at the time of death of the body, kundalini may try to escape through this hole. When Narada explained kundalini's operations to King Prachinabarhi, he said that at the time of death,

Puranjan followed the kundalini through this hole, out of the physical system once and for all.

Initially a student should close the base chakra orifice. The problem is that it is a subtle hole. Those students who think that ashwini mudra anus lock closes this hole are misinformed. It does not. Ashwini mudra in so far as it is a physical action cannot close this hole. It can only close this hole if it is a psychic action. This means that if to you there is no subtle body, no psychic self, then your action of ashwini mudra cannot do what it supposed to do as described in the ancient yogic books like *Hatha Yoga Pradipika*. The reason for closing this hole is that if you infuse energy, kundalini will vent that energy through this base hole. Your infusion will be a waste of time.

Once you master that lock and the energy cannot escape through the bottom, it will accumulate but it will do so inefficiently. This will happen because at this stage you still do not know what you are doing. Still by chance from time to time, the energy will accumulate. It will cause kundalini to rise. Then the next lock which you should master is the neck lock.

When kundalini ascends the spine, it cannot get into the head unless it tunnels through the neck. Hence by applying the neck lock you can restrict its passage so that it passes through the center of the spine and also so that it is regulated as it transits.

But once it gets into the head then what? Then you must apply the mind lock. Once kundalini gets into the head of the subtle body, which is what we conventionally call the mind, it will do what it wants to do. It will not behave like an obedient child merely because you visualized what it should do. It will act independently. You need to know the mind lock. Kundalini is an impulsive involuntary energy.

The sex lock is the next lock to be considered. After practicing for some time, the student will realize that there the hole at the base of the spine is a pin hole in comparison to the hole which is the genitals. If the hole at the base of the spine is such that we can plug it by welding a needle into it, then the one where the genitals are, is so large that even if we get an elephant and force its body through it, it will still not be plugged completely.

When the student sees this, he/she is faced with a dilemma, which is:

If I close this, that action may be counterproductive to my sexual pleasure needs. If I do not close this, that lack of action will cause the practice to be stagnant. The student will go back and forth with these arguments until he/she decides to either cease yoga or satisfy the demands for progress.

Agnisara Advanced Kriyas

During breath infusion practice, Swami Rama came. He was on the subtle side. He showed a diagram with the final procedures concerning the agnisara practice. He entered my subtle body. He did agnisara with it in the base of the trunk area but in specific zones, not haphazardly. Generally, yogis do agnisara as stomach pumps, strenuously agitating the intestinal organs. However, there was a practice which was given by Gorakshnath Mahayogin who began the Nath Yogi lineage.

These yogis specialize in hatha yoga, the extreme type, which concerns complete conquest of kundalini by physical and mystic means. Hatha yoga has come to mean asana postures but that was not its original meaning.

When doing the breath of fire and the agnisara practice, one usually does the breathing either in zone 1, 2 or 3 of the diagrams.

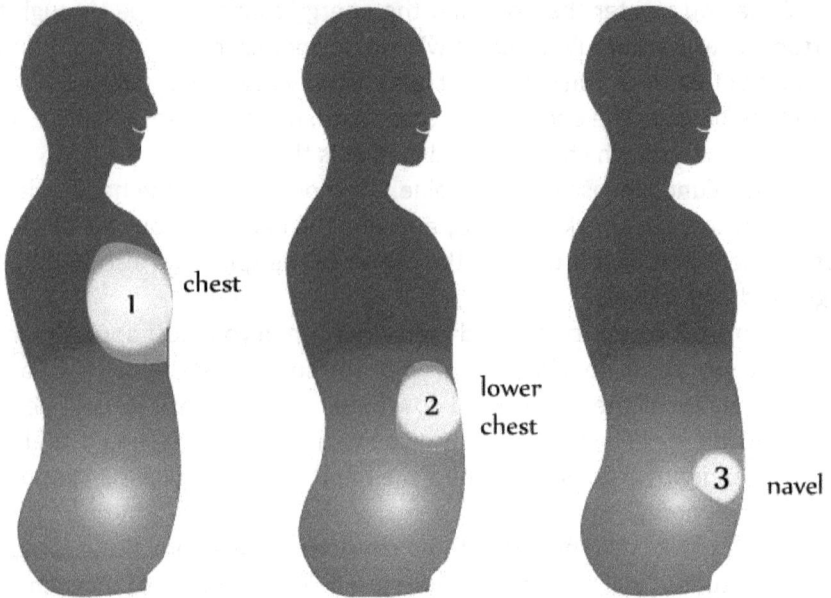

1 chest

2 lower chest

3 navel

If one advanced in the practice, the actions will move into zones 4 and 5 which are the advanced platforms.

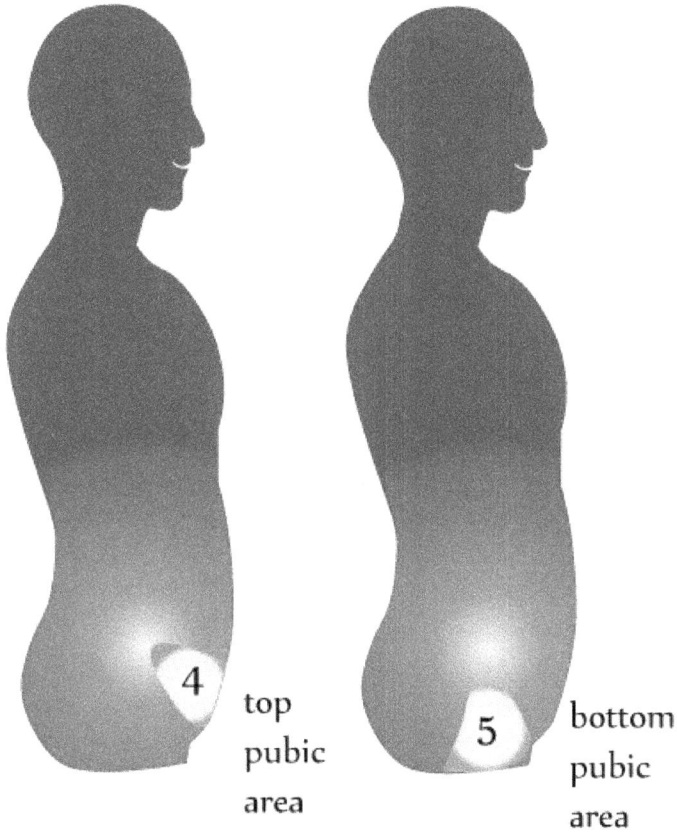

4 top pubic area

5 bottom pubic area

Doing *bhastrika* pranayama usually concerns the lungs but as the yogi proceeds, he/she will be able to use other parts of the body as the source point of the suction and compression of the breathing actions.

At long last one should shift that to stage 5 or 6, so that the mental impetus as well as the diaphragm muscles are operated from urges from these areas. This happens over the course of time of regular practice for some years.

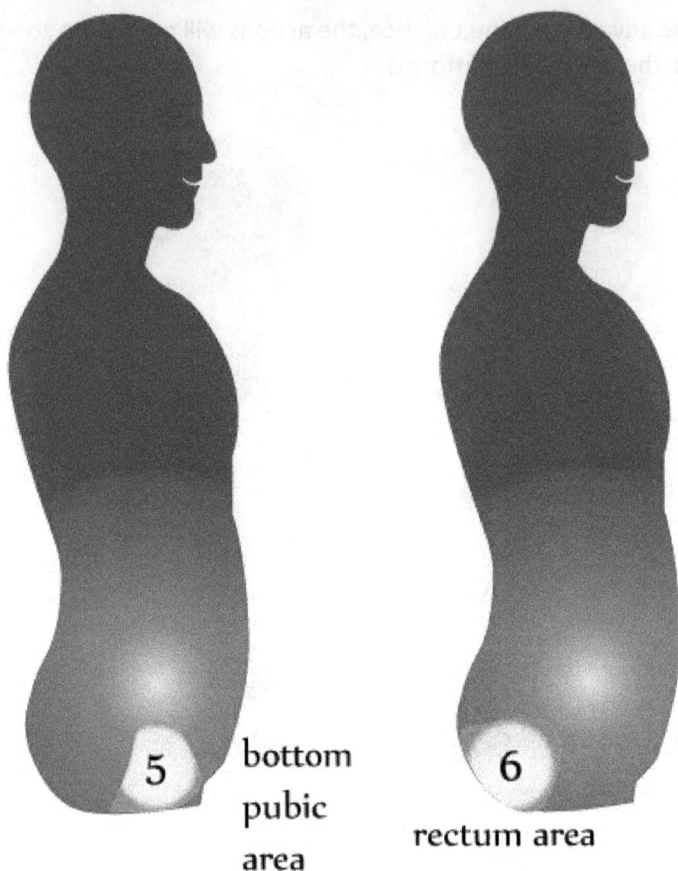

5 bottom pubic area

6 rectum area

Swami Rama advocated the agnisara stomach churning practice with pranayama. This procedure which he released to me, shows that he is proficient.

I practiced this kriya in zones 4, 5 and 6 today. I was surprised at the operations which happened in the subtle body and the effects of this in terms of clearing those areas of every bit of dense energy, even the smallest amount which was hidden here and there in the lower trunk. This also does wonders for energy which hides in the thigh which the yogi has difficulty reaching and removing.

Bhastrika is a rapid breathing process in which air is infused into the blood stream via the lungs. This process is forceful. To be truthful it is unnatural. The only time the body naturally tries to force air into the blood stream, is when the body is exhausted as in the case where a person runs at a high speed.

Then the body realizes that it cannot get sufficient air for basic maintenance of the form. It increases the breathing rate. Note the panting of the athletes at the end of a race. All runners bend over and breathe rapidly then. The system itself involuntarily does this.

Bhastrika is doing rapid breathing when there is no endeavor, so as to artificially increase the fresh air in the system and to extract the used air from it. The normal system is that the body retains a percentage of the used air for certain purposes but when doing *bhastrika* one upsets that process and increases the ration of fresh air to stale air in the system.

Agnisara is a complex system. Initially it means using the diaphragm to churn the intestines and colon vigorously. As one gains mastery one extracts the used air in the cells of the system. This is where doing it during *bhastrika* practice is effective.

After about twelve or twenty rapid breaths, one stops and does the churning. Then again one does twelve or more rapid breaths. Then one does the churning again. This is repeated until one feels that the cells in the intestines and colon, released all stale air (carbon dioxide) which was retained. Usually with agnisara specifically one stops on an exhale.

To do the churning one needs a vacuous area. If one does it on an inhale, there will be air in the lungs which will obstruct the churning action.

Index

A

a little, 69
absolute expressions, 82
absorption limit, 174
accessory association, 87
adjuncts,
    coreSelf, 208
    kundalini effects, 16
    reform, 215
agent of action, 24
agnisara diagrams, 225-229
agnisara flushway, 107
alarm, 24
alert, 199
aliens, 146
ammunition, 220
amrit nectar, 13
anandaSamkocha, 27
anchor, 141
Anu Gita, 66, 195
anuloma, 183
arc point, 76
armpits, 63
ashwini mudra, 211, 225
association,
    accessory, 87
    details, 85
    nonyogic, 68
    requirement, 77
astral escape, 181
astral eyes, 39
astral planes wanderer, 121
astral projection, 67, 100
astral sex, 220
athato, 123
athletes, 229
attachment, transmigration, 28
attention shift, 193
attentiveness, 184
audio diaphragm, 199

author,
    birth circumstance, 86
    death, 183
    parent influence, 150
axial position, 141

B

back of head, meditation, 30, 38
back support, 25
Badrinath, 66
base chakra,
    location, 157
    uproot, 147
bath, 26. 123
Beverford, 110
Beverford, Ojai, 178
bhastrika, details, 16
Bhogavati, 186
Bill of Rights, 186
black out, 16
blindfold, 84, 103, 136, 193
bliss aspect squeeze, 27
bliss, 16, 99
blocks, two, 57
body fall, 151
bones, soft, 59
books, 66
born under captivity, 195
bowels, kundalini, 49
Brahma, deity, 146
Brahma Sutras, 123
brahma yoga, 189
brahman experience, 137
brahman, 16
brahmananda, 211
brahmins, 100
brain,
    lower, 199
    two, 201
brats, 27
breasts, 211

breath infusion,
  bath, 26
  master, 104
  obstacles, 72
  resistance energy, 31
breath of fire, 183
bubble body, 186, 189
bucking the horse, 200
Buddha,
  alien, 146
  kundalini control, 47
  past life, 29
buddhi lila, 59
buddhi yoga, 193

C

camera, 199
captain, 23
carbon dioxide, 137, 194, 224
carriages, 67
cast, 87
cauldron, 172
causal body, 147
celibacy, 77
chakra diagrams, 100
chambermaid, 50
child, 20
children, 160
chin lock, 138
classic yoga, 142
clay, 123
clean bliss, 99
clean energy, 109
coccyx, 121
coin, 43
cold viruses, 207
combatants, 153
commitment, 197
compounded eyes, 180
conductor, 67
confidence, 66
consequential reactions, 186
conspiracy, 199
consumer, 143
contraception, 138
contract, 140

coreSelf,
  direct contact, 208
  enemy, 153
  fusion, 20
  intellect dependent, 174
  isolated, 17
  plural, 16
  position, 141
  power supply, 215
  rim, 16
  turning, 30
  what is it? 20
course charted, 66
cranium light, 47
criminal element, 179
crown chakra, 101
crystals, 81

D

dangerous poses, 84
dark energy, 210
death, author, 183
death zone, 80
deck, 114
deity, grace, 66
desirelessness, 102
desperation, 52
destruction of food brain, 188
detachment, 39
devil of stupor, 181
dharana, 88
Dhruva, 107
dhyana, 88
diaphragm, audio, 199
dignity, 186
discouragement energy, 178
discovery tool, 156
disoriented, 153
distinction, 218
distribution, 104
divine body, 135, 188, 217
dizzy feeling, 153
donut, 136
down spike, 128
downward route, 146
dump, 220

dungeon, 95
Duryodhana, 107
dynamite, 57

E

eagles, 145
effect energy, 180
eka, 86
elderly one, 20
elimination, 143
embryo, kundalini constructed, 185
emotional intelligence, 164
empowerment, 42
enemy of self, 153
enemy squadrons, 104
energy limit, 174
energy pooling, 76
engine system, 143
enjoyer, 20
entry gate, 49
equality, 112
Europeans, 170
evacuating waste, 186
evil genius, 202
extinction, 52
extortion plan, 39
extremities, 95
eye camera, 199

F

fallen brats, 27
father, child, 20
father, supreme, 125
fetishes, 218
fetus, 193
fingernail, 217
flash actions, 84
flirtation, 179
flushway, 107
fly, 180
food, 16
food brain, 188
foot and hands, 7
foundation, 103
frustration, 52
funnel chakra, 67

G

game, 212
garden hose, 78
gender body, 142
genetic tendencies, 187
Genghis Khan, 200
glass shooting, 114
God, not, 188
Goddess Ganga, 146
gold out, 16
golden donut, 136
golden light, 208
grace of deity, 66
gravity of planet, 141
guerrilla, 41
gun, 24
guru competition, 175
guru insult, 178
gut feeling, 164

H

hands, 113
hard word, 186
hatha yoga, 151
headaches, 87, 153
heat bliss, 82
hip, 27
Hiranyakashipu, 47, 107
history, 87
hormonal energy diagrams, 127
horse, 200
hose, 78
hydraulic system, 134

I

ice-cream, 20
infinite self, 174
influenza, 87, 207
infusion, diagram, 159
inhibitions, 181
inner space, 27
insomnia, 177
insteps, 94
instinct, kundalini, 153
insult, 178

intellect,
    agent, 24
    attitude, 7
    extortion, 39
    kundalini hit, 153
    kundalini influences, 22
    perception, 39
    pleasure receptor, 217
    yoga, 102, 193
intensity energy, 178
internal yoga, 27
intruder, 40
invaders, 146
investment, 146
invisibility, 65
island, 137
isolated self, 17

J

Jesus Christ, 146
jivoham, 59
justifications, 63

K

kaivalyam, 214
kanda, 90. 167
Kansas City, 160
kapalabhati,166, 184
karana, 147
karma, 180
ketones, 137
kevalam, 214
kidneys, 186
kill body, 60
king, 186
King Tongue. 171
kinked garden house, 78
kites, 60
kleshas, 41
Krishna, 146
kumblak, 60, 163

kundalini,
    arousal memory, 153
    arrest, 95
    back of head, 22
    blast, 23
    bliss effect, 210
    captain, 24
    control, 9, 46
    criminal, 179
    direct, 192
    elimination, 44, 143
    enemy of self, 153
    extremities, 19
    flash actions, 84
    hard work, 186
    influence, 203
    intentions, 163
    investment, 146
    lila, 59
    lower arousal, 21
    match, 79, 132
    movements, 208
    pattern habit, 157
    person, 47
    posture, 151
    preliminary, 56
    recognition, 161
    sentient, 47
    sex excitement, 157
    sex pleasure, 46
    sexless, 134
    sexually charged, 135
    slant passage, 23
    sleep, 73
    spine diagram, 18
    spontaneous arousal, 114
    struck, 17
    stub, 156, 185
    stub sex organ, 99
    survival intelligence, 116
    swipe back, 204
    trunk, 179
    wayward, 67

Yoga inVision 11

L
lalata chakra, 74
lava, 140
legs, bliss, 98
lessons, 121
liability, 221
liberation, singular, 125
lions, 145
lineages, 184
lips, 211
location, perception tool, 40
lock,
    details, 224
    effects, 58
    redundant, 51
logic, 164
loop, 92-94
loop around attack, 164
lotus, reverse, 25
lower brain 199
lumbar area, 121
lung chakra, 67

M
Mahabharata, 146
Mahabhisha, 146
mahavrata, 197
management, 157
mantras, 27
map, 66
mechanic, 24
meditation resistance, 31
meditation time, 49
memory,
    intellect, 73, 102
    warfare, 41
menthol cream, 43
meter, 164
method, 66, 135, 144
microbeads, 99
miner, light, 75
mist, 21
Mongolia, 200
monitor, 20
moon influence, 111

moral breach, 24, 108
morale, 66
morality, 24
mother, toddler, 215
mothering energy, 188
motiveless, 147
mouth, entry gate, 49
muladhar, chakra attack, 160
mutiny, 24
mystic power, 196

N
naad,
    ejected from, 42
    light, 89
    reference, 141
    sound, 89
Narada, 224
Narayana, 28
nasal alert, 199
Nath sampradaya, 121
navel chakra, fragmented, 165
navel outcrop, 163
navel survival, 142
neck light, 129
neck lock, 138
neti pot, 112
neutral bliss, 109
night club, 20
no mind, 7
nostril imbalance, 111
not God, 28
nothingness, 16, 101, 102
nuclear device, 57

O
obligation, practice, 42
ocular orbs, 53
Ojai, 178
old method, 135
omniVision, 114
oneness, 186
OSI, 113
outcrop, 163

P

package of energies, 98
pain focus, 159
pain, 156
palace, 95
Pali canon, 29
paradise, 14
parallel zone, 90
passenger, 67
past lives, 29
pathogens, 87
pelvis to knees, 20
pepper, 27
Person God, 186
Personality of Godhead, 47
physical body fall, 151
physical body, affects subtle, 123
physical body, subtle mimics, 213
pinching action, 159
pixels, 53
place of excitement, 186
pleasure, interpreted, 41
pleasure, sources, 16
plot, 87
plumber, 79
pollution, subjugation, 84
pond, 105
pores, 81
poses, dangerous, 84
posture, kundalini, 151
postures, pain, 156
potty, 50
power consumer, 143
power supply, 215
Prachinabarhi, 224
prajananda, 211
Pranajogi, 6. 21
pranaVision, 55, 180
pranayama master, 104
pray and sing, 6
prep time, 102
primordial impulse, 111
proficiency, time, 104
prohibitions, 8
psychiatric ward, 46

puberty, 135
Puranjan, 186, 225
Pururavas, 28
pus, 16

Q, R

Quan Ying, 188
queen, 50
rainfall, 103
Ramayana, 24
rat, 168
rational meter, 164
rebellion, 46
receptor, 199
rectum, 49
reference, naad, 141
reluctance, 41
remove viewing, 40
reproduction influences, 141
reproduction, Brahma, 146
resistance energy, 31
rest, subtle body, 181
retention, sex fluids. 220
reverse gravity, 143
reverse lotus posture, 25
reverse sushumna, 133
rib cage, 100
Rishi Singh Gherwal, 113
rose, 120
royal bed, 186

S

sacral cage, 95
samadhi, 17, 88
samyama, 88
self, enemy, 153
sensation focus, 159
sense of identity vision, 39
senses, kundalini influence, 22
sensor, 199
sentient kundalini, 47
severance of umbilical cord, 188
sewage, 108
sex chakra, rose, 120
sex energy, management, 157
sex expression, 141

sex junkie, 132
sex maniac, 58
sex organ chakra, 11. 119
sex organ, components, 213
sex pleasure locations, 218
sex pleasure reference, 11
sex responsibility, 140
sex, astral, 220
sex, enemy, 12
sex, remembered, 99
sexless kundalini, 134
sexual climax, 211
sexual fluids, 16
sexual intercourse, angelic, 27
ship, 23
Shiva, 59, 76, 146
Shivaratri, 197
Shivoham, 59
shoulders, 63
siddhaloka heaven, 13
siddhis, 196
Sisyphus, 96
skirt, 160
slant passage, diagram, 23
slave, 215
sleep,
    essential, 177
    kundalini, 73
    stupor, 181
slip, 158
small of back, 52, 57, 111, 152
snake, 168
social behavior, 25
social detachment, 39
social security, 146
soft bones, 59
specialization, 218
spinal breathing, 105
spiritual body,
details, 79, 81
feelings, 217
perception, 55
split subtle body, 48
squatting posture, 153
squeeze down, 20

stale energy, 175, 210
star, 136
stretches, 156
stub kundalini, 156, 185
stub sex organ, 99
student of a student, 55
student practice, 68
stupor and sleep, 181
subtle body,
    configuration, 80
    domain, 65
    earth bound, 141
    internal state, 123
    morality, 24
    physical mimics, 213
    physical needed, 140
    pleasure craving, 123
    rest, 181
subjective perception, 53
subjugation of pollution, 84
subtle head, turning, 30
sugar binges, 69
sugar, 170
Sugriva, 24
suicide bomber, 41
sun influence, 111
supreme father, 125
surveillance, 40
surya, 220
Swami Rama photo, 110
Swami Rama misconduct, 108
sweets, 20
swipe back, 204
syrup, 27

T

tail, 60
tantric yogi, 58, 188
Taoist masters, 66
Taoist sex practice, 158
taste receptor, 199
teaching, 74
telepathy, 197
teleportation message, 200
tension, 160. 223
termites, 20

testes, 51
theme, 87
thigh,
    authority, 12
    conquest, 176
    function, 126
    merge, 49
    stale energy, 122
    targeted, 44
third eye vision, location, 39, 40
third eye, thought entry, 101
three windows, 39
Tibet, Mongolia, 200
Tibeti Yogi, 44, 98
tight ball, 115
tilak, 100
toes, 95
tongue, supreme, 170
touch sensor, 199
train, 67, 94
trunk, cleared, 171
trunk kundalini, 179
twinkles, 95
U
Uddhava Gita, 28
umbilical cord, 188
unconsciousness, 16
Universal Form, 66
uniVision, 39
urdha reta, 158
urges of energy, 140
urine, 27, 186
Urvashee, 28

V

vacumn draw, 221
villain, 107
viloma, 183
vision, location, 39
visualization, 27, 187
volcano, 140
vrata, 197
vrittis, control, 73

W

wanderer, 121
warfare, memory, 41
wayward energy, 179
wheeling and dealing, 176
windows, three, 39
windshied, 30
wood, 20

X, Y. Z

yesterday, 102
yoga,
    failure, 96
    guru competition, 175
    progress suspended, 14
    wealth, 221
yoga siddha form, 80
yoga siddha reproduction, 126
Yogi Bhajan photo, 160
Yogi Bhajan, Rishi Singh, 113
yogi,
    contact, 66
    past life regression, 72
young adult, 20
Yudhishthira, 213
zone, parallel, 90

About the Author

Michael Beloved (Yogi *Madhvāchārya)* took his current body in 1951 in Guyana. In 1965, while living in Trinidad, he instinctively began doing yoga postures and tried to make sense of the supernatural side of life.

Later in 1970, in the Philippines, he approached a Martial Arts Master named Arthur Beverford. He explained to the teacher that he was seeking a yoga instructor. Mr. Beverford identified himself as an advanced disciple of *Śrī* Rishi Singh Gherwal, an Ashtanga Yoga master.

Beverford taught the traditional Ashtanga Yoga with stress on postures, attentive breathing and brow chakra centering meditation.   In 1972, Michael entered the Denver, Colorado Ashram of *kundalini* yoga Master *Śrī* Harbhajan Singh. There he took instruction in *bhastrika* pranayama and its application to yoga postures. He was supervised mostly by Yogi Bhajan's disciple named Prem Kaur.

In 1979 Michael formally entered the disciplic succession of the Brahmā - Madhava-Gaudiya Sampradaya through *Swāmī* Kirtanananda, who was a prominent sannyasi disciple of the Great Vaishnava Authority *Śrī Swāmī* Bhaktivedanta Prabhupada, the exponent of devotion to Sri Krishna.

However, yoga has a mystic side to it, thus Michael took training and teaching empowerment from several spiritual masters of different aspects of spiritual development. This is consistent with *Śrī* Krishna's advice to Arjuna in the *Bhagavad Gītā:*

Most of the instructions Michael received were given in the astral world. On that side of existence, his most prominent teachers were *Śrī Swāmī* Shivananda of Rishikesh, Yogiraj *Swāmī* Vishnudevananda, *Śrī Bābāji Mahasaya* - the master of the masters of *Kriyā* Yoga, *Śrīla* Yogeshwarananda of Gangotri - the master of the masters of *Rāj* Yoga (spiritual clarity), and Siddha *Swāmī* Nityananda the Brahmā Yoga authority.

The course for kundalini yoga using pranayama breath-infusion was detailed by Michael in the book *Kundalini Hatha Yoga Pradipika.* This current book was composed from meditation and breath-infusion notes which were originally shared in staple bound booklets as Yoga Journals.

Michael's preliminary books relating to this topic are *Meditation Pictorial, Meditation Expertise,* and *Meditation ~ Sense Faculty* (co-author). Every technique (kriya) mentioned was tested by him during pranayama breath-infusion and *samyama* deep meditation practice.

This is a result of over forty years of meditation practice with astute subtle observations intending to share the methods and experiences. The information is published freely with no intention of forming an institution or hogtying anyone as a disciple.

Publications

English Series

Bhagavad Gita English

Anu Gita English

Markandeya Samasya English

Yoga Sutras English

Hatha Yoga Pradipika English

Uddhava Gita English

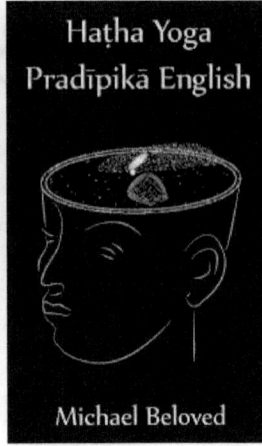

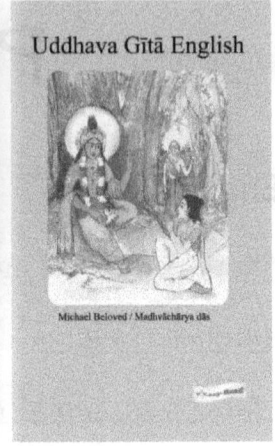

These are in 21st Century English, very precise and exacting. Many Sanskrit words which were considered untranslatable into a Western language are rendered in precise, expressive and modern English.

Three of these books are instructions from Krishna. **In *Bhagavad Gita* English** and **Anu Gita English**, the instructions were for Arjuna. In the **Uddhava Gita English,** it was for Uddhava. *Bhagavad Gita* and Anu Gita are extracted from the Mahabharata. Uddhava Gita was extracted from the 11th Canto of the Srimad Bhagavatam (Bhagavata Purana). One of these books, the **Markandeya Samasya English** is about Krishna, as described by Yogi Markandeya, who survived the cosmic collapse and reached a divine child in whose transcendental body, the collapsed world was existing.

Two of this series are the syllabus about yoga practice. The *Yoga Sutras* of Patañjali is elaboration about ashtanga yoga. Hatha Yoga Pradipika English, is the detailed information about asana postures, pranayama breath-infusion, energy compression, naad sound resonance and advanced meditation. The Sanskrit author is Swatmarama Mahayogin.

My suggestion is that you read ***Bhagavad Gita* English**, the **Anu Gita English, the Markandeya Samasya English,** the *Yoga Sutras* **English,** the **Hatha Yoga Pradipika** and lastly the **Uddhava Gita English**, which is complicated and detailed.

For each of these books we have at least one commentary, which is published separately. Thus one's particular interest can be researched further in the commentaries.

The smallest of these commentaries and perhaps the simplest is the one for the Anu Gita. We published its commentary as the Anu Gita Explained. The *Bhagavad Gita* explanations were published in three distinct targeted commentaries. The first is *Bhagavad Gita* Explained, which sheds lights on how people in the time of Krishna and Arjuna regarded the information and applied it. *Bhagavad Gita* is an exposition of the application of yoga practice to cultural activities, which is known in the Sanskrit language as karma yoga.

Interestingly, *Bhagavad Gita* was spoken on a battlefield just before one of the greatest battles in the ancient world. A warrior, Arjuna, lost his wits and had no idea that he could apply his training in yoga to political dealings. Krishna, his charioteer, lectured on the spur of the moment to give Arjuna the skill of using yoga proficiency in cultural dealings including how to deal with corrupt officials on a battlefield.

The second Gita commentary is the Kriya Yoga *Bhagavad Gita*. This clears the air about Krishna's information on the science of kriya yoga, showing that its techniques are clearly described for anyone who takes the time to read *Bhagavad Gita*. Kriya yoga concerns the battlefield which is the psyche of the living being. The internal war and the mental and emotional forces which are hostile to self-realization are dealt with in the kriya yoga practice.

The third commentary is the Brahma Yoga *Bhagavad Gita*. This shows what Krishna had to say outright and what he hinted about which concerns the brahma yoga practice, a mystic process for those who mastered kriya yoga.

There is one commentary for the **Markandeya Samasya English**. The title of that publication is Krishna Cosmic Body.

There are two commentaries to the *Yoga Sutras*. One is the *Yoga Sutras of Patañjali* and the other is the Meditation Expertise. These give detailed explanations of ashtanga Yoga.

The commentary of Hatha Yoga Pradipika is titled Kundalini Hatha Yoga Pradipika.

For the Uddhava Gita, we published the Uddhava Gita Explained. This is a large book and requires concentration and study for integration of the information. Of the books which deal with transcendental topics, my opinion is that the discourse between Krishna and Uddhava has the complete information about the realities in existence. This book is the one which removes massive existential ignorance.

Meditation Series

Meditation Pictorial

Meditation Expertise

CoreSelf Discovery

Meditation Sense Faculty

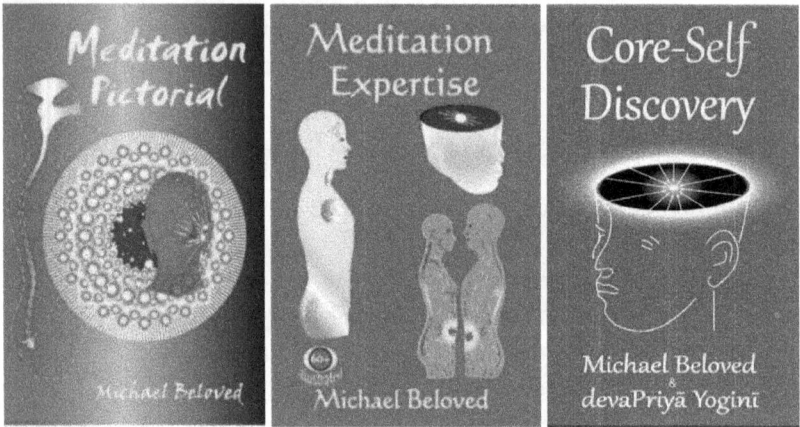

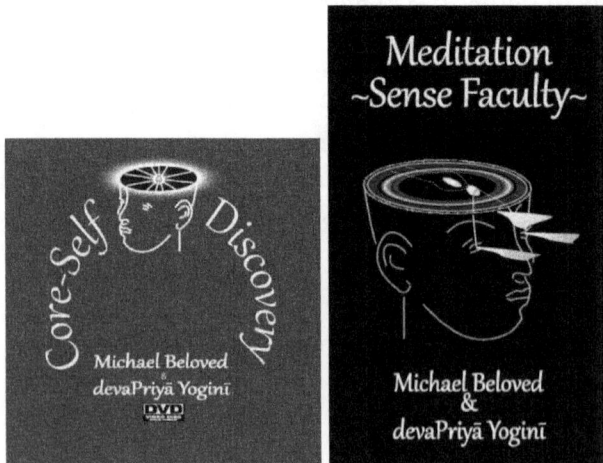

The specialty of these books is the mind diagrams which profusely illustrate what is written. This shows exactly what one has to do mentally to develop and then sustain a meditation practice.

In the **Meditation Pictorial**, one is shown how to develop psychic insight, a feature without which meditation is imagination and visualization, without any mystic experience per se.

In the **Meditation Expertise**, one is shown how to corral one's practice to bring it in line with the classic syllabus of yoga which Patañjali lays out as the ashtanga yoga eight-staged practice.

In **CoreSelf Discovery**, (co-authored with *devaPriya Yogini*) one is taken though the course of *pratyahar* sensual energy withdrawal which is the 5th stage of yoga in the Patañjali ashtanga eight-process complete system of yoga practice. These events lead to the discovery of a coreSelf which is surrounded by psychic organs in the head of the subtle body. This product has a DVD component.

Meditation ~ Sense Faculty (co-authored with *devaPriya Yogini*) is a detailed tutorial with profuse diagrams showing what actions to take in the subtle body to investigate the senses faculties. The meditator must first establish the location and function of the observing self. That self must be screened from the thoughts and ideas which usually hypnotize it.

These books are profusely illustrated with mind diagrams showing the components of psychic consciousness and the inner design of the subtle body.

Explained Series

Bhagavad Gita Explained

Uddhava Gita Explained

Anu Gita Explained

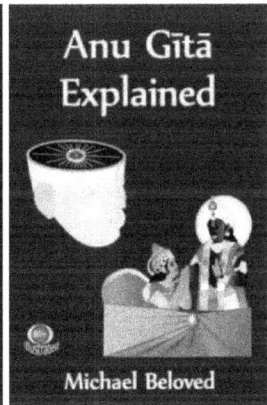

The specialty of these books is that they are free of missionary intentions, cult tactics and philosophical distortion. Instead of using these books to add credence to a philosophy, meditation process, belief or plea for followers, I spread the information out so that a reader can look through this literature and freely take or leave anything as desired.

When Krishna stressed himself as God, I stated that. When Krishna laid no claims for supremacy, I showed that. The reader is left to form an independent opinion about the validity of the information and the credibility of Krishna.

There is a difference in the discourse with Arjuna in the *Bhagavad Gita* and the one with Uddhava in the Uddhava Gita. In fact, these two books may appear to contradict each other. In the *Bhagavad Gita*, Krishna pressured Arjuna to complete social duties. In the Uddhava Gita, Krishna insisted that Uddhava should abandon the same.

The Anu Gita is not as popular as the *Bhagavad Gita* but it is the conclusion of that text. Anu means what is to follow, what proceeds. In this discourse, an anxious Arjuna request that Krishna should repeat the *Bhagavad Gita* and again show His supernatural and divine forms.

However, Krishna refuses to do so and chastises Arjuna for being a disappointment in forgetting what was revealed. Krishna then cited a celestial yogi, a near-perfected being, who explained the process of transmigration in vivid detail.

Commentaries

Yoga Sutras of Patañjali

Meditation Expertise

Krishna Cosmic Body

Anu Gita Explained

Bhagavad Gita Explained

Kriya Yoga Bhagavad Gita

Brahma Yoga Bhagavad Gita

Uddhava Gita Explained

Kundalini Hatha Yoga Pradipika

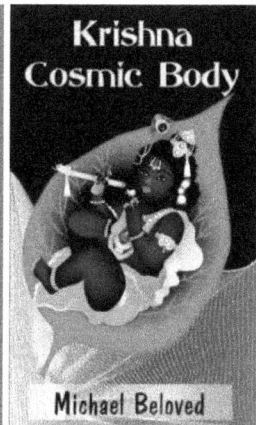

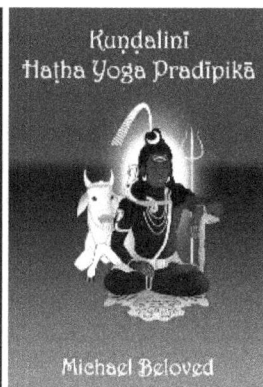

Yoga Sutras of Patañjali is the globally acclaimed text book of yoga. This has detailed expositions of yoga techniques. Many kriya techniques are vividly described in the commentary.

Meditation Expertise is an analysis and application of the *Yoga Sutras*. This book is loaded with illustrations and has detailed explanations of secretive advanced meditation techniques which are called kriyas in the Sanskrit language.

Krishna Cosmic Body is a narrative commentary on the Markandeya Samasya portion of the Aranyaka Parva of the Mahabharata. This is the detailed description of the dissolution of the world, as experienced by the great yogin Markandeya who transcended the cosmic deity, Brahma, and reached Brahma's source who is the divine infant, Krishna.

Anu Gita Explained is a detailed explanation of how we endure many material bodies in the course of transmigrating through various life-forms. This is a discourse between Krishna and Arjuna. Arjuna requested of Krishna a display of the Universal Form and a repeat narration of the *Bhagavad Gita* but Krishna declined and explained what a siddha perfected being told the Yadu family about the sequence of existences one endures and the systematic flow of those lives at the convenience of material nature.

Bhagavad Gita Explained shows what was said in the Gita without religious overtones and sectarian biases.

Kriya Yoga *Bhagavad Gita* shows the instructions for those who are doing kriya yoga.

Brahma Yoga *Bhagavad Gita* shows the instructions for those who are doing brahma yoga.

Uddhava Gita Explained shows the instructions to Uddhava which are more advanced than the ones given to Arjuna.

Bhagavad Gita is an instruction for applying the expertise of yoga in the cultural field. This is why the process taught to Arjuna is called karma yoga which means karma + yoga or cultural activities done with yogic insight.

Uddhava Gita is an instruction for apply the expertise of yoga to attaining spiritual status. This is why it explains jnana yoga and bhakti yoga in detail. Jnana yoga is using mystic skill for knowing the spiritual part of existence. Bhakti yoga is for developing affectionate relationships with divine beings.

Karma yoga is for negotiating the social concerns in the material world. It is inferior to bhakti yoga which concerns negotiating the social concerns in the spiritual world.

This world has a social environment. The spiritual world has one too.

Currently, Uddhava Gita is the most advanced and informative spiritual book on the planet. There is nothing anywhere which is superior to it or which goes into so much detail as it. It verified that historically Krishna is the most advanced human being to ever have left literary instructions on this planet.

Even Patañjali *Yoga Sutras* which I translated and gave an application for in my book, **Meditation Expertise**, does not go as far as the Uddhava Gita.

Some of the information of these two books is identical but while the *Yoga Sutras* are concerned with the personal spiritual emancipation (kaivalyam) of the individual spirits, the Uddhava Gita explains that and also explains the situations in the spiritual universes.

Bhagavad Gita is from the *Mahabharata* which is the history of the Pandavas. Arjuna, the student of the Gita, is one of the Pandavas brothers. He was in a social hassle and did not know how to apply yoga expertise to solve it. On the battlefield, Krishna gave him a crash-course on yogic social interactions.

Uddhava Gita is from the *Srimad Bhagavatam (Bhagavata Purana),* which is a history of the incarnations of Krishna. Uddhava was a relative of Krishna. He was concerned about the situation of the deaths of many of his relatives but Krishna diverted Uddhava's attention to the practice of yoga for the purpose of successfully migrating to the spiritual environment.

Kundalini Hatha Yoga Pradipika is the commentary for the Hatha Yoga Pradipika of Swatmarama Mahayogin. This is the detailed process about asana posture, pranayama breath-infusion, complex compressions of energy, naad sound resonance intonement and advanced meditation practice.

This is the singular book with all the techniques of how to reform and redesign the subtle body so that it does not have the tendency for physical life forms and for it to attain the status of a siddha.

These books are based on the author's experiences in meditation, yoga practice and participation in spiritual groups:

Specialty

Spiritual Master

sex you!

Sleep Paralysis

Astral Projection

Masturbation Psychic Details

Spiritual Master — Michael Beloved

sex you! — michael beloved

Sleep Paralysis — Michael Beloved

Astral Projection — Michael Beloved

Masturbation Psychic Details — Michael Beloved

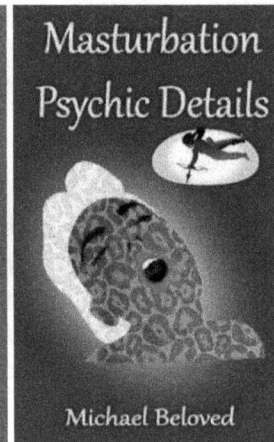

In **Spiritual Master**, Michael draws from experience with gurus or with their senior students. His contact with astral gurus is rated. He walks you through the avenue of gurus showing what you should do and what you should not do, so as to gain proficiency in whatever area of spirituality the guru has proficiency.

sex you! is a masterpiece about the adventures of an individual spirit's passage through the parents' psyches. The conversion of a departed soul into a sexual urge is described. The transit from the afterlife to residency in the emotions of the parents is detailed. This is about sex and you. Learn about how much of you comprises the romantic energy of one's would-be parents!

Sleep Paralysis clears misconceptions so that one can see what sleep paralysis is and what frightening astral experience occurs while the paralysis is being experienced. This disempowerment has great value in giving you confidence that you can and do exist even if one is unable to operate the physical body. The implication is that one can exist apart from and will survive the loss of the material form.

Astral Projection details experiences Michael had even in childhood, where he assumed incorrectly that everyone was astrally conversant. He discusses the lifeForce psychic mechanism which operates the sleep-wake cycle of the physical form, and which budgets energy into the separated astral form which determines if the individual will have dream recall or no objective awareness during the projections. Astral travel happens on every occasion when the physical body sleeps. What is missing in awareness is the observer status while the astral body is separated.

Masturbation Psychic Details is a surprise presentation which relates what happens on the psychic plane during a masturbation event. This does not tackle moral issues or even addictions but shows the involvement of memory and the sure but hidden subconscious mind which operates many features of the psyche irrespective of the desire or approval of the self-conscious personality.

inVision Series

Yoga inVision 1

Yoga inVision 2

Yoga inVision 3

Yoga inVision 4

Yoga inVision 5

Yoga inVision 6

Yoga inVision 7

Yoga inVision 8

Yoga inVision 9

Yoga inVision 10

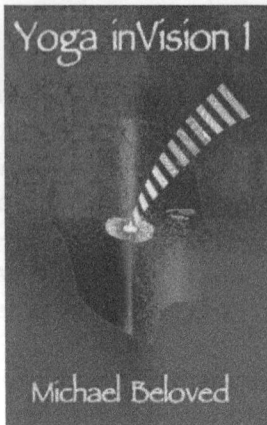

Yoga inVision 1 — Michael Beloved

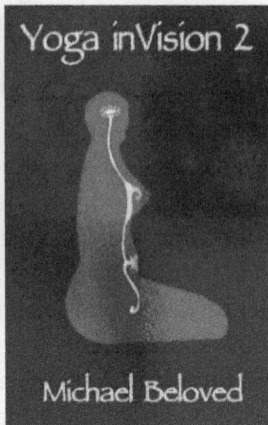

Yoga inVision 2 — Michael Beloved

Yoga inVision 3 — Michael Beloved

Yoga inVision 4 — Michael Beloved

Yoga inVision 5 — Michael Beloved

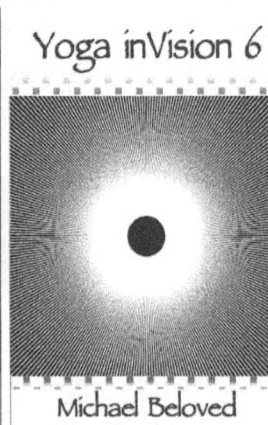

Yoga inVision 6 — Michael Beloved

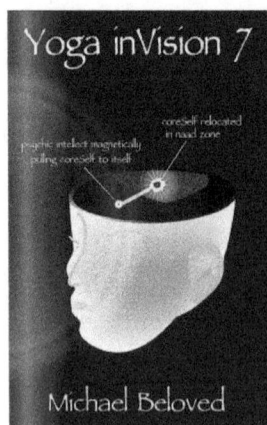

Yoga inVision 7 — Michael Beloved

Yoga inVision 8 — Michael Beloved

Yoga inVision 9 — Michael Beloved

Yoga inVision 1, the first in this series, describes the breath-infusion and meditation practices during the years of 1998 and 1999. There are unique, once in a lifetime as well as recurring insights which are elaborated. inFocus during breath-infusion and the meditation which follows is an adventure for any yogi. This gives what happened to this particular ascetic.

Yoga inVision 2 reports on the author's experiences from 1999 to 2001. Each day the experience is unique, illustrating the vibrancy of practice. Many rare once-in-a-lifetime perceptions are described.

Yoga inVision 3 reports on the author's experiences from 2001 to 2003.

Yoga inVision 4 reports on the author's experiences from 2006 to 2009.

Yoga inVision 5 reports on the author's experiences from 2006 to 2008.

Yoga inVision 6 reports on the author's experiences in 2010.

Yoga inVision 7 reports on the author's experiences in 2011.

Yoga inVision 8 reports on the author's experiences in 2011.

Yoga inVision 9 reports on the author's experiences in 2012.

Yoga inVision 10 reports on the author's experiences in 2012.

Online Resources

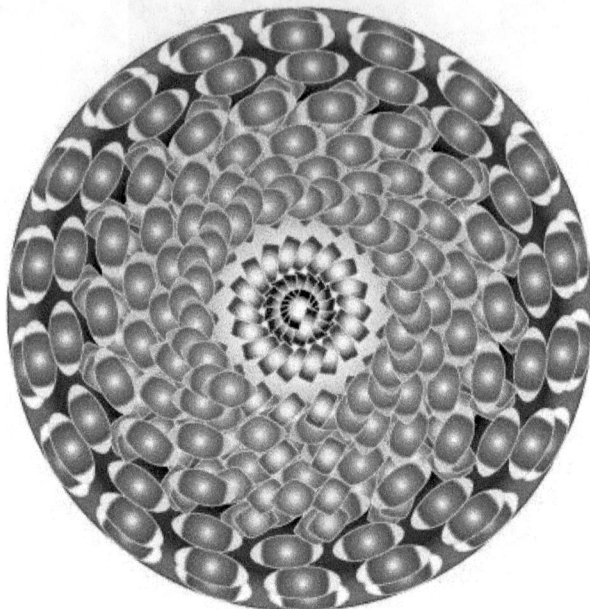

Email:	michaelbelovedbooks@gmail.com
	axisnexus@gmail.com
Website:	michaelbeloved.com
Forum:	inselfyoga.com
Posters:	zazzle.com/inself

www.ingramcontent.com/pod-product-compliance
Lightning Source LLC
Chambersburg PA
CBHW072341090426
42741CB00012B/2881